Acknowledgements

The Vanier Institute of the Family wishes to thank the many people who contributed to this project. Without the tremendous body of knowledge that *Statistics Canada* has created over the years, this project would not have been possible. Our special thanks go to the staff of the *Centre for International Statistics.* Their imagination and creativity in analyzing the data from Statistics Canada and other sources have provided a penetrating examination of demographic, sociological, economic and cultural trends related to Canada's families. Kathy Eisner and Ish Theilheimer of Ruby Communications applied their writing, editorial and interpretive talents to help bring the topic to life. Special thanks go to our colleague, Alan Mirabelli, who first conceived of a book that not only posed the questions Canadians most frequently ask about families but also presumed to answer them. Special thanks are also due to Michelle Greig-Murray for her patience and attention to detail in preparing the final manuscript. We would also like to acknowledge the many authors and commentators whom we have cited and who have added so much to our understanding of today's families.

The Vanier Institute of the Family wishes to acknowledge the generous support of the *National Welfare Grants Division of Human Resources Development Canada* which made this publication possible. The opinions expressed herein are those of the Institute and are not necessarily those of *Human Resources Development Canada*, nor are they government policy.

Robert Glossop, Ph.D.
Director of Programs

Anne Mason
Project Director

Ottawa, Ont.
Canada
January, 1994

The Vanier Institute of the Family

306
.85
0971
P264

Ministry of Education & Training
MET Library
13th Floor, Mowat Block, Queen's Park
Toronto   M7A 1L2

MAY 1 7 1994

Table of Contents

Introduction — xi

So What is a Family, Anyway? — 1

    The things families do — 3
    Why family definitions matter — 4
    Exceptions have become the rule — 6
    Households are not families — 8
    The need for a broader definition of family — 9
    Definitions of family — 10
    The basic functions of families — 12
    Families shifting from direct to indirect provision — 12
    How important is family to Canadians? — 13
    Why is family gaining in importance for Canadians? — 14

Canadian People - Canadian Families — 17

Canada – 28 million people and 7 1/2 million families — 19
    Chart 1: Canadian People – Canadian Families — 19

Baby boom bulging through Canadian population — 20
    Chart 2: Age Structure of the Canadian Population, Males and Females — 20

Canada's first families — 21
    Chart 3: Aboriginal Origins: Métis, Inuit and North American Indian — 21

Ninety-six percent of Canadians come from somewhere else — 22
    Chart 4: Ethnic Origins — 22
    Chart 5: Total Number of Immigrants Admitted to Canada — 23
    Chart 6: Distribution of Foreign-born Population by Region — 23

As Canadian as motherhood and language — 25
    Chart 7: Canadian Population by First Language — 25

Canada's families – Predominately Christian, but church influence is slipping — 26
    Chart 8: Religious Affiliation in Canada — 26

Canadian families – How'r ya gonna keep 'em down on the farm? — 28
    Chart 9: Urban/Rural Location of Canadians — 28

How many Canadians live in families? Numbers are up but percentages are down — 29
    Table I: Changes in Population and the Number of Canadians Living in Families — 29

The Vanier Institute of the Family

Canada's changing families – Diversity is now the norm   30
  Chart 10:   Family Types "Out of 100 Families..."   30

How families look in different provinces and territories   31
  Table II: Provincial and Territorial Family Profile   31

Canadian families are shrinking   32
  Chart 11:   Trends in Family Size in Canada   32

Extended families rare in Canada today   33
  Chart 12:   Percent of Non-elderly Families with at Least One Elderly Member, by Age of Family Head   33

Sandwich generation eaten up between children and aging parents   34
  Chart 13:   Percent of Families with at Least One Dependent Child and One Elderly Member   34

Look who's getting married!   35
  Chart 14:   Marital Status of Canadian Population Age 15 and Over   35
  Chart 15:   Marital Status by Age   35

Marriage – Still in fashion after all these years   36
  Chart 16:   Marriage Rates   36
  Chart 17:   Trends in Marital Status: Population Age 15 and Over   36

The second time around...   38
  Chart 18:   First Marriages and Remarriages as Percentages of All Marriages   38

No hurry to the altar – Canadians are holding off tying the knot   39
  Chart 19:   Average Age at First Marriage   39

Early marriage loses its sheen –
Teens avoiding marriage, first-marriages down   40
  Chart 20:   Age-specific First Marriage Rate for Females in Canada   40
  Chart 21:   Age-specific First Marriage Rate for Males in Canada   40

One in ten "married" couples not married   42
  Chart 22:   Proportion of Population in Common-law Relationship   42
  Chart 23:   Legal Marital Status of Persons Living Common-law   43

Shacking up – a prelude to marriage?   44
  Table III: Proportion of Married Individuals Who Cohabited Together Prior to Marriage, by Age   44

'Til divorce do us part   45
  Chart 24:   Number of Divorces   45

Marriage and divorce – A parallel line dance   47
  Chart 25:   Number of Marriages and Divorces   47

From the basement to the big leagues – Canadian divorce rates jump in comparison with other nations   **48**
     Chart 26:   Divorce Rates – An International Perspective   48

Canadian marriages outlast their American cousins   **49**
     Chart 27:   Divorce and Remarriage: Canada and the U.S.   49

Separate paths to lone parenthood   **50**
     Chart 28:   Marital Status of Lone Parents   50
     Chart 29:   Changes in Marital Status of Lone Mothers   51

Canada's families: Some have children...and some don't   **52**
     Chart 30:   Families With and Without Children   52
     Chart 31:   Families With Children Living at Home:
          Distribution by Age of Children   52

From boom to bust – Fertility rates sagged to record lows before staging mini-rally in late '80s   **54**
     Chart 32:   Total Fertility Rate   54

The greying of Canada   **55**
     Chart 33:   The Aging of the Population   55
     Table IV: Median Age and Proportion of the Population
          0 - 14 and 65 and Over   56

Move over, motherhood – Canadian women increasingly postpone marriage and child rearing   **57**
     Chart 34:   Average Age of Mother for 1st and 2nd Births   57

Hanging up the shotgun – Births to not-married women on the increase   **58**
     Chart 35:   Births to Not-married Women as a Percentage of Total Births   58
     Chart 36:   Births to Not-married Women by Age   58

Adoption – More applicants, fewer kids   **60**
     Chart 37:   Domestic Adoptions: Public and Private   60

Mine, yours and ours – Big families are often blended families   **61**
     Chart 38:   Blended and Non-blended Families by Number of Children   61

Canadian Families: Making Ends Meet...or Not   63

No one home during the day   **65**
     Chart 39:   Labour Force Participation Rates,
          Males and Females Age 15 and Over   65

Most women have two careers – At home and on the job   **67**
     Chart 40:   Labour Force Participation Rates,
          Men and Women by Marital Status   67

The Vanier Institute
of the Family

Women on the job – A steady climb since 1941   69
       Chart 41:   Female Labour Force Participation Rates by Marital Status   69

Children keep us working   70
       Chart 42:   Labour Force Participation Rates, Adults 15 - 64   70

How times change! Both parents employed in 7 of 10 families, up from 3 in 10 twenty years ago   71
       Chart 43:   Employment Status of Husbands and Wives With Children Under 19 Years of Age   71

Who's minding the kids?   72
       Chart 44:   Female Labour Force Participation Rates by Age of Youngest Child   72
       Chart 45:   Labour Force Characteristics of Women by Age of Youngest Child   72

Bringing home the bacon... together   74
       Chart 46:   Earners in Husband-Wife Families   74

More than "pin money" but...   75
       Chart 47:   Contribution of Wife's Earnings to Overall Family Income   75

Working more for less? After big gains in the '70s, family incomes flatten off despite more earners per family   76
       Chart 48:   Trends in Average Family Income and Average Family Size   76

Family incomes going nowhere fast   77
       Table V: Average Family Income by Family Type   77

Middle class not dead yet – Most Canadian families are "middle-income"   78
       Chart 49:   Percentage Distribution of Families by Level of Family Income   78

Family incomes vary from sea to sea to sea   79
       Table VI: Average Family Income in Constant (1990) Dollars, Canada, Provinces and Territories   79

As men and women age, the income gap grows   80
       Table VII: Number of Married Men and Women by Age, Showing Proportion With Employment Income and Average Earnings   80

Divorce a good career move for women?   82
       Table VIII: Number of Divorced Men and Women by Age, Showing Proportion with Employment Income and Average Earnings   82

Single mothers are struggling   83
       Chart 50:   Percentage Distribution of Male and Female Lone-parent Families by Level of Family Income   83

The short end of the stick – Women much worse off than men after separation and divorce — **84**
    Chart 51:   Child Support and Alimony as a Percentage of Recipient's Total Income by Recipient's Family Type — 84

Many teens working too — **86**
    Table IX: Employment and Average Earnings of Teenagers (Aged 14 - 17) Living With Parents — 86

Family Poverty – Seniors escaping, single moms sinking — **87**
    Chart 52:   Poverty Rate Among Canadian Families — 87
    Chart 53:   How Poor is Poor? — 88

No progress on child poverty — **89**
    Chart 54:   Child Poverty Rates by Family Type — 89

Most poor children live in two-parent families — **90**
    Chart 55:   Who Do Poor Children Live With? — 90

Making ends meet — **91**
    Table X: Average Expenditure of Urban Canadian Households on Selected Goods and Services — 91

Baby needs new shoes – Couples with children lead family spending race, lone parents left in the dust — **92**
    Chart 56:   Average Yearly Expenditures by Family Type — 92

How come we've got no money left? — **93**
    Table XI: Where Did The Money Go? — 93

Children are big-ticket items — **94**
    Table XII: The Cost of Raising a Child — 94

Place roof over four walls – Add love and/or children — **96**
    Chart 57:   Percentage of Family Households Owning Their Home — 96
    Chart 58:   Percentage of Family Households Renting Their Home — 96

Ours and the bank's – One third of Canada's families have mortgages, another quarter of them rent — **98**
    Chart 59:   Family Households by Tenure — 98

Canadians plugged in to bare necessities — **99**
    Table XIII: The Luxury Goods Canadian Families Own — 99

The more things change...Despite changed attitudes, women still do the lion's share of household work — **100**
    Chart 60:   Percentage of Women and Men Who Participate Daily in Selected Household Chores — 100

A woman's work is never...valued — **102**
    Chart 61:   Average Value of Household Work: Men and Women — 102

The Vanier Institute of the Family

Doing our bit – Volunteering in Canada on the rise despite increase in dual-earner families — **104**
    Chart 62:   Where do People Volunteer? — 104

Canadian Family Life Today – How It Feels   105

A day in the life   107

The time crunch   108
    Table XIV: Percentage of the Respondents Agreeing With Statements on Perceptions of Time — 108

Employed women get small slice of the time-use pie   109
    Chart 63:   Average Weekly Time Use: Employed Women — 109
    Chart 64:   Average Weekly Time Use: Employed Men — 110
    Chart 65:   Average Weekly Time Use: Female Homemakers — 111

Who cares for the kids?   112
    Chart 66:   Primary Child Care Arrangement for Children 0 - 5, Whose Parents are Employed — 112
    Chart 67:   Primary Child Care Arrangement for Children 6-12, Whose Parents are Employed — 113
    Chart 68:   Parental Child Care Preferences and Proportion Using Those Preferences — 114

Licensed care – Not much, not cheap   115
    Chart 69:   Number of Children With Mothers in the Labour Force and Number of Licensed Child Care Spaces — 115
    Chart 70:   Average Monthly Day Care Fees, Licensed Centres — 116

A place for grandparents   117
    Chart 71:   Living Arrangements of Seniors — 117

"Sandwich Generation" boxed in   118

Most people with disabilities live with their families   119
    Chart 72:   Distribution of Adults With Disablities by Family Status — 119

With a little help from our friends...and family   121
    Chart 73:   Percent of Seniors Who Provide Unpaid Help to Family Outside Their Household, by Type of Help Provided — 121
    Chart 74:   Percent of Seniors Who Provide Unpaid Help to People Outside Their Household, by Type of Help Provided — 122

Families helping families   122
    Chart 75:   Percent of Canadians Who Provide Unpaid Help to People Outside Their Household, by Type of Help Provided — 122
    Chart 76:   Percent of Canadians Who Provide Unpaid Help to Family Outside Their Household, by Type of Help Provided — 123

Families in motion   **124**

     Chart 77:   Mobility Status of Canadians   124

That long-distance feeling   **126**

     Chart 78:   Distance Children and Mothers Live Apart
                    Distance Children and Fathers Live Apart   126

     Chart 79:   How Often Mothers and Children Visit
                    by The Distance Between Them   127

     Chart 80:   How Often Fathers and Children Visit
                    by The Distance Between Them   127

     Chart 81:   How Often Grandparents and Grandchildren
                    Visit With One Another   129
                    How Often Grandparents and Grandchildren
                    Phone and Write to one Another   129

     Chart 82:   How Often Siblings Visit With One Another
                    How Often Siblings Phone and Write to One Another   130

Troubled homes: The down side of family   **131**

     Families and abuse   131

     Wife assault   132

     Elder abuse   133

     Child abuse   133

     Child sexual abuse   134

And in the end...Supporting family life in Canada   **135**

Chart References   **137**

End Notes   **141**

The Vanier Institute
of the Family

The Vanier Institute
of the Family

x

Introduction

Family is one of the deepest and most abiding of human needs. Few things matter more to most of us than the well-being of our families. Collectively, families remain the foundation of society whatever the age, whatever the changes with which they must contend.

Profiling Canada's Families identifies significant trends and forces affecting Canada's families and the changes they are undergoing. Through a process of asking questions about what family is: how, where and with whom Canadians live; how they get by; and what it actually feels like to live in Canadian families, *The Vanier Institute of the Family* goes beyond the raw numbers to examine more closely the textures of Canadian family life as it is lived today. In the course of this examination, the Institute has uncovered some remarkable facts and disposed of a number of persistent misconceptions.

This book examines the details of Canadian family life by presenting charts and graphs coupled with written explications of the numbers and trends. Many of the research findings presented here have been previously unavailable. It then looks more closely at the numbers, asking the question: "And so what?" What do these numbers and data mean to our families, our communities, our work places and our governments?

In this, the International Year of the Family 1994, it is appropriate that people be able to ask good questions and apply a well-grounded perspective to the task of answering them. It is the hope of *The Vanier Institute of the Family* that this book will stimulate thoughtful, informed discussion and debate throughout 1994 and well beyond.

The Vanier Institute of the Family

The Vanier Institute
of the Family

SO WHAT IS A FAMILY ANYWAY?

The Vanier Institute of the Family

So what is a family, anyway?

The things families do

Families and their members generate a lot of activity. They serve one another and themselves. They earn, purchase and consume. They save and spend, care and nurture, borrow, share and give. Here are some glimpses of family members as they fulfill some of the basic functions of families.

Physical maintenance and care of family members
A tired lone mother spending a sleepless night with a sick baby who can't quite fall asleep

A teenage boy going to the store for Uncle Arnold, who fell off the porch and sprained his ankle

Father and daughter putting up storm windows and then taking half of them down and washing them again because they are smudged

A young father learning to iron shirts properly and clean behind toilets

Addition of new members
Nervous, expectant parents attending birthing classes

Couples with infertility mastering the fine points of basal thermometers

A childless couple waiting at the airport for the arrival of an adoptive baby from abroad

Socialization of children
Two parents puzzling over the latest math teaching technique with their ten-year old

A father and mother taking turns getting up at 5 a.m. to take their son to hockey practice

A 14-year old going with his folks to visit his grandparents on Sunday when he'd really rather be skateboarding

Social control of members
A young girl apologizing – under parental orders – to the neighbours for breaking a window

A teenager bringing her boyfriend home to meet the folks for the first time

Three adult siblings worrying over coffee about the woman their elderly father plans to marry

Production, consumption and distribution of goods and services
A young father putting in a day on the production line

A 45-year old single mother working as a teller at the local bank

A family of five burdened with bags of groceries, clothes and hardware forgetting where their car is parked at the shopping mall

An elderly couple welcoming the working mother delivering meals-on-wheels

Love and affective nurturance
Two new parents spending an entire day gazing at their newborn – and leaving the phone unplugged

Middle-aged newlyweds spending an entire day in bed – and leaving the phone unplugged

A teacher calling in sick so she can take the day off to spend with her dying mother – and leaving the phone unplugged

The Vanier Institute of the Family

Why family definitions matter

For most people, the word "family" means precisely the kind of family that they, themselves, grew up in.

For many, that family consisted of a husband who worked outside the home, a homemaker wife, and children. This family unit is sometimes called the "traditional" family. Most older adults in Canada grew up in families like this, which may explain why so many opinion leaders, most of whom are older adults, refer to it as traditional.

This family structure, however, was a fairly recent development, and it never was universal. Many Canadian adults did not grow up in such families. Twenty, forty, or sixty years ago, there were many Canadians growing up with two parents that worked, or with only one parent, or with step-parents and step-siblings. Today, two-parent, one-earner families are in the minority. So when it comes to the traditional family, tradition is a matter of perspective.

How we define family can have far-reaching implications. It affects such matters as government planning, employers' personnel policies, pension plans, the procedures of schools and other public institutions, and, of course, relationships within families. Who is considered a dependent for tax purposes? Who is allowed to visit a dying patient in a hospital? Into whose care is a school allowed to deliver a student who must be sent home on account of illness? Who belongs to "our" family: the live-in lover? the step-child? the former in-laws or grandparents? Confusion over the definition of family can lead to tension, controversy and unhappiness.

Family living also means different things to different people. Families are amazingly diverse. Life experiences vary greatly for individuals, depending on cultural traditions, heritage and family types. These different family types are distinguished from one another by both their structures and by how they function.

Sometimes family is defined by reference to a marriage, sometimes by reference to biological relatedness of individuals. Sometimes it depends on whether individuals live under the same roof. For other purposes, family seems to be defined on the basis of relationships of dependency or inter-dependency. Some definitions include only family units that have or have had children.

Each of these definitions serves a specific purpose or reflects a particular interest in one aspect of family life. For example, the Province of Quebec has a definition that is consistent with the compelling interests of the government in protecting the rights and interests of children. To the extent that its definition emphasizes the parent-child relationship, it is also consistent with the province's interest in ensuring the reproduction of its distinct language and culture. It may leave out, however, the interests of childless couples, both married and common-law, and their kinship networks or extended families.

The definition used by statisticians and demographers may be useful for counting the number of people who live together in a household and are related in some way. It cannot do justice, however, to the family commitments of individuals not living together.

When the term "family" appears in the statistical profiles in this book, it refers to the Statistics Canada definition of family. This defines family as **a currently-married or common-law couple with or without never-married children, or a single parent with never-married children, in the same dwelling.** In other words, for Statistics Canada, family is people living under the same roof who are either a couple, a couple with children who have never married, or a single parent and one or more children who have never married.

This definition may be adequate for counting households, but it is both limited and limiting in that it does not reflect the familial relationships of a diverse collection of familial groups such as:
- adult siblings who live together
- divorced or widowed people who live with their parents
- related persons who do not live under the same roof but support one another
- people who may not be immediate relations but who do live under the same roof.

Definitions of family are important because they can serve either as an appropriate or misleading basis for public policies and other attempts to support families. We need a notion of family that accurately reflects the real experiences of individuals and the intimate relationships that they establish and attempt to sustain over time. Our definition of family must also acknowledge how families evolve and change.

It would be far easier for all of us if we could simply say "OK, this is what a family is, they all look like this." Every time we wanted to support families, we would only have to say that this policy or this program or this therapeutic intervention has this kind of effect on families. But that would ignore the different needs of mother-led families, father-led families, common-law couples with and without children, married couples without children, "blended families," and so on. We can't do that. Defining family is all the more difficult because we're dealing with a number of populations - cultural, ethnic, linguistic, regional - not simply one. This diversity is acknowledged by Margrit Eichler in what she offers as a realistic, even if not very useful or satisfying, definition of the family:

> A family is a social group that may or may not include adults of both sexes (e.g. lone-parent families), may or may not include one or more children (e.g. childless couples), who may or may not have been born in their wedlock (e.g. adopted children, or children by one adult partner of a previous union). The relationship of the adults may or may not have its origin in marriage (e.g. common-law couples), they may or may not share a common residence (e.g. commuting couples). The adults may or may not cohabit sexually, and the relationship may or may not involve such socially patterned feelings as love, attraction, piety, and awe.[1]

To arrive at a definition, we need to be sensitive to and in touch with family life as Canadians live it. This is a very different view from simply trying to promote any one idealized image of families.

If we are to arrive at a family definition that is relevant, we must do two things. The first is to acknowledge that there are a lot of different types of families out there. Second, we must look at the social environment within which people live. If we are going to understand how people can actually maintain and sustain their family commitments, we must assess the broader patterns of social, political, economic, technological and cultural change within which they, as individuals and family members, are embedded.

More concretely, how we define family is crucial because the definitions will entitle certain family members to various kinds of benefits while denying them to others. This is especially true when it comes to the distribution of property when marital relationships break down, and where questions arise about the exercise of responsibilities over the children of former spouses. These definitions matter a lot when a government introduces tax policies that affect single-earner families differently from dual-earner, or married couples differently from cohabiting couples.

There was a time when marriage was the key criterion to designate whether groups of people were or were not families. In recent years there has been a marked increase in the number of common-law or cohabiting relationships. This lifestyle was frowned upon twenty or thirty years ago, but it enjoys wider acceptance today. Currently there are many people living as family that are not married. Should they not be acknowledged and respected as family members?

Another concrete example is the tendency of commentators to look at how new government budgets or other programs affect "the average family." If the family is defined as the "traditional" family of the 1950s, we will have inaccurate information about how budgetary provisions affect other kinds of families. Recently, analysts have become a little more astute. Some newspaper accounts, for example, compare the effects of new government programs on single-parent and two-parent families. Still, there's not a lot of sophistication about how, for instance, a budget will affect a single wage-earning family differently from a dual wage-earning family.

On the legal front, there are challenges being made by various people who feel that they have been denied rights and benefits accorded to other families simply because they are not married. There are disputes within law as to what constitutes a spouse as, for example, in the case of same-sex couples who have sought to be recognized as families. Although there have been various legal challenges to date, this area of law remains very grey.

The conclusion is that in a lot of public policy analysis there is an implicit image or definition of the family. If that image is limited or has only one kind of family in mind, it is likely to be discriminatory. It can have the effect of entitling certain people and certain family members to various kinds of benefits while denying them to others.

Exceptions have become the rule

Some argue that society should not make legal exceptions. They say that we shouldn't call people family if they knowingly choose to live in non-traditional relationships that aren't legally certified. "That's their business," say those who hold this view, "and they should accept the consequences." This view, however, overlooks many realities of family life today.

For example, a woman may get married with all the expectations of a lifelong commitment. Then a separation or divorce dramatically changes her circumstances. Should her future or the future of her children be put in jeopardy because her family unit no longer corresponds to certain definitions now that she heads a single-parent family? Her single-parent family needs to be acknowledged and supported even if it departs from what people in the past have said was a family or even from her own original aspirations.

Marriage is not the same as family. A marriage can be dissolved quite readily, but the obligations that family entails cannot be dissolved. And therefore, like it or not, families are forever.

Two individuals may decide to have a non-traditional relationship. Their decision does not really affect anyone else and it may be acceptable socially. It gets more complicated, however, if there are children involved. The state has a compelling interest in the needs of those children. With children on hand, it may be necessary or useful to treat those individuals in the same way that the state would treat two married individuals. In making policies that affect families, the needs of children are of central concern.

Sharing money, income and the resources that family members purchase or produce is one of the most important aspects of family life. In a marriage, economic benefits such as income, services and products are provided by each partner and also received by each partner by virtue of their relationship. This economic interdependence is disrupted when a marriage breaks up, along with the break-up of joint residence, sharing of assets, and so on.

The dependence of some family members on others, however, does not end so cleanly. Nor do other familial relationships, commitments and obligations. Therefore, it is in the interests of both the individuals whose lives will remain intertwined, and in the interests of the state, that particular members of the family be protected. This is especially so in the case of women, children and other potentially vulnerable family members.

What if an unemployed adult moves in with her elderly mother and the mother's second husband in order to assist them with their daily living needs? This grouping would not fall into many traditional definitions of family, yet they certainly fulfill many of the functions that families have always fulfilled - nurturing, mutual support, companionship and love.

We very often tend to think of families as groups of people who live under the same roof. Yet family commitments extend beyond the front door. They extend to other generations and to other kin within the community. They may extend, for example, to former spouses and children that were the progeny of a relationship that is now ended. Therefore it's important when we're talking about family not simply to stop at that front door but to acknowledge that there are many people who may be, in strict statistical terms, living alone, but who are, in fact, carrying family responsibilities for children who no longer live with them. Similarly there are people who carry family responsibilities, either physical, economic, or psychological, for aging relatives who may be living on their own or in institutions.

The extended family living in a single household such as might have been found in a rural community of the last century has given way to the smaller households typical of a modern urban society (See diagram on p. 8). Family does not come to an end when children leave home and establish their own households. Siblings may continue to support one another. Grandparents are often quite important in the lives of their grandchildren, although fewer live in the same household with them as they might have on yesterday's rural homestead. Others, such as divorced spouses and former in-laws may be important family members despite remote physical location.

So, we have much the same group of people in today's mobile, changing families as in yesterday's more stable ones. Their roles and relationships are nearly identical. They are merely living in separate households now. To respond to all the realities of today's family relationships, we need definitions of family that include those non-household relationships.

Households are not families

The family leaves home, at least...

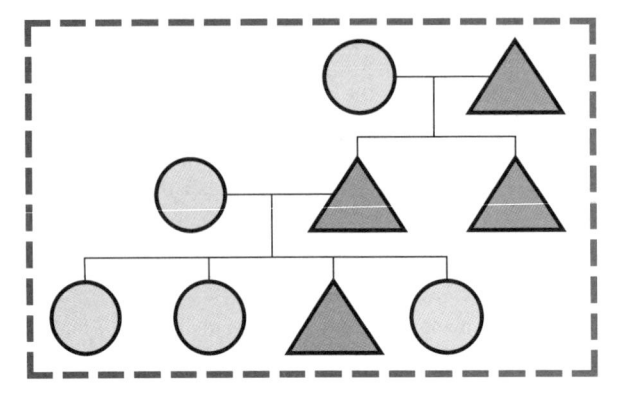

... it is no longer necessarily located within a single household, under one roof. This extended family is in a single household (represented by the dotted line) such as might have been found in a rural community of the last century.

The same people, the same family, but living in the smaller households typical of a modern urban society.

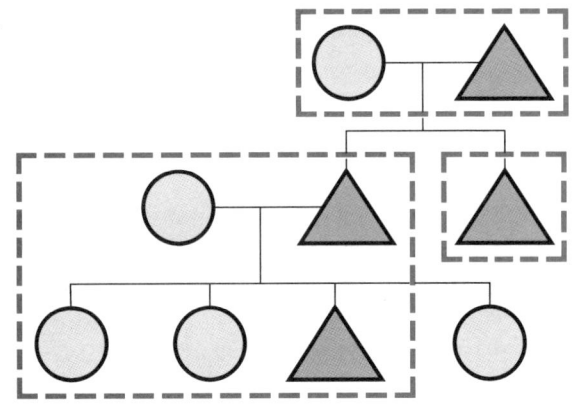

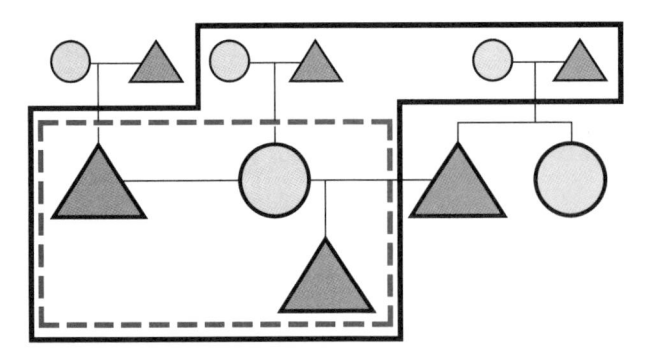

This family takes into account resources of the mother's parents and former parents-in-law (the grandparents of her son) when planning. In reality, this family includes all of the people enclosed by the solid line including three households.

Demographic Review Secretariat[2]

The need for a broader definition of family

There is a need to acknowledge the diversity of various family forms to avoid subordinating various family members within a presumably all-encompassing notion of families. The interests of women, children, and the elderly need to be distinguished within a broader definition of family that does not subordinate their individuality.

Ultimately, it is easier, fairer and more practical to define families by what they do rather than what they look like. We need to respect all these different kinds of families and to develop a definition that is inclusive rather than exclusive of them. As a result, family cannot be defined simply by reference to structure. It's not whether there are two parents and kids, or three generations or whatever. Given the incredible diversity of today's families, what is it that all their structures have in common? What are the common functions that families perform to the benefit of both the individual members of families and to the benefit of the larger society?

Over the past twenty years, a more inclusive definition has been welcomed and largely accepted by the majority of Canadians, implicitly or explicitly. There are relatively few groups who would refuse today to acknowledge the young, unmarried single mother and her child as a family. There are few who would deny that in certain circumstances at least, divorce is the best resolution. And there are also few who would deny that when someone with children divorces and remarries, a new kind of family with distinct characteristics is created. There are few who would deny that the extended family of the First Peoples or of Maritime outports are indeed legitimate forms of family.

Although a broader definition has not found favour with all groups in society, it is gaining acceptance in many areas. It is, for example, now evident in many family law provisions. Family law is trying as best it can to protect the interests of individual women and children following separation or divorce.

Researchers are looking more and more closely at the characteristics of different types of families. Over the last fifteen to twenty years, family counsellors have faced the need to find ways of lending support to different kinds of families, ways that are sensitive to their different structures. It remains tricky, however, for policy-makers, educators and family professionals to deal effectively with the diversity that families represent today.

Canadians are by no means alone in struggling over family definitions. Definitions of family and family policy played a major role in the 1992 U.S. presidential elections, for instance. The debate goes on almost universally. Throughout the industrialized world, people are discussing and debating how to deal with the diversity of families.

Definitions of family

"Family is defined as any combination of two or more persons who are bound together over time by ties of mutual consent, birth and/or adoption/placement and who, together, assume responsibilities for variant combinations of some of the following:
- physical maintenance and care of group members;
- addition of new members through procreation or adoption;
- socialization of children;
- social control of members;
- production, consumption and distribution of goods and services; and
- affective nurturance - love."

The Vanier Institute of the Family[3]

"Refers to a now-married couple (with or without never-married sons and/or daughters of either or both spouses), a couple living common-law (again with or without never-married sons and/or daughters of either or both partners), or a lone parent of any marital status, with at least one never-married son or daughter living in the same dwelling."

Statistics Canada[4]

"...the family is referred to as the basic unit of society; it is appreciated for the important socio-economic functions that it performs. In spite of the many changes in society that have altered its role and functions it continues to provide the natural framework for the emotional, financial and material support essential to the growth and development of its members, particularly infants and children, and for the care of other dependents, including the elderly, disabled and infirm. The family remains a vital means of preserving and transmitting cultural values. In the broader sense, it can, and often does, educate, train, motivate and support its individual members, thereby investing in their future growth and acting as a vital resource for development."

The United Nations[5]

"A parent-child group bound by many and varied ties of mutual, lifetime support and for furthering the development of persons and societies at their source."

Government of Quebec[6]

"For the purposes of this program, the term "family" refers to a grouping of individuals who are related by affection, kinship, dependency or trust."

Social Sciences and Humanities Research Council and Health and Welfare Canada's joint initiative on Family Violence and Violence Against Women[7]

"Today's stay-at-home mother is tomorrow's working mother. Today's career woman is soon pregnant and thinking about how she can quit her job to stay home for a while. One day, the Ozzie and Harriet couple is eating a family meal at the dining room table; the next day, they are working out a joint custody arrangement in a law office."

Barbara Dafoe Whitehead[8]

"There is a lot of talk about family these days, a lot of hand-wringing over its demise. But even those most distressed about threats to the family have few ideas about how to strengthen it. Some cling to the form, wishing that somehow we could promote marriage or encourage parents to better enforce rules in the home.

"But families aren't marriages or homes or rules. Families are people who develop intimacy because they live together, because they share experiences that come over the years to make up their uniqueness - the mundane, even silly, traditions that emerge in a group of people who know each other in every mood and circumstance. It is this intimacy that provides the ground for our lives."

Frances Moore Lappé[9]

"...'the family' is not an institution, but an *ideological, symbolic construct* that has a history and a politics."

Judith Stacey[10]

The basic functions of families

Families perform vital functions for society and for their members. Society as we know it would be simply unimaginable without them. Researcher Shirley Zimmerman[11] has listed six basic functions of families that demonstrate how important and far-reaching these functions are:

- *Physical maintenance and care of family members.* Within healthy families, children, adults and seniors all receive the care and support they need: food, shelter, clothing, protection and so on. Where families are not available or are unable to provide these services, family members suffer and substitutes, usually inadequate ones, must be found.
- *Addition of new members through procreation or adoption and their relinquishment when mature.* Society renews itself through families. For this function, there is, literally, no substitute.
- *Socialization of children for adult roles.* Families prepare their children for life. Most do a fairly good job of it, teaching skills, values and attitudes that equip them to learn, work, form friendships and contribute to society.
- *Social control of members...the maintenance of order within the family and groups external to it.* Within families, individuals learn positive values and behaviour and receive criticism for negative ones.
- *Maintenance of family morale and motivation to ensure task performance both within the family and in other groups.* In this regard, families provide the glue that holds society together and keeps it functioning. Beyond providing mere social control, families, through love and spiritual leadership, inspire their members and others to keep trying.
- *Production and consumption of goods and services.* Families provide for their own by producing goods and services like food, home maintenance and health care. As they strive to fulfill the needs of their members, they play a vital role in the national economy.

In the words of one Ontario grandmother speaking at a focus group session in 1993, "I don't know how anyone gets along without a family." A grandfather said that "a sense of belonging is critical - if you don't have that, you don't have anything."[12]

Families shifting from direct to indirect provision

As our society has moved from agricultural to industrial to post-industrial, the role of families has shifted. In the past, families met the needs of their members fairly directly, producing food, clothing, transportation and other basics on their own. As society became more industrial, families began to purchase more of the goods and services their members needed. In recent decades, the shift of family needs from direct provision to indirect provision has touched new areas. More meals are eaten outside the home or are prepared outside. More child care is provided outside the home. This has been matched by the shift of peoples' activities from within to outside the family. These shifts do not, however, imply that people are not focused on their families.

Some worry that the role of families has become less important because families no longer produce directly to meet their own needs. Yet today's families do something just as important. As they have always done, they acquire and collect or save resources. They then *allocate* resources to meet the needs of their own members. By understanding the vital role of families in deciding how these resources will be deployed to accomplish their responsibilities, families can again be understood as essential. The only change has been that the family now produces indirectly what it formerly produced directly.

The family continues to exist and absorbs much of the time and effort of all of us. We make a fundamental error when we ignore the family's role in production and assume that "the economy" is just the market economy to which people relate strictly as individuals.

How families allocate resources is not always fair, of course. Women, for instance, have generally received an inferior share of family resources. Debates continue over how best to protect their interests or the interests of other family members, particularly weaker ones such as old people and children.

How important is family to Canadians?

Some people believe that family is losing importance in the lives of Canadians. As proof, they point to the rising incidence of divorce and separation, single-parent families, and children being born out of wedlock. They point to other trends to support an argument that the family is threatened or under attack. For example, a majority of married women with children are now in the labour force, and families increasingly purchase services such as child care and food preparation that used to be performed in the home. Common-law marriage is at an all-time high in Canada. Many people feel that our society is growing more violent. The growing awareness of the violence and abuse that takes place in too many families serves to confirm these fears, whether they are well grounded or not. Taken together, the alarmists say that all these trends are signs that family is losing importance or place.

Despite these warnings, public opinion research consistently shows that family is tremendously important to Canadians. If anything, its importance is on the increase.

In 1987 for example, the magazine *Maclean's* surveyed Canadians to find out how they felt about family. The poll showed that Canadians see their families as increasingly important in their lives. Seventy-seven percent of respondents said that family was more important to them than career which scored just 17% - or religion (5%). Eighty-one percent said that family is becoming a "more" or "much more" important part of their lives. Only 7% said that family was becoming less important to them.

Young people seem just as unequivocal as adults on the importance of family. Despite the prevalence of divorce - and their considerable experience of it - young people "are anything but disillusioned with marriage." That's what Reginald Bibby and Donald Posterski found in 1992 when they surveyed nearly 4,000 Canadian high school students. In their book *Teen Trends*, the researchers reported that at least 85% of the teens said they planned to marry. Nine of ten of the marriage-bound planned to have "a church wedding," although only two of ten teens are weekly churchgoers.

Most teens - 86% - expected a lifelong marriage of their own. This group included 78% of those teens whose parents had not stayed together. Most (84%) also expected to have children.

This is not to say that youth have "old-fashioned" notions of what family life should be like. Few young men expect to support a stay-at-home wife. Most young women expect to work outside the home and know that having a skill or profession is their best insurance against marriage break-up. And while Bibby and Posterski report that the majority of Canadian youth approved of premarital sex, they also felt strongly about marital fidelity. Only 10% approved of sex outside marriage.

At the same time, Canadian youth, like adults, saw little wrong with having children without being married. Four in five Quebec teens approved, as did two out of three teens in the rest of Canada. Neither did most young people object to cohabitation. Nearly nine of ten teens approved of unmarried couples living together. Yet while most teens find cohabitation acceptable, the vast majority still plan, eventually, to marry and have children. For youth as for adults, cohabitation is seen as a prelude to marriage, rather than as a substitute.

Why is family gaining in importance for Canadians?

Why is family rising in importance when so many trends seem to point to its downfall?

Perhaps it is because difficult economic times are forcing people to rely on one another more than in more prosperous times. With rising unemployment and poor job prospects, it has become increasingly common for youth to delay leaving home. At the same time, many young adults are returning to the family home in the wake of job loss or the break-up of their own marriages. Many older workers have lost their jobs in recent years and must depend on help from their families and friends. With higher living costs and cutbacks in some government services, seniors are also looking to others for support and assistance. Young or old, people usually turn first to family for help, support and love. Hard times underscore the many ways in which we depend on one another.

Another reason for the increased importance of family is that family time is at a premium. Family members spend much more time at paid labour and away from the home than they have at any time in the recent past. Canadians express strong opinions to pollsters on their need for more family time and more flexibility to help them balance the demands of paid employment and family.

In 1992, *Magazine Affaires Plus*, a French-language magazine for business people and professionals asked 4,000 of its readers for their views on love, work, sex and family. Nearly half of respondents said they felt stressed by the demands of their professional, family and marital lives. Only half felt that they devoted enough time to their spouses. Half the mothers and 57% of fathers said they find it hard to reconcile their family and working lives.

How to balance work and family responsibilities has become a major preoccupation for Canadians. The poll found that nearly two in three respondents were willing to compromise career advancement in order to devote more time to their personal, marital or family lives. And half said they would consider a new, less demanding job in order to preserve their family and personal lives. These results are consistent with those of other recent surveys.

There may also be generational reasons for the increasing importance of family in the minds and lives of Canadians. The post-war baby boom generation came of age at a time of sweeping social change. As a group, they postponed marriage and having children until much later in life than their parents had. After the "Baby Bust" - a period of low birth rates that lasted for nearly two decades - they have now started to have children of their own.

Today's youth may have other reasons for valuing family. The generation now coming of age is the first one to grow up in the period ushered in by the "Sexual Revolution" and the liberalization of divorce laws in the late '60s. Many of them have direct experience of divorce and separation. Almost all of them have friends who have experienced family difficulties. Perhaps this explains why so many Canadian youth fervently want to form stable, loving families of their own.

There are other, more universal reasons why the family enjoys such strong support. People recognize its fundamental importance to individuals and to society at large.

Profiling Canada's Families - A guide to discussion

In recent years Canadians have witnessed dramatic changes in their own personal family lives, in the decisions and aspirations of their children, and in the lifestyles and attitudes of their neighbours and co-workers. Today's families are smaller than at any time in the past. Most children are growing up with fewer siblings. People are living longer and staying healthier. The once-typical male breadwinner family has been displaced by the now-typical two-wage-earner family. Marriage rates have declined while the number of people living together outside of marriage has grown.

Some of the changes are quite disturbing. Divorce rates have increased, and close to half of all children born today will likely see their parents separate or divorce. Far too many women, children and elderly persons are subjected to abuse or violence in their homes. The number of children growing up in poverty is tragically high.

These and other trends have preoccupied Canadians and have generated much discussion and debate. Often these discussions suffer from a lack of accurate information. It is the intention of this book to provide Canadians with a reliable basis upon which they may assess the current status, needs and prospects of their families.

Debate over family is nothing new. A century ago, popular magazines published alarming articles about what people *then* saw as a breakdown among families. Families have survived many changes in society since then, as well as before. In every age, families have adapted and helped their members to adapt, cope and thrive. However we define it, family appears likely to continue as a dominant and, for most Canadians, a positive force in our lives and society. To show our true concern for families, we can understand and help them do what they've always done - for themselves, for their members, and for all of us.

The Vanier Institute
of the Family

CANADIAN PEOPLE
CANADIAN FAMILIES

The Vanier Institute of the Family

Canada – 28 million people and 7 1/2 million families

1. Canadian People — Canadian Families
(1991)

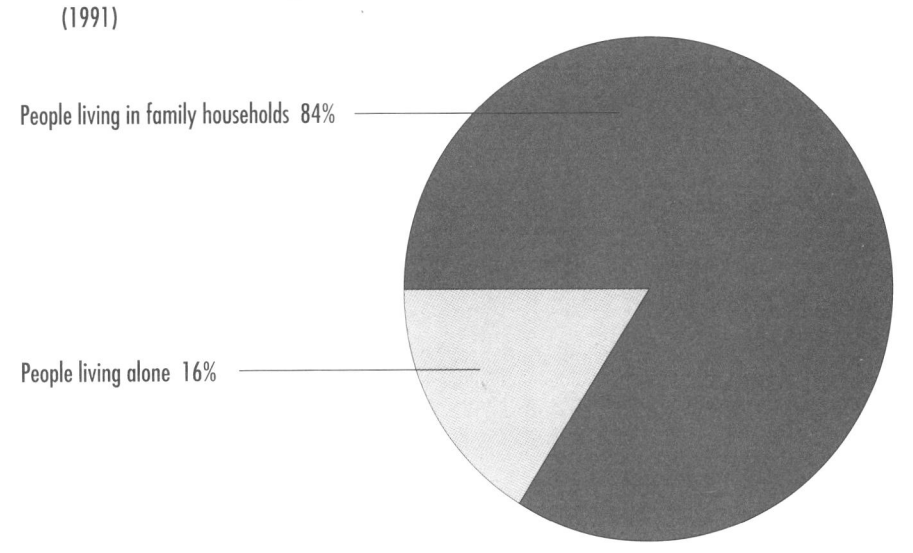

People living in family households 84%

People living alone 16%

Prepared by The Vanier Institute of the Family

In 1991, 26.7 million people lived in Canada, according to the Census. A vast majority of them (84%) lived in the nation's seven and a half million families. We are diverse in language, religion and ethnic background. As a result, our families display a tremendous mix of family types, structures, living arrangements and lifestyles.

Note: The 1991 Census counted approximately 26.7 million people living in Canada. In 1993, Statistics Canada estimated a total population of 28,753,000, which includes those not originally counted in the Census.

The Vanier Institute of the Family

...family is a work in progress, a never-ending renovation job that begins with tidy, visionary blueprints and ends in plaster dust and daily chaos.
    Marnie Jackson[13]

...the family is a fixed point in a changing landscape. Who knows where they will be living or working, who their friends, neighbours, or colleagues will be in twenty years, but a sister is always a sister. Marriages may end, but children are forever. These relationships may be close or distant, loving or not, easy or tense. But they do not go away. They cannot be divorced, quit, annulled, fired, or dissolved. An estranged sister is still a sister.
    Barbara Katz Rothman[14]

...the family is the adaptive mechanism in society that helps us get over the rough spaces as we move from one era to another. It provides elasticity in the social order so we can stretch and contract, make shifts in size, grouping and organizational patterns. The family is a setting in which we can create the other, the different, the alternative. It is both the adapter and the creator of the new. The family is an instrument for imaging futures.
    Elise Boulding[15]

Baby boom bulging through Canadian population

2. Age Structure of the Canadian Population, Males and Females
(1991)

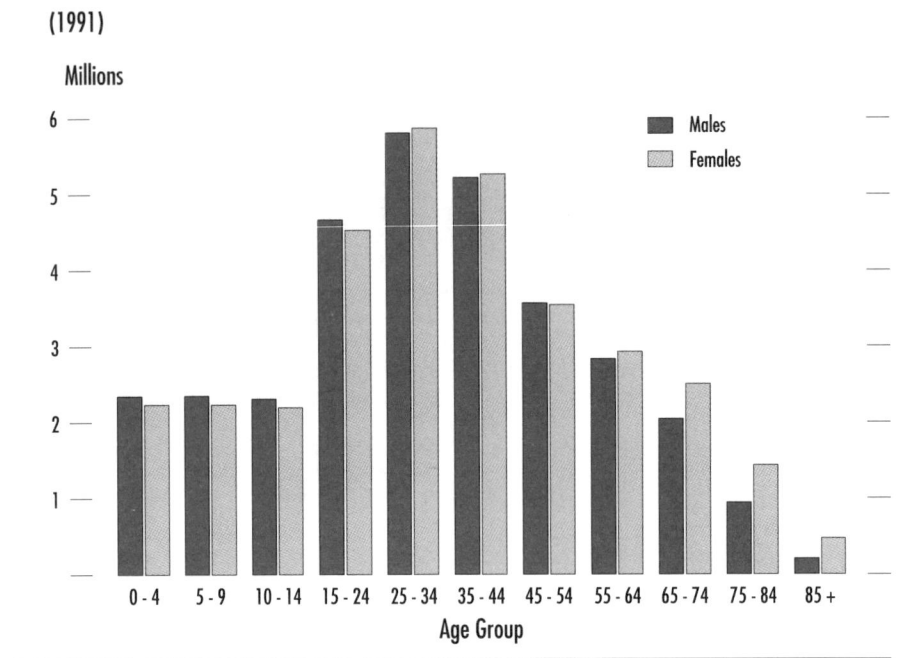

[Bar chart showing population in millions by age group (0-4, 5-9, 10-14, 15-24, 25-34, 35-44, 45-54, 55-64, 65-74, 75-84, 85+) for Males and Females]

Prepared by the Centre for International Statistics

A huge bulge dominates any graph of the age structure of the Canadian population. It's the baby boom, the great wave of people who were born between the late 1940s and the early 1960s. They outnumber both the generation that came before them and the one that came after.

For many years, birthrates in Canada have been much lower than when the Boomers were children. This is consistent with trends in other industrialized nations. As a result, it is likely that as the years pass, that bulge will simply move to the right on the chart.

And so what?

There are so many baby boomers that they have dominated our society all their lives. When they were children, most popular entertainment focused on parents and children. When they were young adults, the world swayed to their groovy beat. The expansive '80s, in some ways, celebrated their growing power and self-confidence. Now in the '90s, they are hunkering down. They have most of the good jobs. They are coming into control of much of the economy. Most politicians today are Boomers.

How does this look to the senior, the university graduate, or the high school student? It would be easy for their interests to be overlooked due to demands from the biggest and most self-absorbed generation ever.

Canada's first families

Even before the first European settlers arrived, this land we call Canada was home to diverse peoples: the Naskapi, Gitksan, Dene, Ojibway, Dakota, Micmac, Huron, Inuit, Cree, Salish, Innu, Mohawk, Tlingit, Maliseet, Gwich'in, Saulteaux, and many others. Hundreds of years later, in 1991, one million Canadians reported Aboriginal origins.

3. Aboriginal Origins:
Métis, Inuit and North American Indian

Non-Aboriginal origins 25,991,370 — 96%

Aboriginal origins 1,002,675

North American Indian only	365,375	= 36%
North American Indian and non-Aboriginal	379,470	= 38%
Métis only	75,150	= 8%
Métis and non-Aboriginal	99,560	= 10%
Inuit only	30,085	= 3%
Inuit and non-Aboriginal	12,915	= 1%
Other	40,120	= 4%

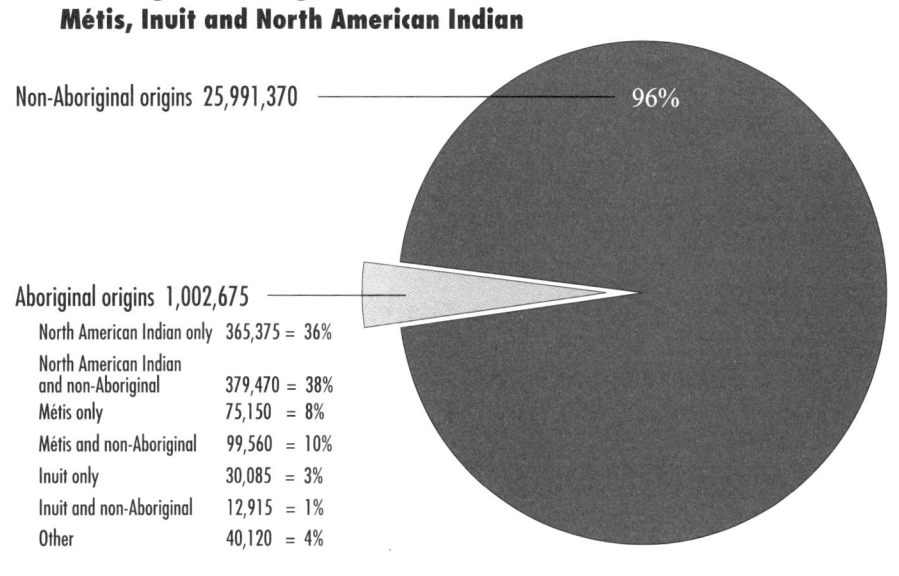

Prepared by the Centre for International Statistics

Over 470,000 Canadians reported a single Aboriginal origin. Of these, 78% were North American Indians, 16% were Métis and 6% were Inuit. Another 532,000 Canadians reported an Aboriginal origin in combination with other origins (most often non-Aboriginal, but sometimes another Aboriginal origin). Again, the majority of these had North American Indian origins. The Inuit were the least likely of the three groups to report mixed or multiple origins. In fact, the Inuit were the only one of the three groups to have more single-origin respondents than multiple-origin respondents.

The Vanier Institute of the Family

Ninety-six percent of Canadians come from somewhere else

Four percent of Canadians today report Aboriginal origins. All the rest - 96% - stem from all over the world.

The influence of Canada's two founding nations still strongly influences our national character and heritage. Sixty-nine percent of Canadians claim at least some British or French blood. In 1991, 28% of the population reported British-only origins, while 23% reported French-only origins.

An increasing proportion of the population report ethnic origins that are neither French nor British (31% in 1991 up from 25% in 1986). Ethnic origins other than Aboriginal, British and French include European only (15%), Asian only (6%), and other (6%), which include African, Latin, Central and South American, Caribbean and other multiple origins.

4. Ethnic Origins
(1991)

British 28%
British and French 4%
French 23%

British and/or French and other 14%
European 15%
Asian 6%
Aboriginal 4%
Other 6%

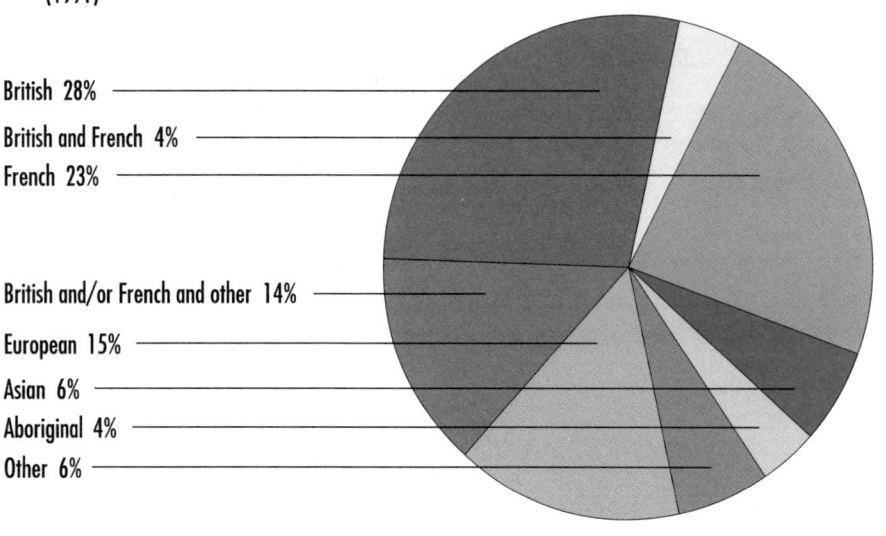

Prepared by the Centre for International Statistics

Immigration has accounted for about 20% of the growth in population since the beginning of this century. Policies over the years have set limits restricting the number and type of immigrants admitted to Canada.

In the mid-1960s immigration to Canada was enthusiastically favoured. However, by the mid-1970s, when large cohorts of baby boomers joined the work force, the need for immigrants was questioned. Currently, a target level for immigration is set by the immigration minister in consultation with the provinces regarding demographic and labour market needs. In 1991, over two hundred thousand immigrants were admitted to Canada, bringing the total number of foreign-born immigrants to 4,342,890, or 16% of the total population.

The origin of immigrants to Canada has changed. In the late 1960s, almost one third of all new immigrants came from European countries. U.S. born immigrants accounted for 9.3% of newcomers. Today, only 2.4% of new immigrants are U.S. born and about one out of four of them are from Europe. The majority - 53% - come from Asian countries, most notably Eastern Asia.

5. Total Number of Immigrants Admitted to Canada

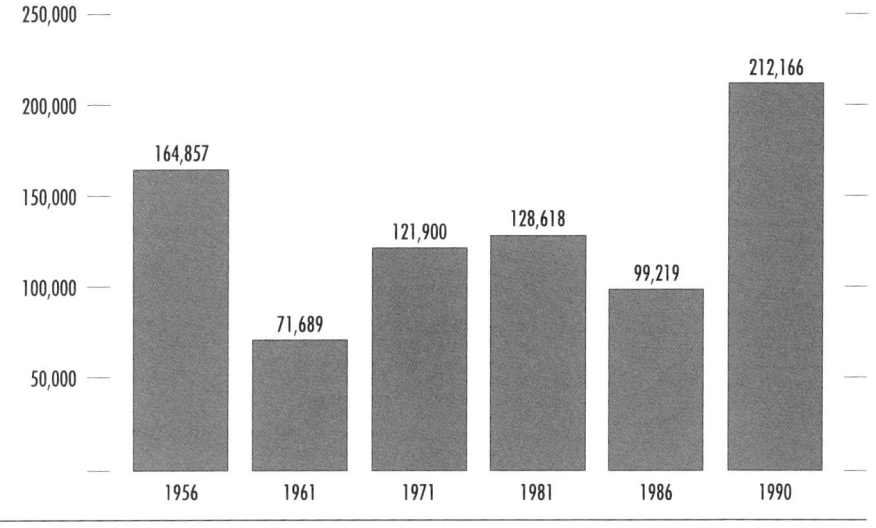

Year	Immigrants
1956	164,857
1961	71,689
1971	121,900
1981	128,618
1986	99,219
1990	212,166

Prepared by the Centre for International Statistics

There were 4.3 million people living in Canada in 1991 who had been born outside of Canada. Of these, more than half (54.6%) lived in Ontario, most in the Greater Toronto area. Only a very small proportion resided in the Atlantic provinces (1.7%) or in either of the Territories (0.1%). Some provinces attract far more immigrants than others. Ontario, for instance, has 37% of Canada's total population, but 54.6% of first generation Canadian residents. Quebec, on the other hand, has 25% of Canada's population but just 13.6% of its immigrants. Almost one in four Ontario residents (23%) was born outside Canada. In Atlantic Canada, just 3.3% of residents are first generation immigrants.

6. Distribution of Foreign-Born Population by Region

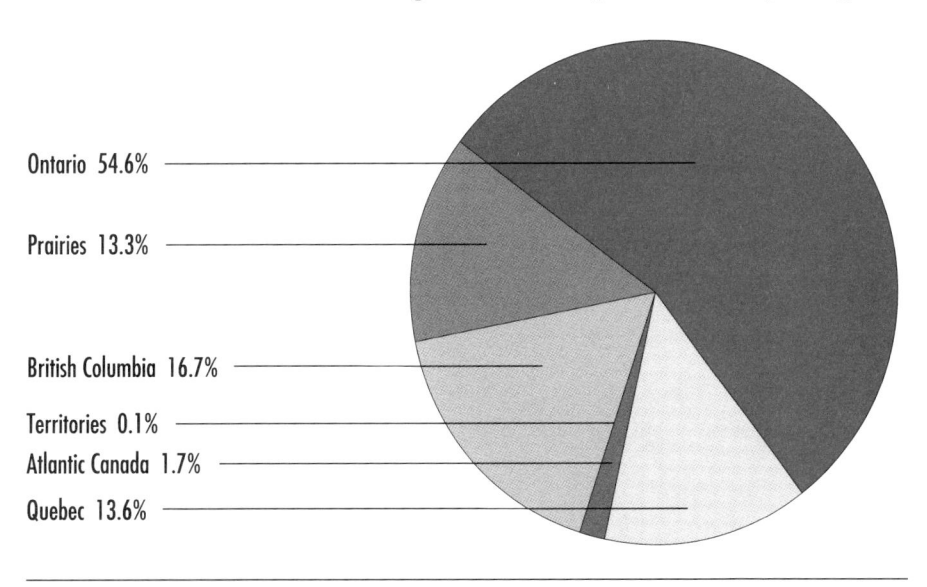

- Ontario 54.6%
- Prairies 13.3%
- British Columbia 16.7%
- Territories 0.1%
- Atlantic Canada 1.7%
- Quebec 13.6%

Prepared by the Centre for International Statistics

All immigrants, however, face a transition period during which they become familiar with Canadian culture and institutions and they have to learn a new language. The provision of services to assist new immigrants through this period will likely present a variety of challenges to Canadians and the government.
Jane Badets[16]

The Vanier Institute
of the Family

And so what?

Next to language, customs involving family may be the most notable identifying features of any culture. Cultures develop strong codes on family matters. Canada's population is mobile and dynamic, with a constant influx of new customs, traditions and styles. Established residents may worry over new ways that become part of everyday life. Immigrants may worry their children won't learn the ways of their ancestors. Our increasingly diverse people bring a rich variety of perspectives to the issues that lie at the heart of family responsibilities.

As Canadian as motherhood and language

7. Canadian Population by First Language

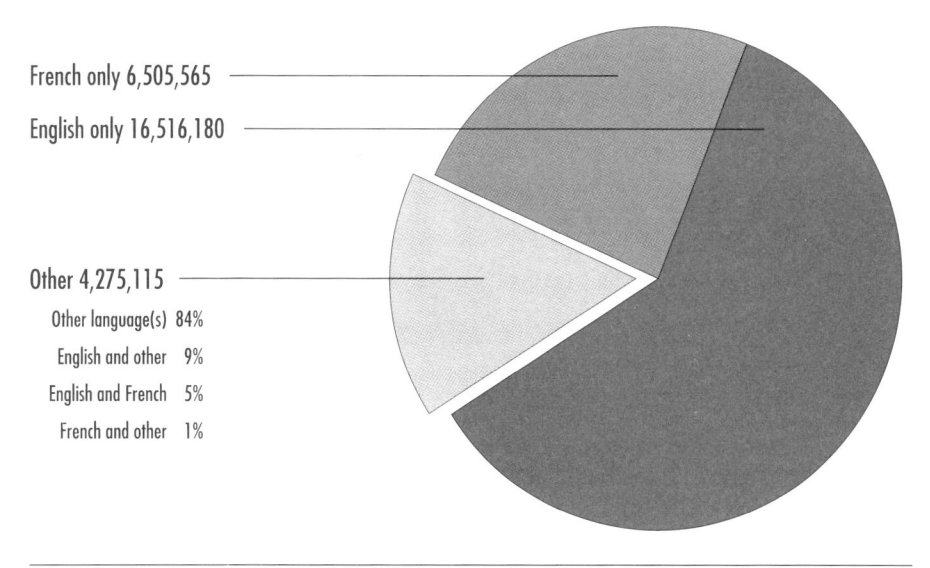

French only 6,505,565
English only 16,516,180

Other 4,275,115
- Other language(s) 84%
- English and other 9%
- English and French 5%
- French and other 1%

Prepared by the Centre for International Statistics

Language is at the heart of Canada's cultural identity. Beyond their two official languages, Canadians communicate in an impressive number and variety of languages. In the 1991 Census, 61% of Canadians reported English and 24% reported French as their only first language. The remainder of the population reported non-official languages or a combination of languages as their first language. An individual's "first language" is the one first learned at home in childhood and that she or he still understands. In some families, the children learn two or more languages simultaneously and thus report more than one first language.

In Quebec, 81% of the population reported French as their first language. Two percent reported French as one of their first languages.

Less than 1% of Canadians (245,740 people) claimed both official languages as their first. A non-official language was reported as the only first language of 13% of the population. Among these, Italian, Chinese and German were the most common. An additional 2% reported a non-official language as one of their first languages. Aboriginal languages were reported by less than 1% of the population. Some Indian reserves, however, were not completely enumerated in the 1991 Census, so this figure is approximate.

The Vanier Institute of the Family

Slightly over half (54%) of the population reporting a non-official language as their mother tongue were living in Montreal, Toronto or Vancouver.
Statistics Canada[17]

The family is the place where language is first learned; it is also the place where we learn our basic values and attitudes, traditions and customs, many basic skills, our way to assess and handle the world around us; and it is the place where we first learn to learn.
The Vanier Institute of the Family[18]

Canada's families
Predominantly Christian, but church influence is slipping

8. Religious Affiliation in Canada

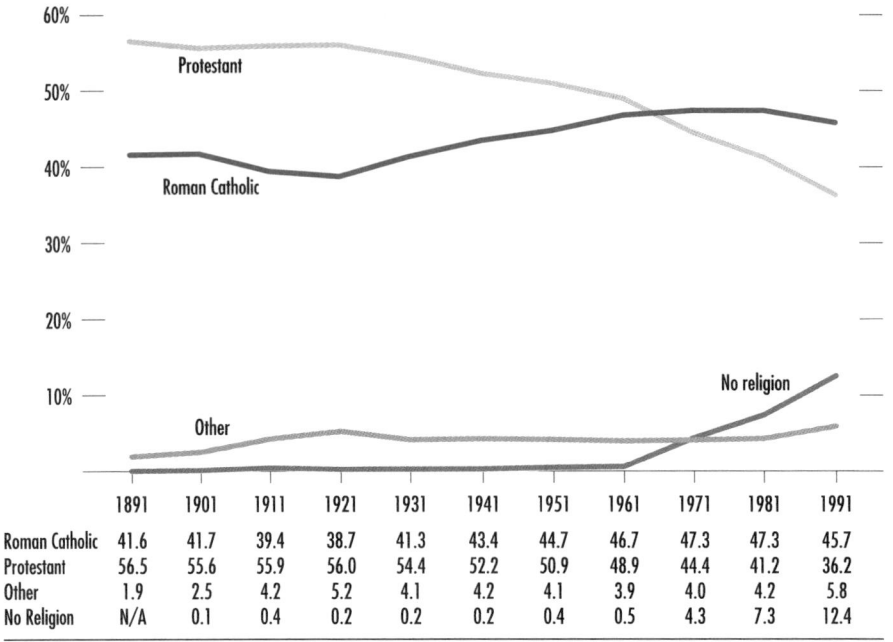

	1891	1901	1911	1921	1931	1941	1951	1961	1971	1981	1991
Roman Catholic	41.6	41.7	39.4	38.7	41.3	43.4	44.7	46.7	47.3	47.3	45.7
Protestant	56.5	55.6	55.9	56.0	54.4	52.2	50.9	48.9	44.4	41.2	36.2
Other	1.9	2.5	4.2	5.2	4.1	4.2	4.1	3.9	4.0	4.2	5.8
No Religion	N/A	0.1	0.4	0.2	0.2	0.2	0.4	0.5	4.3	7.3	12.4

Prepared by the Centre for International Statistics

Among the young people who currently say they have no religious preference, 47% will be looking to religious groups for baptisms and the like, 69% for weddings, and 77% for funerals!
    Reginald Bibby[19]

As it has for over 100 years, Canada remains predominantly Christian. The mix of Christian denominations is changing, however, and Christianity's preeminence in Canadian life is weakening.

In 1991, eight out of ten Canadians were either Roman Catholic or Protestant. Until 1961, Protestants outnumbered Catholics. The year 1971 marked the first time since Confederation that Catholics outnumbered Protestants. Today, Catholics, at 46% of the population, make up the largest religious group in Canada.

Other religions, however, have been practiced here since before Canada existed. Aboriginal peoples were excluded from the earliest census collections, and therefore, their religions were not included. Even so, in 1891, almost 2% of Canadians reported religions other than Christian. In 1991, almost 6% of Canadians were affiliated with other religions. "Other" Canadian religions include Eastern Orthodox (387,000 people), Jewish (318,000 people), Eastern non-Christian religions such as Buddhism, Islam, Hindu, and Sikh (a total of 747,000 people), and para-religious groups (28,000 people).

The number of people reporting no religious affiliation continues to increase steadily. In 1991, 12.4% of the population indicated no religious affiliation, a 90% increase since 1981.

And so what?

Three decades ago, Christianity influenced many aspects of Canadian life. Practices and regulations concerning alcohol sales, store openings, prayer in the schools, sexuality, contraception, marriage and divorce all reflected this influence.

Religious involvement was once the norm; in the 1950s, 85% of Roman Catholics and 40% of Protestants attended services every week. Canadians today, though, want religion "*à la carte,*"[20] not the full dinner. In general, they choose the observances and services they want. Less than three in ten Canadians attend services weekly. And while young Canadians told a survey in 1987 that they remain religious in their beliefs, only a small number of them attended religious services regularly, and they reported low enjoyment of religion. Even so, three out of four young Canadians said they would turn to religious groups for birth-related ceremonies in the future, and four in five said the same about weddings.

Canadian families
How'r ya gonna keep 'em down on the farm?

9. Urban/Rural Locations of Canadians

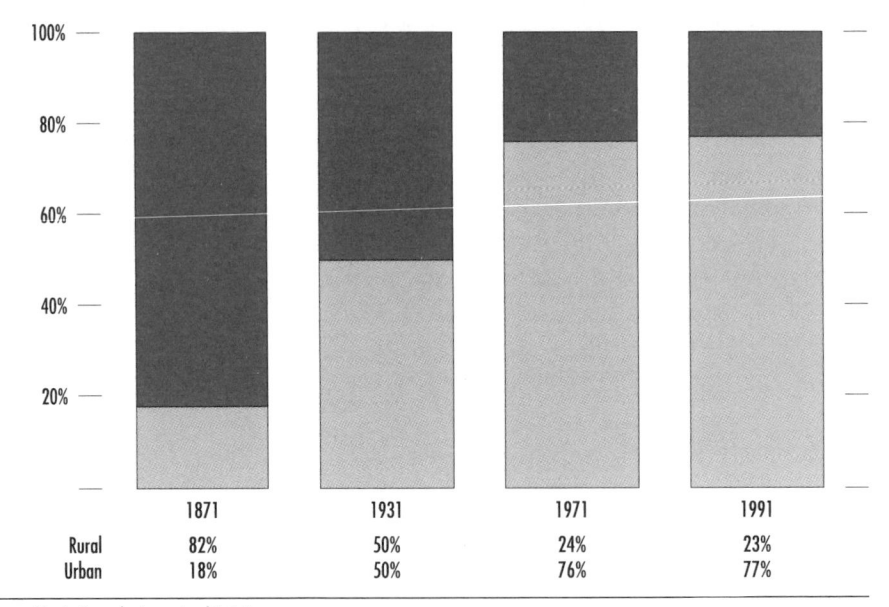

	1871	1931	1971	1991
Rural	82%	50%	24%	23%
Urban	18%	50%	76%	77%

Prepared by the Centre for International Statistics

Among Canadians who are employed full-time, the average commuting time is 48 minutes.

Take just the nine largest cities in Canada: Vancouver, Edmonton, Calgary, Winnipeg, Hamilton, Toronto, Ottawa-Hull, Montreal and Quebec City. In 1931, they had less than one third of the population. Now they house about half of it.

John Kettle[21]

Contrary to our back-woodsy reputation, three quarters of Canadians are now urban dwellers. And more than 30% of all Canadians live in the three largest cities: Toronto, Montreal and Vancouver.

There has been little change in the percentage of city-dwellers over the last twenty years. Prior to 1971, however, the change was swift and overwhelming. In 1871, only two out of every ten Canadians lived in urban areas. In 1931, the population was divided evenly between rural and urban areas. By 1971, three out of four Canadians lived in cities. Immigration has been a factor in the increase as well as people leaving the farms and rural communities for city life.

And leave the farm they did. In 1941, 27% of the population (over 3 million Canadians) lived in farm families; by 1991, there were 867,000 people living on farms, representing only 3.2% of the total population.

And so what?

Many of our images of family date back to the "good old days" when most Canadians lived on farms. Back then, families supplied most of their own needs, and every member of the family played a role in producing food, making clothes, building shelter and so on. Family members were interdependent on one another for their very survival. Today, the interdependence is still there, but families do not directly provide for as many of their own needs, particularly as more and more family members are employed outside of the home. Instead, they purchase an increasing number of the goods and services that they consume. This shift from rural to urban living is reflected in virtually every nation worldwide. In turn, it has given rise to many of the other great social changes and challenges of our times such as smaller families, higher divorce rates, social mobility, greater anonymity and less cohesive communities.

How many Canadians live in families?
Numbers are up but percentages are down

Table I – Changes in Population and the Number of Canadians living in Families

	1971	1981	1991	percent change 1971-1991
Total population in private households*	21.0	23.8	26.7	27%
Number of people living in families*	18.8	20.6	22.5	
Percent	89%	87%	84%	20%
Number of people not living in families*	2.2	3.2	4.2	
Percent	11%	13%	16%	88%
Number of families*	5.0	6.3	7.4	46%

* In millions

Note: Statistics Canada defines a family as a currently-married or common-law couple with or without never-married children, or a single-parent with never-married children, in the same dwelling.

Prepared by the Centre for International Statistics[22]

A vast majority of Canadians live in families. Over the last 20 years, however, the proportion of all Canadians living in family households has decreased substantially, from 89% in 1971 to 84% in 1991. This trend is due to a combination of factors, including an aging population with a larger number of elderly people living alone, an increase in the divorce rate, and a larger number of younger people postponing marriage until later in life.

And so what?

Marriage and family remain popular. Over the past two decades the number of families has increased by 46%. At the same time, however, the number of people *not* living in families has increased even more rapidly. Combined with the drop in the proportion of Canadians living in families, the figures tell us that families are getting smaller and that more of us, whether by choice or by circumstance, now live alone.

Whether it is through marriage, cohabitation, remarriage, parenting, or caring for kin, almost all Canadians, including those who live alone, have chosen to commit themselves to others in the context of their families. Time and again, Canadians declare that it is their families that are most important to them. Accordingly, the interests of individuals cannot be well served if our public policies and institutions do not respect the roles and responsibilities we assume as fathers and mothers, sons and daughters, brothers and sisters, grandparents and grandchildren, cousins, aunts and uncles.

The Vanier Institute of the Family

The rhetoric of family crisis has persisted as a theme in our culture for more than a century.
Arlene Skolnick[23]

One of the oldest human needs is having someone to wonder where you are when you don't come home at night.
Margaret Mead[24]

Although Canadian families experience many problems, for better or worse, the majority of Canadian marriages do last for a lifetime.
Robert Glossop[25]

The Vanier Institute of the Family

Family is content, not form.
   Gloria Steinem[26]

We tend to assume either that our own family experiences are typical or that other families approach some kind of ideal and our own is an exception.
   Alison Hayford[27]

The family patterns of the 1950s are as much in need of explanation as are the departures from them that have occurred since then.... In fact, the decade stands out as an unusual one for twentieth-century family life, whose historical trends have been falling birth rates, rising divorce rates, and later ages of marriages.
   Arlene Skolnick[28]

Canada's changing families
Diversity is now the norm

10. Family Types "Out of 100 Families..."

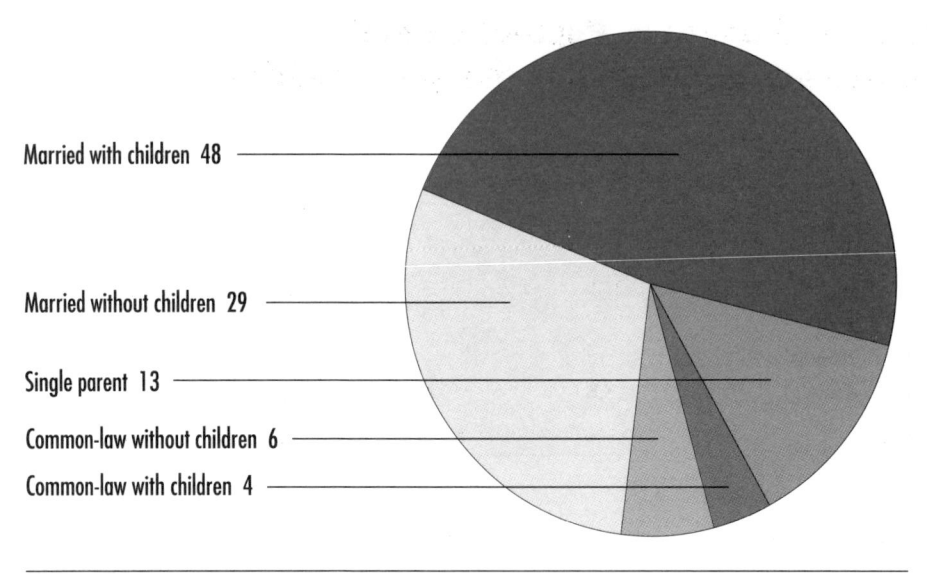

Married with children 48
Married without children 29
Single parent 13
Common-law without children 6
Common-law with children 4

Prepared by the Centre for International Statistics

The balance has tipped in the make-up of Canada's families. In 1986, 52 out of every 100 Canadian families consisted of married couples with never-married children living at home. By 1991, the combination of all other family types outnumbered these families. The second-largest family type in both 1986 and 1991 was married couples without children living at home. This group is composed of childless couples and empty-nesters.

Almost 9 out of 10 Canadian families (87.1%) were husband-wife families in 1991. Lone-parent families accounted for 13 of every 100 families in both 1986 and 1991 (10.7% of families were female lone-parent families and 2.3% were male lone-parent families). The biggest increase was in common-law families, which grew from seven to ten of every 100 families between 1986 and 1991. Four out of ten common-law families have children living at home.

And so what?

We have to be very sure what we mean when we say the word "family." By making assumptions about what a family is "supposed" to look like, we can overlook the needs and realities of Canada's diverse families. Such assumptions can result in all kinds of problems. Why doesn't a particular town's building code allow "granny flats?" Why do some schools assume there will always be a mother at home during the day if the child gets ill? Why do some politicians make single mothers nervous when they talk about "old-fashioned family values?"

The make-up of Canada's families is changing, much as families are changing around the world. Businesses, organizations and governments have no choice but to adjust to these changes and adapt to the diverse circumstances and needs of today's families.

How families look in different provinces and territories

Table II – Provincial and Territorial Family Profile (1991)

	Total Number of Families	Total Families Without Children* Number	%	Total Families With Children* Number	% of all	% two-parent	% lone-parent
CAN	7,356,170	2,579,850	35	4,776,320	65	80	20
NF	150,715	37,775	25	112,945	75	84	16
PE	33,895	10,285	30	23,610	70	81	19
NS	244,610	82,650	34	161,960	66	80	20
NB	198,010	63,105	32	134,900	68	80	20
QC	1,883,235	642,060	34	1,241,175	66	78	22
ON	2,726,735	954,015	35	1,772,725	65	81	19
MB	285,935	102,380	36	183,550	64	80	20
SK	257,560	94,400	37	163,155	63	81	19
AB	667,985	230,205	34	437,780	66	81	19
BC	887,660	358,070	40	529,590	60	80	20
NT	12,725	2,595	20	10,130	80	80	20
YT	7,105	2,305	32	4,805	68	78	18

* Never-married child(ren) of any age living at home.

Prepared by the Centre for International Statistics[31]

Just over one third of families in Canada do not have children living at home. British Columbia has the highest proportion of such families, while families in the Northwest Territories and in Newfoundland are the most likely to have children living at home. Newfoundland also has proportionally fewer lone-parent families.

Generally, however, the proportion of lone-parent and two-parent families remains fairly consistent across the country. Lone-parent families account for between 12% and 16% of all families (those with and without children) in every province and territory. Nationally, 13% of all families are lone-parent families. Of families with children, one in five is headed by a lone parent.

The Vanier Institute of the Family

[Families have] weathered combinations of step, foster, single, adoptive, surrogate, frozen embryo, and sperm bank. They've multiplied, divided, extended and banded into communities. They've been assaulted by technology, battered by sexual revolutions, and confused by role reversals. But they are still here...playing to a full house.
— Erma Bombeck[29]

...Whether truncated by death or divorce or by the departure of grown children, we don't stop being a family. And a family doesn't need two parents to make a family.
— Letty Cottin Pogrebin[30]

Canadian families are shrinking

11. Trends in Family Size in Canada

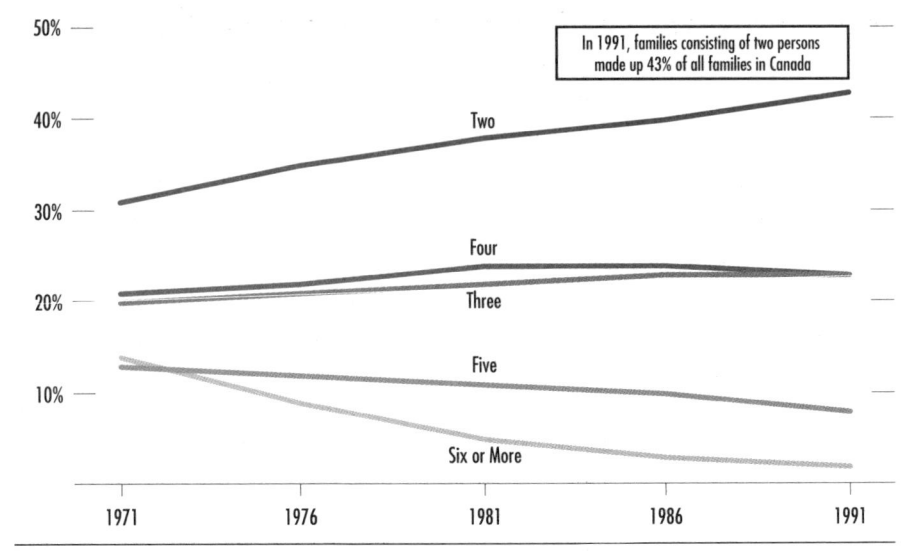

In 1991, families consisting of two persons made up 43% of all families in Canada

Prepared by the Centre for International Statistics

Canadian families have decreased in size in the last two decades from an average of 3.7 persons to 3.1 persons in 1991. The smaller average size is due largely to a sharp increase in the number of two-person families. In 1971, three out of ten families were two-person families. By 1991, it was four in ten. Increases in the number of lone-parent families and childless couples including "empty nesters" contributed to this trend. During the same period, the number of large families (six or more persons) decreased sharply - from 14% of all families down to fewer than 3%.

And so what?

The "downsizing" of Canadian families has affected every facet of society. We now see nearly-empty large houses that were once homes to large families. Businesses now sell products and services designed for the needs of two or three, rather than five or six or more. Smaller families also mean smaller kin networks – fewer siblings, cousins, wedding guests and so on.

As Arlene Skolnick has observed, in the nineteenth century: "Because people lived shorter lives and had more children, a woman could expect to live her entire life with children in the home. Today, the average woman can expect to live more than 33 years after her last child has left the house."[32]

In addition, Marvin B. Sussman notes that "Caring for one's own has had a long history and persists today in both expectations and practices. Family members are the major caregivers to their dependent members. The growing requests from care receivers come at a time when there is a paucity of women to assume traditional caregiving roles, because they are settled in careers and jobs. Also, fewer caregivers will be available as a consequence of lower birthrates of the post-World War II baby boom cohort. Ethical, moral and legal issues regarding the extension of life of the older population; living without quality; care of the ill and disabled; best investment of dollars in medical care and social services will be assiduously debated in the following years."[33]

...the decision to have children is increasingly based on economic, social and psychological factors and less on religious beliefs or a sense that having children is the 'right' thing to do.

In 1945, 60% of Canadians said the ideal number (of children) was four or more. By 1985, an almost identical proportion said that two or less was ideal.

A growing proportion of new babies have no brothers or sisters. About half of all new babies born now are first children compared with about 40% in 1971.

Roger Sauvé[34]

Extended families rare in Canada today

12. Percent of Non-elderly Families* With at Least One Elderly Member, by Age of Family Head

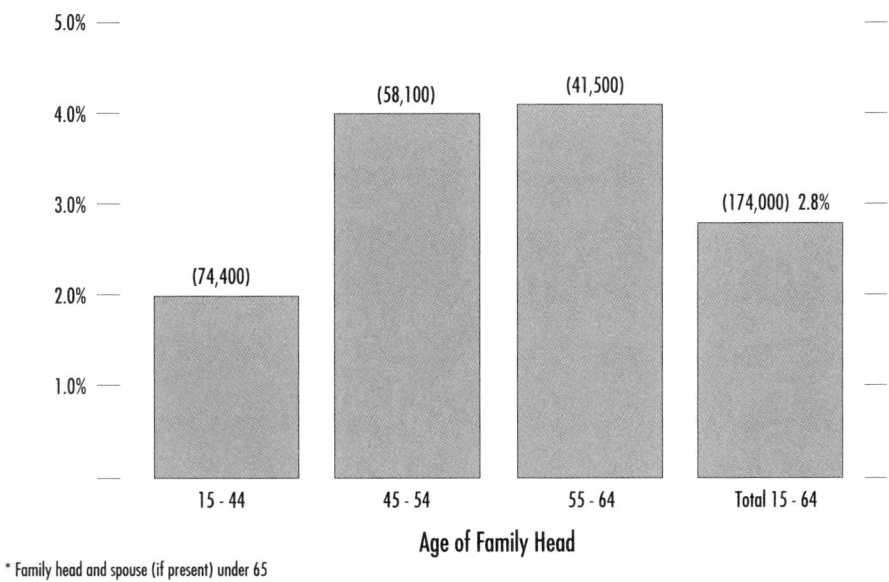

Age of Family Head	Percent	Count
15 - 44	2.0%	(74,400)
45 - 54	4.0%	(58,100)
55 - 64	4.0%	(41,500)
Total 15 - 64	2.8%	(174,000)

* Family head and spouse (if present) under 65

Prepared by the Centre for International Statistics

In 1991 there were 174,000 non-elderly families – defined by Statistics Canada as those with both the family "head" and spouse (if present) under 65 years of age – with an elderly relative living with them. Only 2% of younger families – those with the head of the family under 45 years of age – have an elderly relative living with them. Approximately 4% of all other non-elderly families – those with the head of the family aged from 45 to 64 years of age – have an elderly relation in their home.

And so what?

Whether by choice or necessity, most seniors do not live with their children today. As a result, when they need assistance, they often must turn to people outside their families, either on a voluntary or a paid basis. Seniors who must pay for home maintenance, cleaning and other support services require more income than those who live with their extended families.

By the same token, these seniors are not available to render services to younger family members. In extended families, many seniors are often able to help their children and grandchildren by providing child care, cooking, and doing maintenance and other household chores. Some may also provide direct financial assistance to the household.

One wonders if more families will be caring for their elders in their homes as the proportion of seniors in the population increases in the coming years.

The Vanier Institute of the Family

The most common type of extended family in Canada includes a nuclear family plus a widowed parent unable to live alone. In 1986, 7 percent of women aged 65 and over compared with 3 percent of elderly men lived in extended family situations...
— Maureen Baker[35]

The extended family... remains important in Canada and in many other countries as a support group. Relatives who do not share a residence, may try to live in the same neighbourhood, visit regularly, telephone daily, assist each other with child care, provide economic and emotional support, and help find one another employment and accommodation... This kind of living arrangement has been called the MODIFIED EXTENDED FAMILY.
— Maureen Baker[36]

Sandwich generation eaten up between children and aging parents

13. Percent of Families With at Least One Dependent Child and One Elderly Member

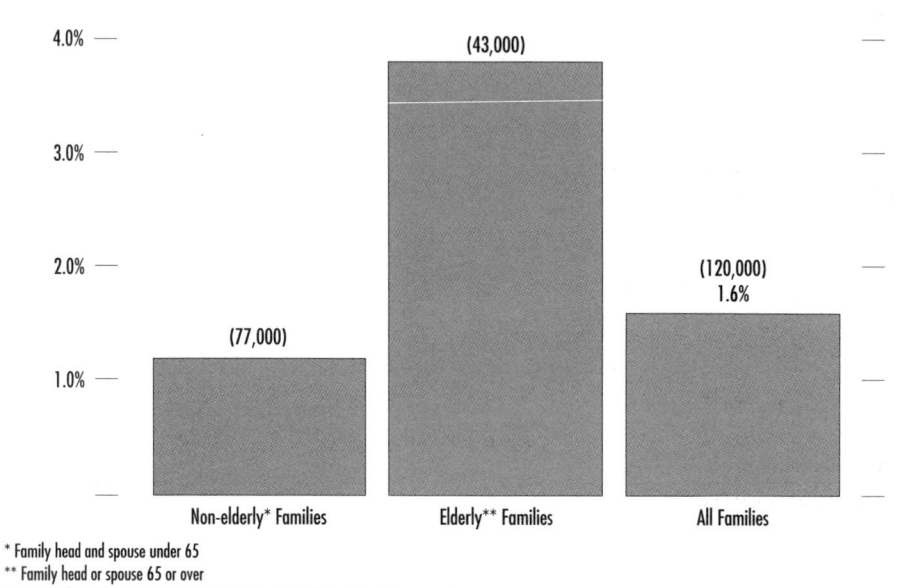

[Bar chart showing:
- Non-elderly* Families: ~1.2% (77,000)
- Elderly** Families: ~3.8% (43,000)
- All Families: 1.6% (120,000)]

* Family head and spouse under 65
** Family head or spouse 65 or over

Prepared by the Centre for International Statistics

Because middle-aged people could have children and even grandchildren who require attention, as well as parents who require personal assistance, they have been called the SANDWICH GENERATION... Some adult children invite elderly parents to live with them, but more often help them to maintain their own homes. Children may shop for aging parents, cut lawns or shovel snow, visit, and provide companionship and emotional support. They also may help elderly parents to identify and access available social services, purchase home care, or move into new accommodation more convenient to their needs.
Maureen Baker[37]

As the baby boomers age, more and more of them are assuming responsibility for both their dependent children and their aging parents. Caught in the middle as they are, they are known as the "sandwich generation."

Despite their dual responsibilities, few of them actually live with their parents. Only 77,000 non-elderly families, 1.2% of the total number of non-elderly families, had at least one dependent child and at least one elderly family member living with them. At the same time, 43,000 elderly families (3.8% of the total number of elderly families) had at least one dependent child living with them.

And so what?

While it is relatively rare for families with children to live with older family members in Canada, responsibility for aging parents is not so rare. And while it is most common for seniors and their spouses to live on their own without younger family members, many still look to younger family members for support of various kinds.

The Vanier Institute of the Family

Look who's getting married!

14. Marital Status of Canadian Population Age 15 and Over
(1991)

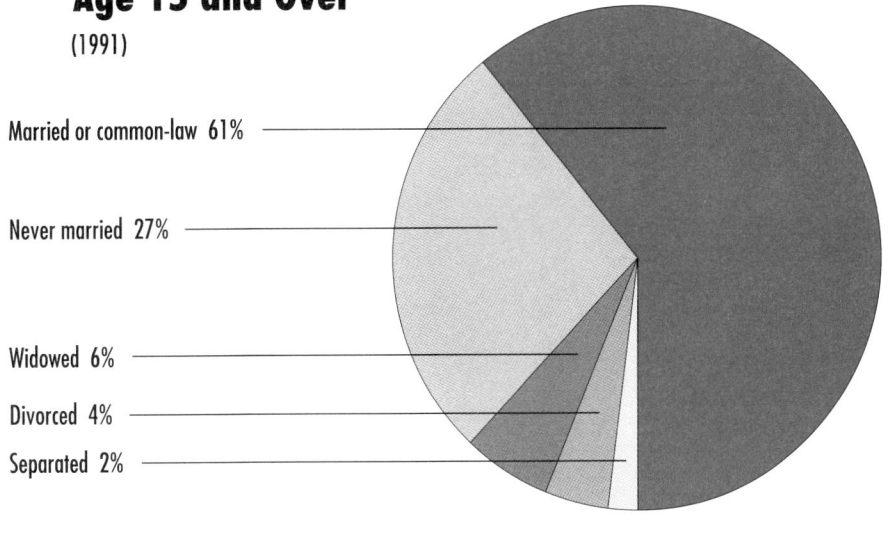

- Married or common-law 61%
- Never married 27%
- Widowed 6%
- Divorced 4%
- Separated 2%

Prepared by the Centre for International Statistics

Most Canadians (61%) aged 15 and over are married or living with a common-law spouse. Another 26% have never been married, while 6% are widowed. Only a very small proportion of Canadians are at any one time separated (2%) or divorced (4%). Of course, many more who have been divorced have remarried and many of those who today are married will, sometime in the future, separate from their spouse.

15. Marital Status by Age
(1991)

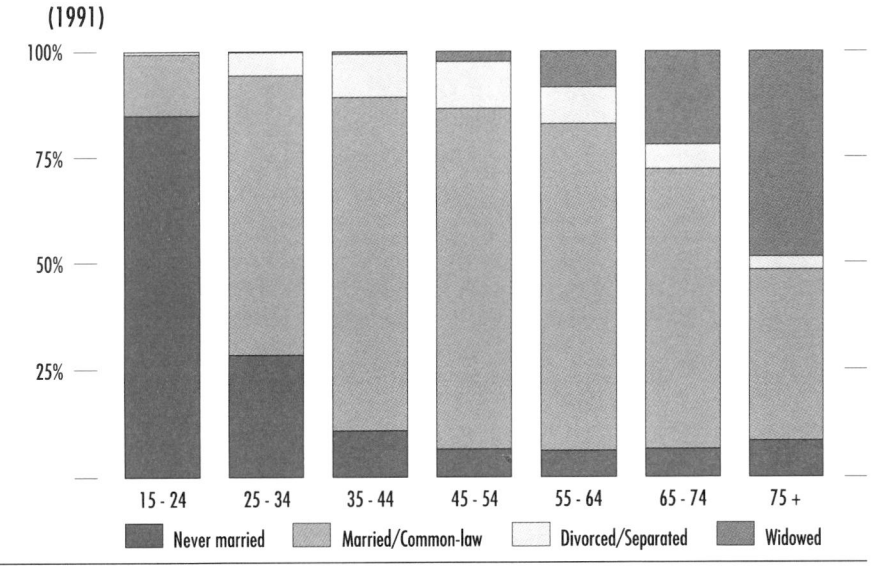

Age groups: 15-24, 25-34, 35-44, 45-54, 55-64, 65-74, 75+

Legend: Never married | Married/Common-law | Divorced/Separated | Widowed

Prepared by the Centre for International Statistics

This chart tends to confirm what we intuitively know about the relationships between marital status and age. For example, very young adults are likely to have never been married, and older Canadians are more likely to be widowed.

Most Canadians under the age of 24 have never been in a marriage or common-law relationship. From the age of 25 onwards, however, Canadians who are married or living common-law outnumber the combined total of all other Canadians in that age range. There are substantially more people in marriages and common-law relationships in every age group except the very youngest (under 24) and the very oldest (75 and over).

The 35-44 age group has the greatest number of married/common-law Canadians, *and* the greatest number of divorced or separated Canadians.

The Vanier Institute of the Family

Quebec, on the other hand, had the highest proportion of women aged 75 and over who had never married (15% compared with the national average of 9%).
  Gordon Priest[38]

The Vanier Institute of the Family

Marriage
Still in fashion after all these years

16. Marriage Rates

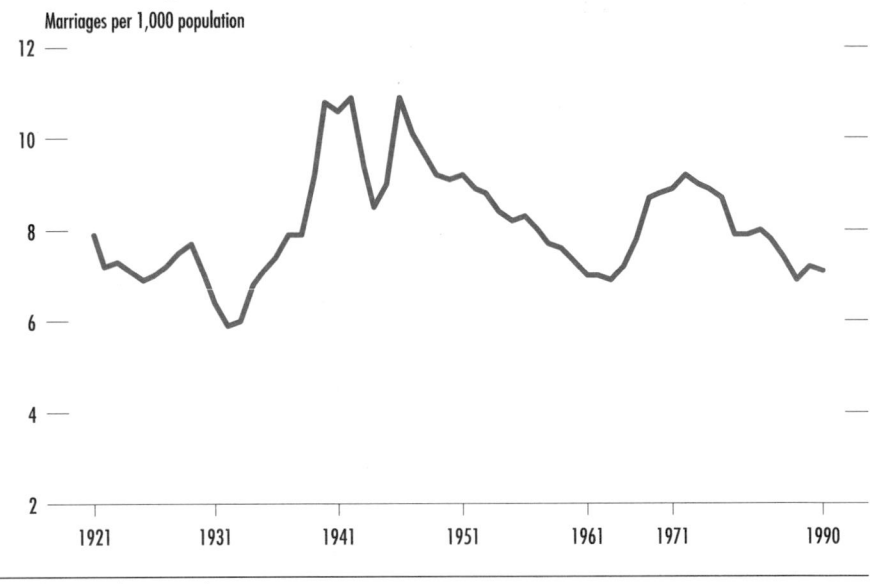

Marriages per 1,000 population

Prepared by the Centre for International Statistics

17. Trends in Marital Status: Population Age 15 and Over

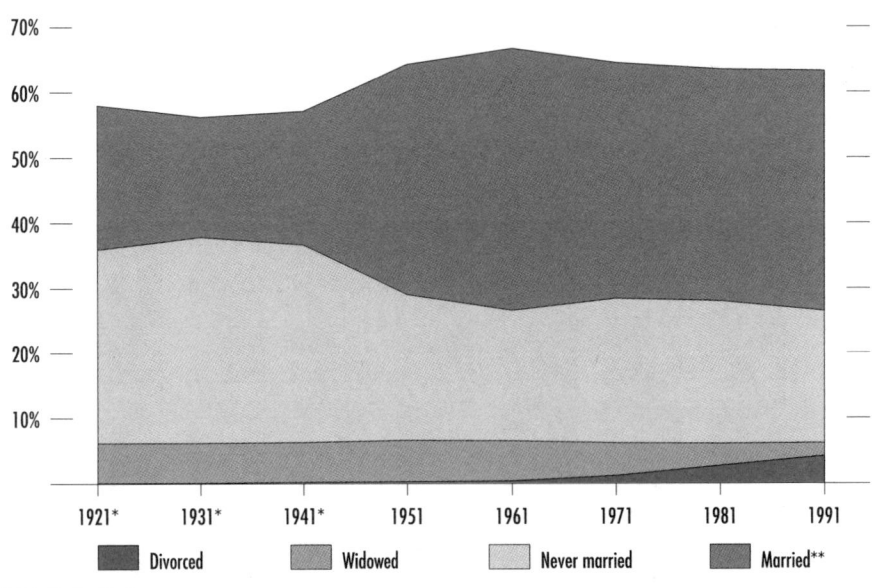

■ Divorced   ■ Widowed   ■ Never married   ■ Married**

* Excludes Newfoundland
** Includes common-law and, except for 1921, includes legally married but separated

Prepared by the Centre for International Statistics

Legal marriage is still the preferred lifestyle for the majority of adult Canadians. Even so, legal marriage is happening later and a growing percentage of adults are not marrying at all.

The latest information suggests that 14 percent of women and 17 percent of men will never marry. For both sexes, the proportion who will never marry has risen by about 6 to 7 percentage points since the early 1970s.

Those who are 'tying the knot' for the first time in a legal marriage are increasingly delaying the event.

— Roger Sauvé[39]

Marriage is about as popular as ever. In spite of more divorces, more Canadians (63%) now are legally married (married or separated) or living common-law than in 1921 (58%). After a steep rise after World War II, the proportion of married Canadians peaked in the 1960s, with two-thirds of Canadians married or living common-law. And while the proportion of divorced Canadians has increased since the '60s, it remains the lowest of all marital statuses. Just 4% of Canadians over 15 are currently divorced.

The fluctuating marriage rate of the last 70 years shows how economic and social circumstances influence the decision and timing of marriage. The rate began to decline in the middle of the 1920s due to a worsening economic situation. During the Depression, it dipped to an all-time low of 5.9 marriages per 1,000 population in 1932. Many young Canadians with no jobs and money put off marriage plans. After 1932, the marriage rate began to rise along with the economy.

The Second World War created a stampede to the altar – a reaction to the uncertainty of life in wartime. There was also a more pragmatic reason – single men were drafted before married men. During the Conscription Crisis in 1942, marriage rates peaked at 10.9 per 1,000 population. In 1946, the marriage rate hit 10.9 again as the returning war veterans rushed to make up for lost time. After the mid-1940s, the marriage rate declined for 20 years. In 1951, more than 100 women out of a thousand between the age of 15 and 59 married for the first time. When the baby boomers came of marrying age, it received a boost for a few years in the early 1970s.

By 1990, however, the marriage rate, at 7.1, was similar to that of the 1920s. Only 60 out of a thousand women were marrying for the first time and just 47 out of a thousand men were, possibly reflecting an uncertain job market and the growing acceptance of single lifestyles and common-law marriage.

And so what?

While the marriage rate has had its ups and downs over the years, people are marrying today at about the rate of 75 years ago. The big change is that many more marriages today are remarriages. The first-marriage rate, as distinct from the overall marriage rate, has steadily declined for the last 40 years. And those who are marrying are waiting until they are older.

The Vanier Institute of the Family

As a result of current marriage trends...the proportion of adult life spent married is currently declining. Compared with women in 1945 - 1950, women today spend approximately 20 percent less of their adult lives married (Espenshade, 1985).
Teresa M. Cooney[40]

Love comes after marriage.
Inuit proverb[41]

The Vanier Institute of the Family

The original plot goes like this: first comes love. Then comes marriage. Then comes Mary with a baby carriage. But now there is a sequel: John and Mary break up. John moves in with Sally and her two boys. Mary takes the baby Paul. A year later, Mary meets Jack, who is divorced with three children. They get married. Paul, barely two years old, now has a mother, a father, a stepmother, a stepfather, and five stepbrothers and stepsisters – as well as four sets of grandparents (biological and step) and countless aunts and uncles. And guess what? Mary's pregnant again.
Barbara Kantrowitz and Pat Wingert[42]

Remarriage is the triumph of hope over experience.
Samuel Johnson[43]

The second time around...

18. First Marriages and Remarriages as Percentages of all Marriages

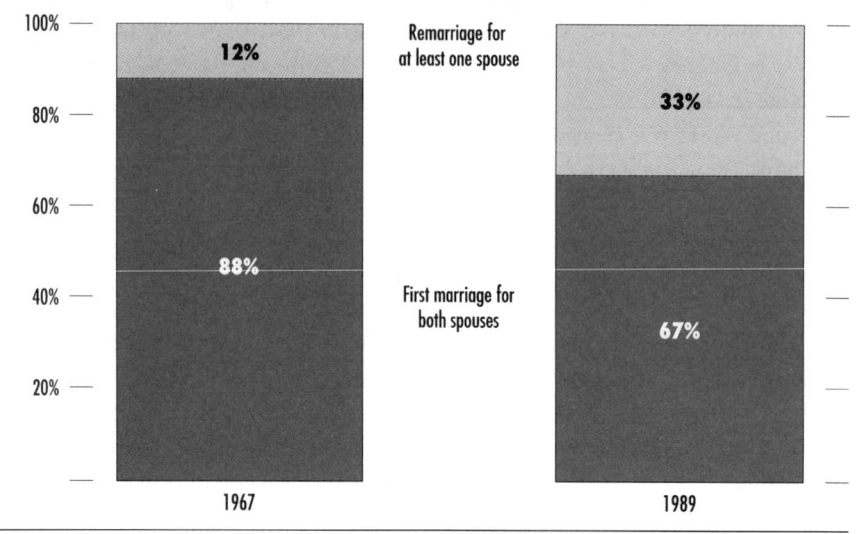

[Bar chart showing: 1967 — 88% First marriage for both spouses, 12% Remarriage for at least one spouse; 1989 — 67% First marriage for both spouses, 33% Remarriage for at least one spouse]

Calculated by the Centre for International Statistics

In 1967, almost nine out of ten newlyweds were tying the knot for the very first time. By 1989, however, a third of all marriages had at least one partner with previous experience in marriage. While the number of all marriages increased, the number of first marriages for both spouses declined slightly and remarriages tripled. Marriages between two previously-married persons almost quadrupled in number between 1967 and 1989. Divorced men tend to be older at remarriage than their female counterparts by more than three years. In 1990, the average age of remarriage for divorced men was 41.1 years, and for women, 37.5 years. The gap is even greater for widowed persons remarrying. In 1990, widowed men remarried at an average age of 60.8, and women, at an average age of 54.1.

What factors have sparked these sharp changes?
- The population is aging – there are just not as many young people today – either proportionately or absolutely – as there were in 1967.
- Changes in the divorce laws in 1968 and 1985 made divorces easier to get and remarriage more possible.
- People are living longer and are healthier at an older age. They have more time to remarry.
- Remarriage may be more socially acceptable.

And so what?

Today's high rates of separation, divorce and remarriage have helped to make it necessary to distinguish between family and household. People may leave their spouses, but the family ties they have forged continue in most cases.

Today's "blended families" illustrate the complex ties that occur as remarriage becomes more prevalent. In addition to children and step-children, family bonds develop between in-laws, grandparents and grandchildren, and other family members, regardless of whether the marriage remains intact. It is now not uncommon for children to have multiple sets of grandparents, parents, step-parents, step-siblings, half-siblings and so on. Family names, family holidays, and gift-giving are just a few examples of formerly simple traditions that can get exceedingly complex for "blended" or "recombined" families.

No hurry to the altar
Canadians are holding off tying the knot

19. Average Age at First Marriage

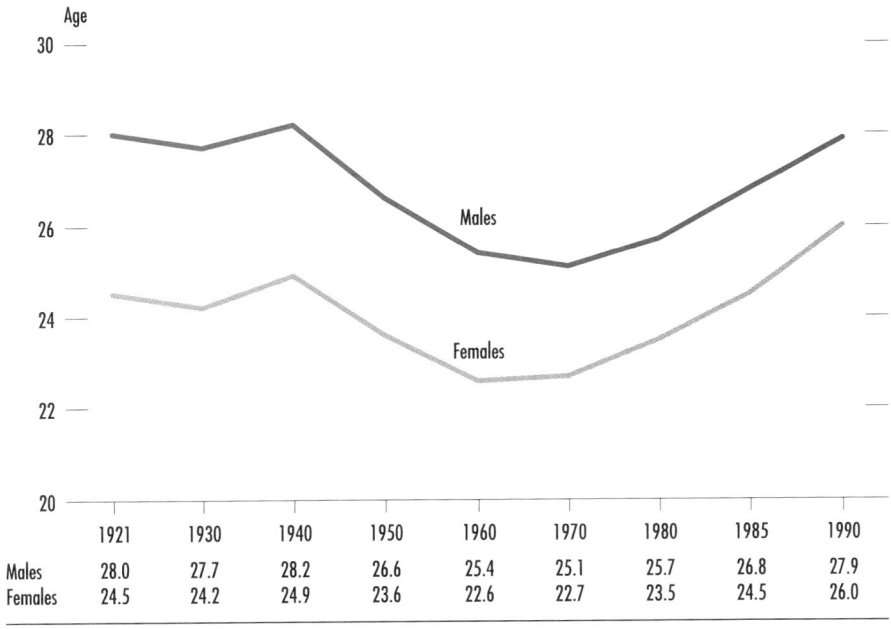

	1921	1930	1940	1950	1960	1970	1980	1985	1990
Males	28.0	27.7	28.2	26.6	25.4	25.1	25.7	26.8	27.9
Females	24.5	24.2	24.9	23.6	22.6	22.7	23.5	24.5	26.0

Prepared by the Centre for International Statistics

The average age at first marriage has been increasing for both men and women over the last twenty years as people delay marriage for various reasons: to finish their educations, establish careers, save some money, cohabit, or simply explore their options. In 1990, the average age of first-time brides was 26 years, and the average age of first-time grooms was 27.9 years. Those figures are up from 22.7 years for women and 25.1 years for men in 1970.

First-time marrying males are, on average, older than first-time marrying females by two to three years. Although this age gap is slowly shrinking, the tendency for men to marry at an older age than women has persisted as a strong societal norm characteristic of both first marriages and remarriages.

And so what?

The implications of women marrying at a younger age than men are immense. Given the combination of women's higher life expectancy and their tendency to marry older men, women are more likely to experience the death of a spouse, and often live considerable portions of their lives in widowhood. Most women, especially older ones, are not economically independent. The average earnings of women in the labour force are much lower, on average, than mens'. Thus the years of widowhood are, for a great number of women, years of poverty as well.

Perhaps most significantly, the increase in the average age at marriage suggests that it is not likely that birth rates will increase substantially.

The Vanier Institute of the Family

Women don't want to start having children as early as they used to, and generally don't want to marry until they're ready to have children.
John Kettle[44]

Early marriage loses its sheen
Teens avoiding marriage, first-marriages down

20. Age-specific First Marriage Rate for Females in Canada

Rate (per 1,000 never-married females)

Prepared by the Centre for International Statistics

21. Age-specific First Marriage Rate for Males in Canada

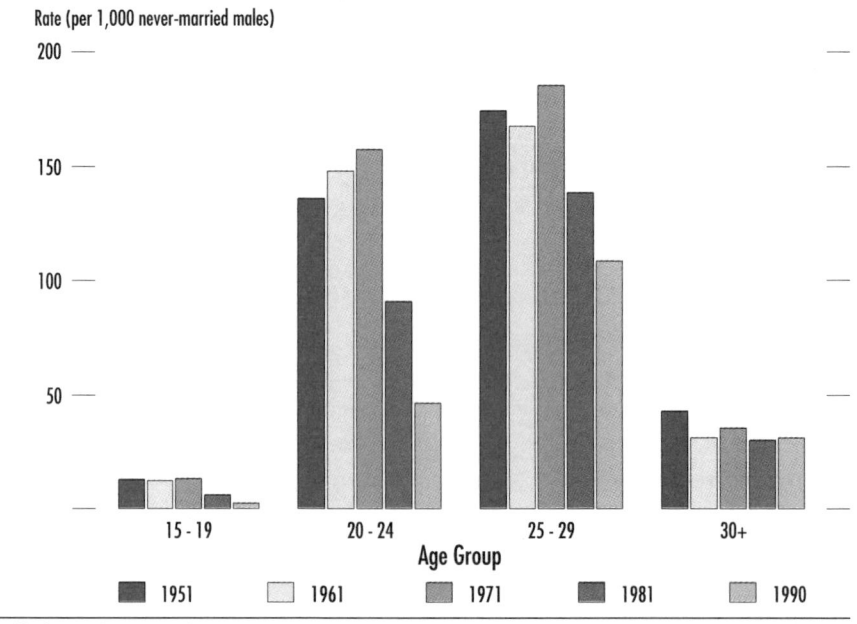

Rate (per 1,000 never-married males)

Prepared by the Centre for International Statistics

Canadians over thirty are more likely to marry for the first time than are teenagers. This is not new for men, but it is for women. In 1951, sixty-six out of a thousand teenage women married, by 1990 only 11 out of a thousand married.

First-marriage rates for women in their early twenties plunged as well, from 223 per thousand in 1961 to 88 in 1990. Women in their late twenties, rather than early twenties, are now the most likely to marry for the first time. Also, the data suggest that while many women are postponing marriage, a substantial number of women are foregoing marriage altogether.

Not surprisingly, first-marriage rates for men in all age groups have also dropped – most notably for men in their early twenties. In 1971, among men aged 20-24, 157 per thousand married; in 1990, only 46 did. Today, men over the age of 50 are much more likely to marry for the first time than are men under the age of 20. Fewer than three males in a thousand between the ages of 15 and 19 married in 1990, down from 13 in 1971.

First-marriage rates for men over the age of 30 have remained more stable than for other age groups over time.

And so what?

The trend toward later first marriages has wrought major changes. For example, it has contributed to lower fertility rates, higher population mobility, later household formation, and changing patterns of consumption of consumer goods and services. Another implication is that couples are waiting longer to become parents, so parents are, on average, older than those of previous generations. This can be advantageous in several ways. Parents may be more mature and their careers better established, so they may be able to offer better living standards to their children than their parents could to them. On the other hand, they may be more tired, more set in their ways, less healthy and less able to accommodate the rigors of parenting than previous generations.

One in ten "married" couples not married

22. Proportion of Population in Common-law Relationship
(1991)

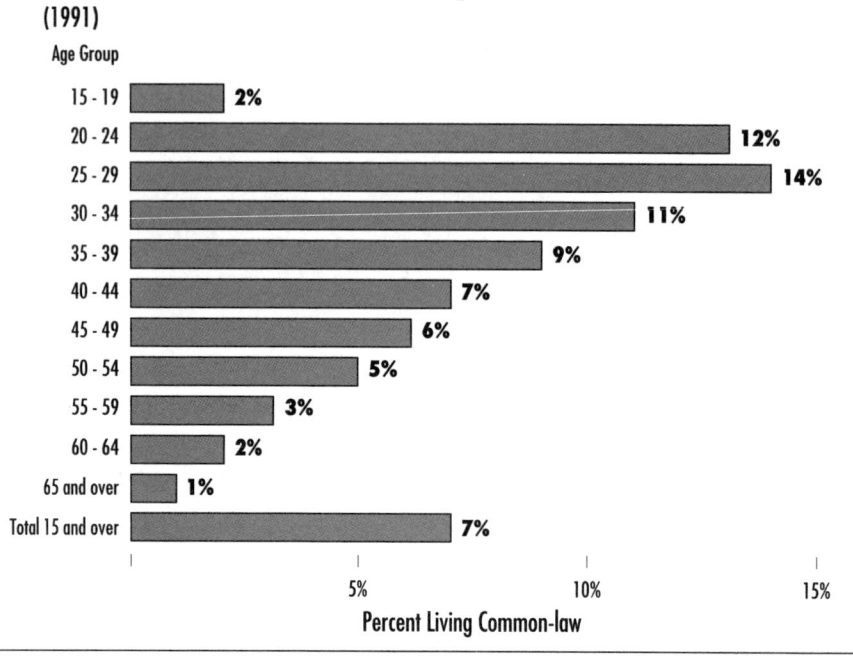

Age Group	Percent Living Common-law
15 - 19	2%
20 - 24	12%
25 - 29	14%
30 - 34	11%
35 - 39	9%
40 - 44	7%
45 - 49	6%
50 - 54	5%
55 - 59	3%
60 - 64	2%
65 and over	1%
Total 15 and over	7%

Prepared by the Centre for International Statistics

Of all Canadians over the age of 14 in 1991, 7% were living in common-law relationships. These common-law unions represented 10% of all Canadian families in 1991. Such relationships were most prevalent among young adults, with 12% of those in their early twenties and 14% of those in their late twenties living common-law. The proportion declines with each successive age group, to a low of 1% among senior citizens. Only a very small proportion of teenagers (2%) live in common-law relationships. Canadians over the age of 50 are more likely to be living common-law than are Canadians under the age of 20.

23. Legal Marital Status of Persons Living Common-law
(1991)

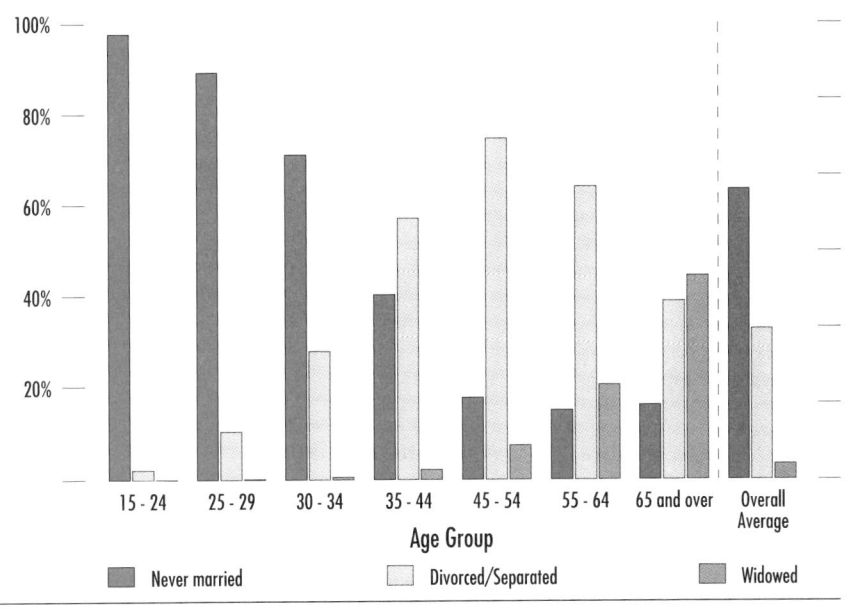

[Bar chart showing percentages by Age Group (15-24, 25-29, 30-34, 35-44, 45-54, 55-64, 65 and over, Overall Average) with categories: Never married, Divorced/Separated, Widowed]

Prepared by the Centre for International Statistics

People under the age of 35 who are living common-law typically have never been married. Between the ages of 35 and 64, most people living common-law are legally separated or divorced, whereas most seniors in common-law relationships are widowed. From examining the patterns, we see that among people in common-law relationships, the never-marrieds decrease with age, the widowed increase with age, and the divorced and separated component peaks in the middle of the age scale.

Overall, six in ten people (about 62%) in common-law relationships have never been married, about one third (32%) are divorced or separated, and the remainder are widowed.

And so what?

"Increasingly, couples are living together without going through a wedding ceremony although most of these will eventually marry, especially those who intend to have children. Young people who come from divorced families and older divorced adults are often reluctant to enter into legal marriage without some previous knowledge of what it is like to live with their partner. Living together may become more socially acceptable in the future as a "courtship pattern" or preliminary stage to marriage. In addition, those who are ideologically opposed to traditional marital roles will continue to see common-law relationships as an alternative to legal marriage."

Maureen Baker[46]

Co-vivant. Partner. Significant Other. Common-Law Spouse. Society has attempted to identify a name for people who, for a variety of reasons, opt to live within a relationship without the formality of marriage.
Judge J. Wilma Scott[45]

Close to one third of young couples 25 years of age and under are living in a common-law relationship.
Roger Sauvé[48]

Young couples are still forming 'first unions' as early as their parents and grandparents did. The delay in legal marriages is being offset by a dramatic increase in cohabitation or common-law relationships.
Roger Sauvé[49]

Shacking up
A prelude to marriage?

Table III – Proportion of Married Individuals Who Cohabited Together Prior to Marriage, by Age
(1990)

Age	Number Married*	Number Cohabited*	Percent Cohabited
20 - 29	1,432	533	37%
30 - 39	2,951	837	28%
40 - 49	2,550	318	12%
50 +	4,046	145	4%
All ages	11,009	1,833	17%

*In thousands

Calculated by the Centre for International Statistics[47]

Common-law unions are often a prelude to marriage rather than an alternative to it. Younger Canadians are nine times more likely than older Canadians to have cohabited before marriage. Thirty-seven percent of married Canadians in their twenties "tried it out" before exchanging vows. Only 4% of the over-fifty married population had lived with their spouses prior to marriage. This difference between age groups may reflect a change in the prevailing social attitudes. What has become a common and largely acceptable choice for many was once widely considered to be beyond the pale. Have the changing attitudes that have affected younger people carried over into the older population as well?

And so what?

Marriages that have been preceded by cohabitation have not proved, statistically, to be more stable than other marriages. However, the rise of cohabitation has had a decided impact on Canadian society. As common-law couples and their out-of-wedlock children have become more numerous and accepted, demands have grown for recognition of their rights and needs by the courts, lawmakers, employers and the community as a whole.

'Til divorce do us part

24. Number of Divorces

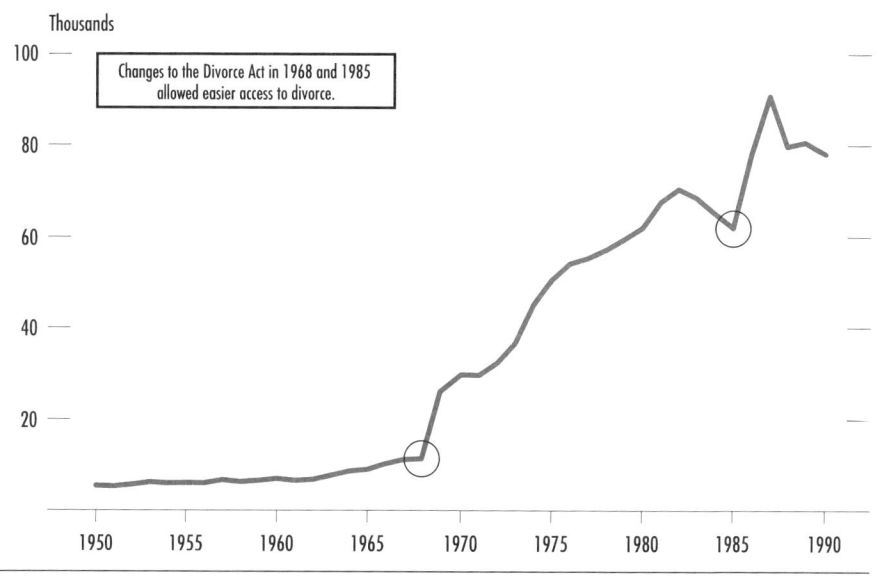

Thousands

Changes to the Divorce Act in 1968 and 1985 allowed easier access to divorce.

Prepared by the Centre for International Statistics

Before 1968, it was difficult to obtain a divorce in Canada. A divorce was granted only if it could be proven that one spouse had committed adultery. In 1968, grounds for divorce were expanded to include marital breakdown and marital offenses. Marital breakdown included desertion, imprisonment, or separation for at least three years, while marital offenses included physical or mental cruelty.

In 1985, further changes in the *Divorce Act* made marital breakdown the sole ground for divorce. This was defined to include separation of not less than one year, adultery, and/or physical or mental cruelty. In the first year after the change, 91% of the divorces obtained under the new act cited separation as the cause for divorce.

The increase in the number of divorces granted (11,000 in 1968 compared with 78,000 in 1990) is due, in part, to the growth in the number of married couples and, in part, to the changes in the *Divorce Act*. In the years immediately following the changes, the number of divorces jumped considerably, especially in 1986 when "no fault" divorce provisions came into effect. This suggests that many couples delayed divorcing in anticipation of the changes to divorce laws.

And so what?

More liberal divorce laws represent the Great Divide in the history of Canada's families. Although couples have always separated, the easy availability of divorce, combined with related social changes, has totally altered how we look at marriage, having children and almost every aspect of family life. In turn, our new attitudes spill over into every other aspect of life – work, inheritance, sexuality and relationships of all kinds. Before 1968, a marriage, whether good or bad, was forever for most people. To terminate it was difficult and frowned-upon. Just 25 years later, it can be staggering to contemplate the differences between life today and how it was before divorce laws changed.

It is difficult to determine the exact number of children affected by divorces in Canada because there is no official information about out-of-court custody decisions. In 1990, approximately 34,000 children were involved in divorce cases in which the courts made custody decisions. In eight out of ten such cases, custody was awarded to the mother.

The Vanier Institute of the Family

The wonder is not that divorce rates are so high today, but that so many marriages and families and relationships survive and even thrive.
Arlene Skolnick[50]

The last fifty years have apparently changed the marriage relation from a permanent and lifelong state to a union existing for the pleasure of the parties. The change...is... revolutionary.
- *an American writer in 1887 warning of threats to the family*[51]

...it is not 'the family', but one, HISTORICALLY SPECIFIC, system of family life that has broken down, and this has had diverse effects on people of different genders, races, economic resources, sexual identities, and generations. Some have benefited greatly; others have lost enormously; most have won a few new rights and opportunities and lost several former protections and privileges.
Judith Stacey[53]

Joint custody is a question of involvement, not residence.
Phillip Epstein[54]

What is less difficult to determine is that women and children often find themselves living in poverty following separation and divorce. Three quarters of those not receiving alimony or child support live in poverty. And even more disturbing is the fact that approximately two thirds of those who do receive such support still have total incomes below the poverty lines.[52]

Outcomes of divorce for children

A child's adaptation to divorce is influenced by a number of stressors in addition to...developmental and cognitive factors...

Typical life changes that affect child adjustment are:
- negative economic consequences (especially in the child's primary residence),
- erratic contact or no contact with the non-residential parent,
- ongoing parental conflict,
- parental dating or remarriage,
- less availability of the residential parent (i.e. returns to the workforce full-time),
- continued exposure to psychologically disturbed parent(s),
- changes in residence and related factors (i.e. loss of peer group, change in school), and
- reactions of family and friends....

Several factors are predictive of more positive outcomes. Based on her clinical observations, Wallerstein (1983b) suggests that children's coping with changing family circumstances is shaped by:
- the extent to which parents resolve or set aside their conflicts,
- the quality of the residential parents' relationship with their children and their capacity to parent,
- the extent to which children do not feel rejected by non-residential parents,
- assets, capacities, and deficits of individual children,
- availability of support networks and children's ability to use them,
- the absence of children's continued anger or depression,
- how events are defined, and
- developmental needs.

Rhonda Freeman[55]

Marriage and Divorce
A parallel line dance

25. Number of Marriages and Divorces

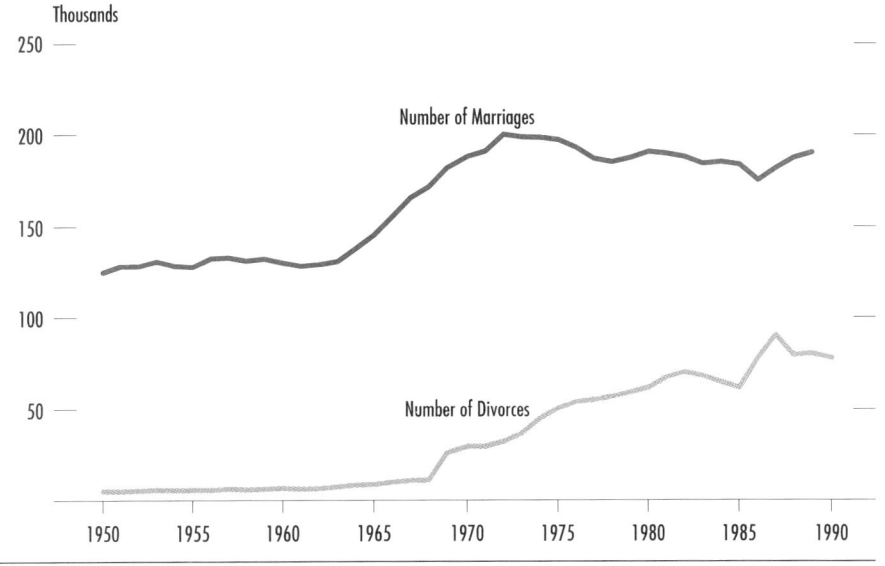

Prepared by the Centre for International Statistics

Over the past four decades, marriages have outnumbered divorces by as much as 168,000 in 1972 and as little as 91,000 in 1987. In general the difference has stayed in the range of 100,000.

The big change is the ratio of divorces to marriages. In 1951, one couple divorced for every 24 couples that married. In 1987, as marriages dipped and divorces peaked, this ratio reached a low of one couple divorcing for every two couples marrying. Since 1987, the gap has widened each year, and in 1990 one couple divorced for every 2.4 that married.

The length of marriage before divorce has become shorter since the *Divorce Act* changes of 1968 and 1985. In 1969, the median duration of marriages ending in divorce was almost 15 years. Under the new act, couples who divorced in 1986 had been married a median of 9.1 years. Marriages ending between 1968 and 1985 lasted a median of 11.2 years.

And so what?

That divorce is more common today than three decades ago is not news. What may be surprising, however, is the healthy lead that marriage has managed to maintain over divorce. Whether it's because people like it, or because it's convenient and practical, marriage continues to hold its own in an age of social mobility, casual relationships and easy divorce.

The Vanier Institute of the Family

Because most who divorce remarry or 're-partner', there are few sociologists who see this high rate of divorce as any indication of a loss of commitment to marriage and family though, for many, these institutions are defined rather broadly. Indeed, it appears that, for most people, involvement in familial life styles, if not traditional forms of marriage and family, matter immensely. Thus, as we have broadened our conception of family, we have also come to recognize that divorce does not signify the end of familial relationships but rather a reorganization of them.

If divorce is a social problem, it is so largely and in the long run in its economic consequences and not in its threat to the future of marriage and family.
    C. James Richardson[56]

The Vanier Institute of the Family

It may be that Canada has simply lagged behind some of the other industrial societies, notably the United States, in the speed at which certain cultural changes have taken place, and this is reflected in the now-accelerated pace with which our divorce rate has risen during the 1980s.
C. James Richardson[57]

From the basement to the big leagues
Canadian divorce rates jump in comparison with other nations.

26. Divorce Rates: An International Perspective

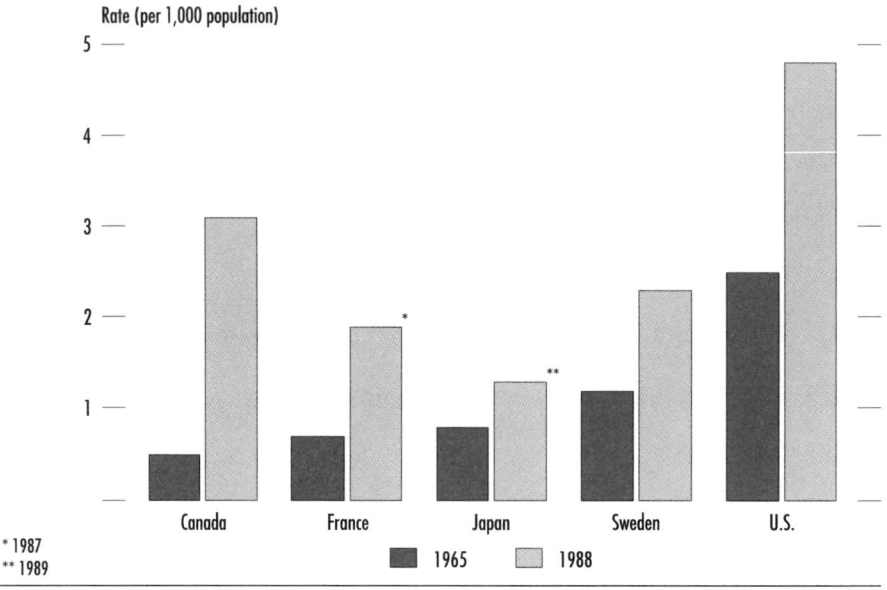

Rate (per 1,000 population)

* 1987
** 1989

■ 1965   □ 1988

Prepared by the Centre for International Statistics

Between 1965 and 1988, Canada moved from having one of the lowest divorce rates to having one of the highest among industrialized nations. For most of these nations, divorce rates rose sharply between 1965 and 1975 but increased more moderately between 1975 and 1986. The U.S. stands out with the highest divorce rate throughout the years, while Japan continues to show a relatively low rate of divorce.

And so what?

The increase in divorce that Canadians have experienced is in line with the experiences of our neighbours. Similar trends have affected all industrialized nations over the past few decades. Trends such as greater social mobility, increased women's labour force participation, more liberal attitudes regarding sex, a less dominant role for organized religion, changing views about relationships, lower birthrates, and the movement for equal rights for women have produced great upheaval. The institution of marriage has not been immune.

Canadian marriages outlast their American cousins

27. Divorce and Remarriage: Canada and the U.S.

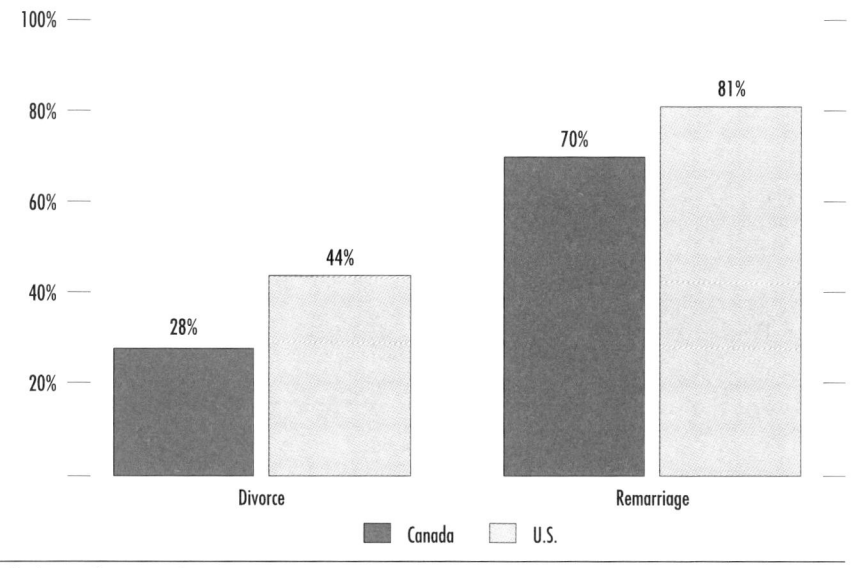

[Bar chart showing Divorce: Canada 28%, U.S. 44%; Remarriage: Canada 70%, U.S. 81%]

Prepared by the Centre for International Statistics

While marriage rates in Canada and the U.S. are similar, divorce rates are not. Fully 44% of American marriages end in divorce, compared with 28% of Canadian marriages. Divorce does not appear to erode people's faith in the institution of marriage. Eight out of ten divorced Americans and seven out of ten divorced Canadians remarry.

Although Canadians and Americans spend roughly the same proportion of their lives in marriage, Canadians marry less often and for longer periods. The average Canadian marriage lasts 31 years, compared with 24 years for the average American marriage.

And so what?

It's worthwhile to ponder why Canadians marriages, on average, last so much longer than those of Americans. Is it a more traditional, conservative style? More generous social programs that help keep families from dire poverty? A less mobile, less dynamic culture with less diversity? Stronger, more compassionate communities?

The consequences of this difference are worth considering as well, especially the impact on children. Divorce can be a positive and necessary step, and it is possible to minimize its negative effects on children. As a group, however, children of divorce may have a harder time in life.

Whatever is keeping Canadians married longer than Americans may be worth identifying and preserving.

The Vanier Institute of the Family

Divorce rates [in the United States] have climbed throughout most of the 20th century. In the early 1940s, only about one in seven women could anticipate experiencing a divorce; by 1980, the odds had increased to about 50%....

Teresa M. Cooney[58]

The Vanier Institute of the Family

...lone parenthood is more pervasive than current statistics indicate. About 500,000 women were lone parents in 1984 but another 900,000 had passed through this status.
Maureen Moore[59]

The 1931 level of lone-parent families has yet to be surpassed...
Maureen Moore[60]

Separate paths to lone parenthood

28. Marital Status of Lone Parents
(1991)

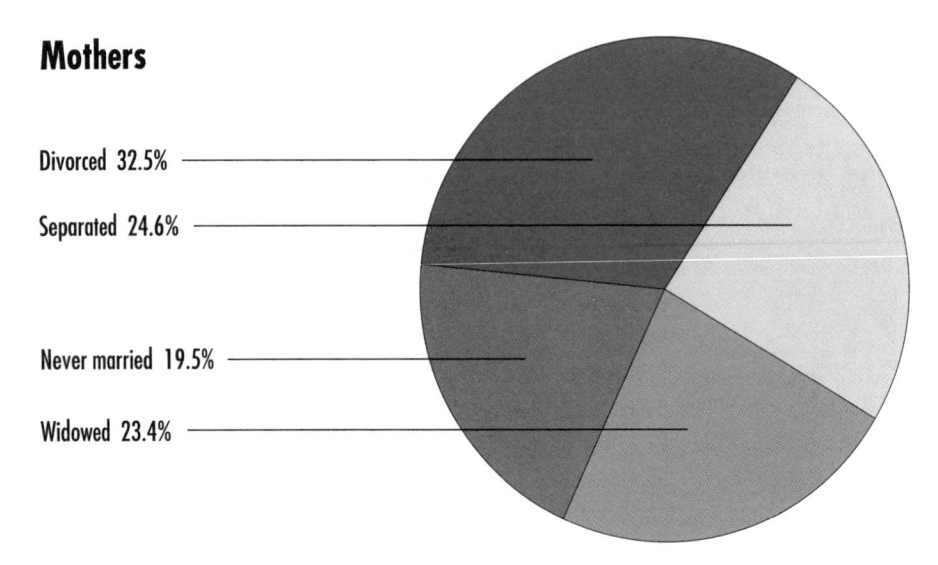

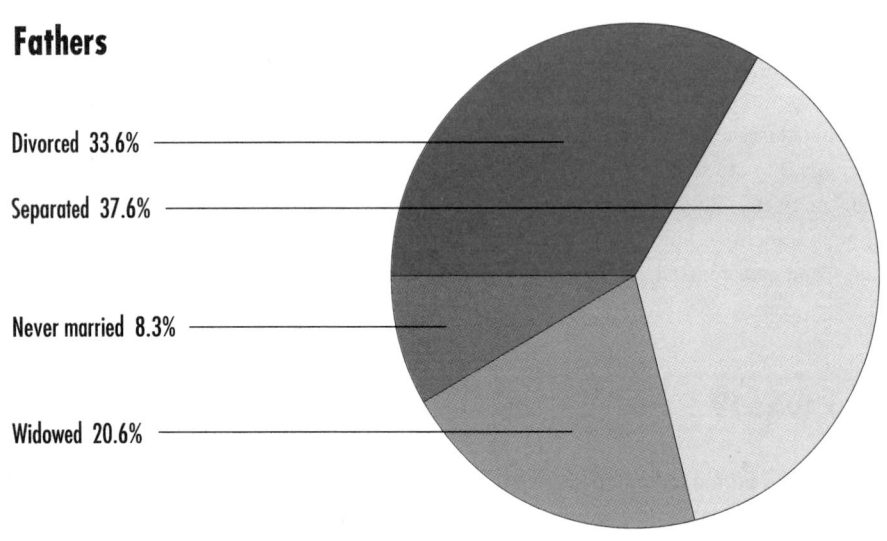

Mothers

Divorced 32.5%
Separated 24.6%
Never married 19.5%
Widowed 23.4%

Fathers

Divorced 33.6%
Separated 37.6%
Never married 8.3%
Widowed 20.6%

Prepared by the Centre for International Statistics

There are close to one million lone-parent families in Canada. That represents 12.9% of all families and one in five of all families with children. As long ago as 1931, 13.6% of all families were lone-parent families. The proportion dropped to an all-time low of 8.2% in 1966. While the vast majority (82%) of today's lone-parent families are led by lone mothers, there are a significant number of lone fathers (170,000).

Today, divorce and separation are the leading cause of lone parenthood for both men and women. Forty years ago, two thirds of lone-parents were widows or widowers. By 1991, three quarters of mothers raising children on their own were either separated, divorced or unmarried.

29. Changes in Marital Status of Lone Mothers

1951

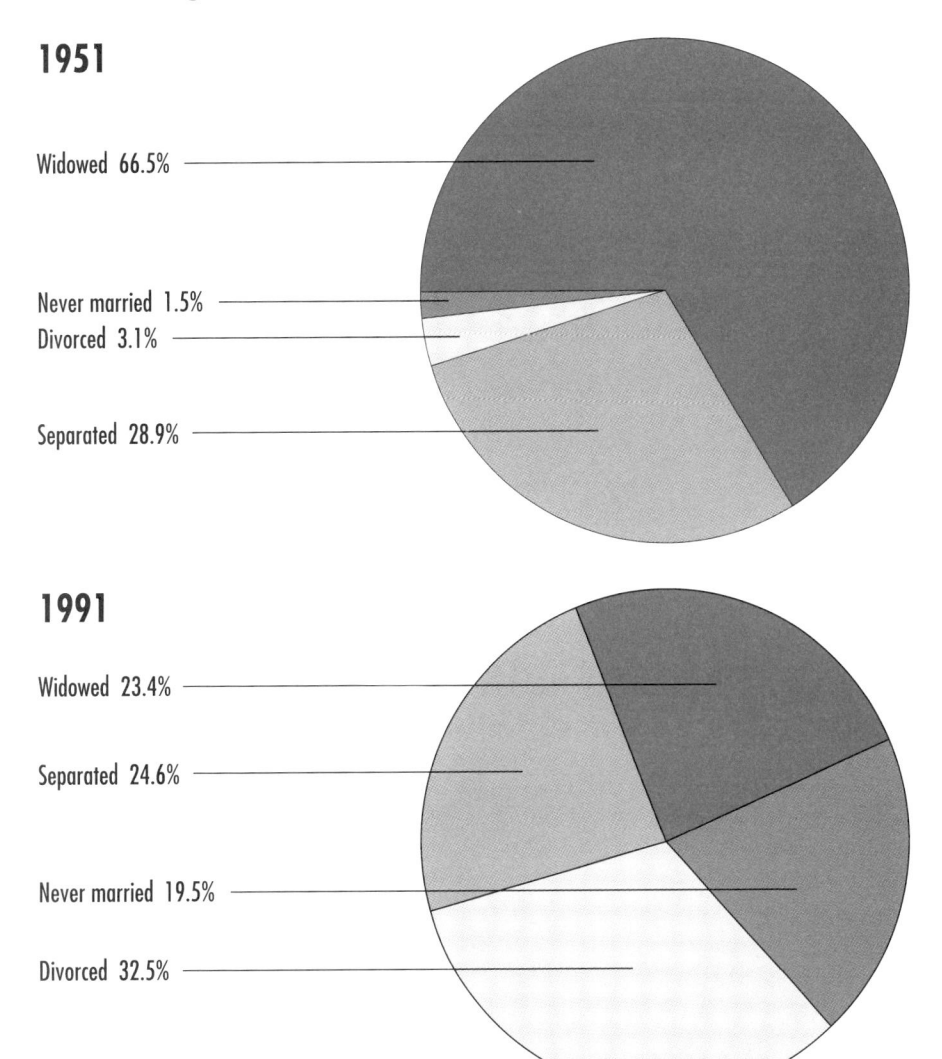

Widowed 66.5%

Never married 1.5%
Divorced 3.1%

Separated 28.9%

1991

Widowed 23.4%

Separated 24.6%

Never married 19.5%

Divorced 32.5%

Prepared by The Vanier Institute of the Family

And so what?

In the past, there was a strong social stigma attached to being a lone parent. Even today, some people are inclined to pass judgment on lone parents, especially single mothers.

The true story of how people become lone parents offers a different view. Most people enter lone parenthood not through choice but as a result of circumstances – death of a spouse, an abusive relationship, desertion or a marriage that just didn't work.

The Vanier Institute of the Family

...it appears possible that 42% of children born between 1971 and 1973, and 45% of those born between 1975 and 1977 will have seen their parents separate by the time they reach twenty.
Nicole Marcil-Gratton[61]

What is certain is that, already, one woman in four will be a single parent at some time in her life.
Charles Jones, Lorna Marsden, Lorne Tepperman[62]

The Vanier Institute of the Family

Canada's families
Some have children...and some don't

30. Families With and Without Children*
(1991)

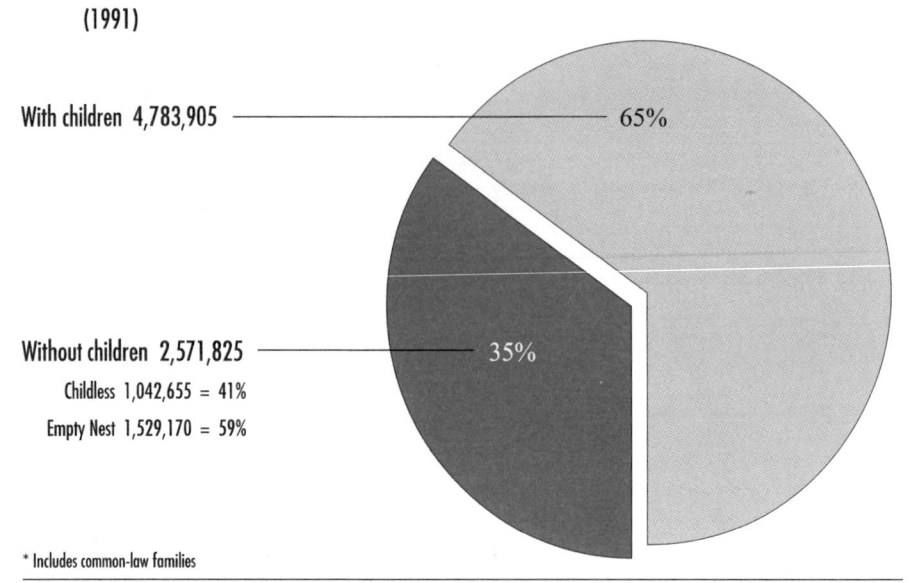

With children 4,783,905 — 65%

Without children 2,571,825 — 35%
 Childless 1,042,655 = 41%
 Empty Nest 1,529,170 = 59%

* Includes common-law families

Prepared by the Centre for International Statistics

For the first time in history, the average couple has more parents living than it has children. It is also the first era when most of the parent-child relationships take place after the child becomes an adult.
— Arlene Skolnick[63]

31. Families With Children Living at Home: Distribution by Age of Children

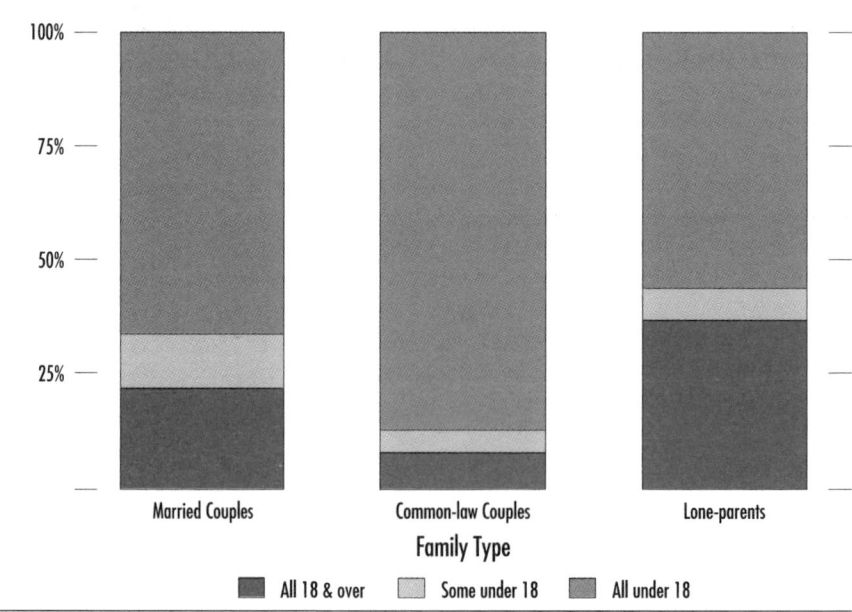

Family Type: Married Couples, Common-law Couples, Lone-parents

Legend: All 18 & over | Some under 18 | All under 18

Prepared by the Centre for International Statistics

Stages of life that scarcely existed a hundred years ago have become part of the average person's experience: adolescence, middle age, empty nest, retirement.
— Arlene Skolnick[64]

Most kids live with two parents. In 1991, more than eight out of ten children lived with two parents; only about 14% lived with a lone parent.

But does a family always include children? No. Though the majority of Canadian families (65%) include children living at home, the proportion of families without children is on the rise. In 1981, 32% of all Canadian families had no children at home. Just ten years later, families without children, including families that are intentionally or unintentionally childless and those couples whose children have left home, made up 35% of all families.

The largest and fastest growing proportion of these families without children are the "empty nesters." As the population with its large baby boom contingent ages, this trend is expected to continue.

There are even more empty nesters than the chart suggests because lone parents never become statistical empty nesters. Once the last child leaves home, a lone parent is no longer considered a family; he or she becomes instead, for statistical purposes, an "unattached individual." Thus, while single parents are included in the calculation for "all families," they are excluded from the "families without children" category.

Married couples with children are almost three times as likely as common-law couples with children to have all of their at-home children aged 18 years or older. The reason for this difference is simple. Since common-law relationships are more likely among younger people, they are also more likely to have young children.

And so what?

The life course of families keeps changing. Most families have children, but they pass through their life courses differently from in the past. They have children later, they have fewer of them, and they live longer without them than do past families. But children remain central to their existence.

More than a third of Canada's families do not have children in the house. The proportion might even be higher if other familial groupings such as adult children moving back with widowed parents, groups of close friends, or gay couples were included in the statistical definition of family. The trend toward smaller families and longer life expectancies has resulted in more couples living in empty nests and living in them longer.

Yet children remain a reality for most families. The family ties and responsibilities continue, regardless of where a family's children at their various ages may reside.

To be born out of wedlock no longer means to be born without a family, as common-law marriage is becoming a lifestyle that does not preclude parenthood.
Nicole Marcil-Gratton[65]

The vast majority of young adults who could soon become parents do plan to have children eventually.
Nicole Marcil-Gratton[66]

The Vanier Institute of the Family

Despite personal sacrifices, the lack of sleep and the pain, adults require children in their lives. Without children, we have no commitment to the future. We become a society without heart.
Robert Couchman[68]

When women delay childbearing beyond their mid-30s, the chances are that they will bear either one child or no children at all.
G. N. Ramu[69]

...the number of women in their 30s will reach a peak in 1994 or 1995 and by the end of the decade will be down to or below today's numbers. The ammunition for a new baby boom is nearly expended. The chance that births will ever again reach 500,000 a year is remote; that they will reach 450,000 is highly unlikely.
John Kettle[70]

A new baby boom? Not by any historic standard. In fact, Canada's need for new people will still have to lean most heavily on immigration in the foreseeable future. And will still come up short.
John Kettle[71]

Although voluntary childlessness has received considerable media and social science attention since the 1970s, it is not a new phenomenon in Canada. A high 17.7% of ever-married women born between 1906 and 1911 were childless.... It is projected that 16% of the present generation may voluntarily forego maternity....
Emily M. Nett[72]

From boom to bust
Fertility rates sagged to record lows before staging mini-rally in late '80s

32. Total Fertility Rate

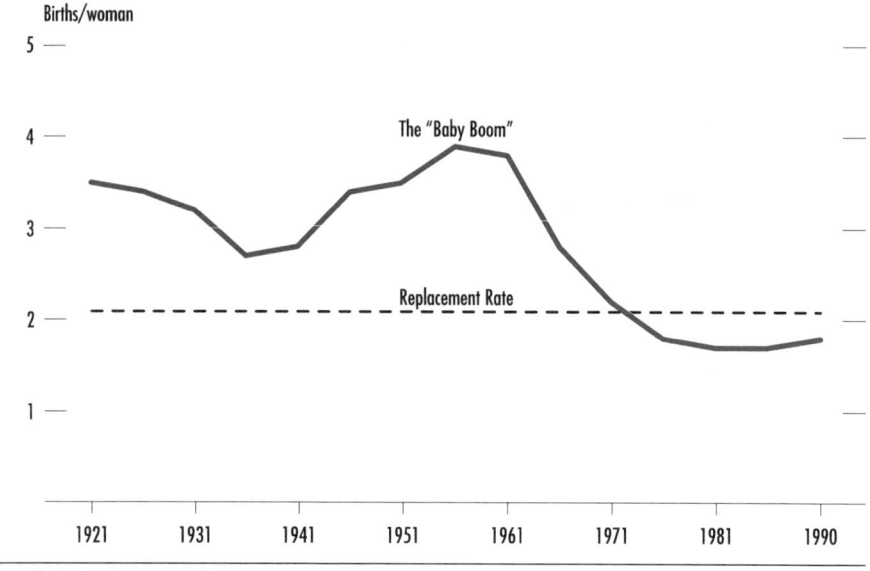

Births/woman

The "Baby Boom"

Replacement Rate

1921 1931 1941 1951 1961 1971 1981 1990

Prepared by the Centre for International Statistics

Marriage rates have gone up and down but remain historically fairly steady. The fertility rate, on the other hand, has plummeted since its high in 1959. We have gone from baby boom (1945-1960) to baby bust. And we went quickly. The total fertility rate (the number of children a woman would have during her lifetime if she were to follow the fertility patterns of the time) dropped from 3.9 in 1960 to 2.3 in 1970. By 1981 it was down to 1.7 – well below the replacement rate of 2.1 births per woman. More than any other factor, this low birthrate is responsible for the phenomenon we now call "the aging society". At this rate the replacement of the current generation is not assured.

Babies may be starting to make a comeback, however. The fertility rate has crept up from its low of 1.65 in 1987 to 1.8 in 1990.

Childlessness – Intentional and unintentional

Some researchers have estimated that as many as 16% of Canadian women currently in their childbearing years will remain childless. It is impossible to know for sure. It is also impossible to know how many of these women are childless by choice and how many are involuntarily infertile. Recently, the Royal Commission on New Reproductive Technologies surveyed Canadians and found that 7% of couples married or living together for at least two years were infertile.[67]

And so what?

Lower fertility now affects almost every industrialized nation. Along with it come myriad changes and dilemmas: How will we replace today's work force when the baby boomers near retirement age? How will governments raise sufficient tax revenues from the next generation to pay for programs if that generation is much smaller than today's? Where will tomorrow's consumers come from, and what will businesses do if there are far fewer of them? What will we do with houses that are too big and schools with too many classrooms? Who will care for the baby boomers when they get old? How will we replace today's population, and should we? Clearly, lower fertility is at the heart of many of the social and economic questions that bedevil business people, communities, planners and lawmakers.

The greying of Canada

33. The Aging of the Population

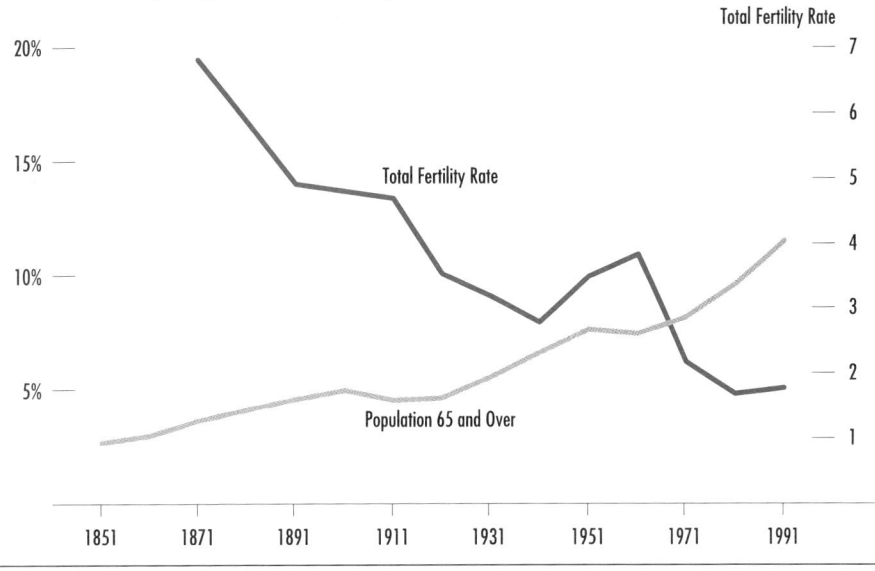

Chart showing Total Fertility Rate and Population 65 and Over from 1851 to 1991

Prepared by The Vanier Institute of the Family

Canada is an aging society. This means that as the years go by, the proportion of older people in Canada grows larger. Some say this has occurred as the baby boom has aged, but the facts don't bear this out. Instead, societal aging is mostly a factor of a steady decline, over time, in fertility. Women are having fewer children. The baby boom was, in reality, a Baby Blip, a temporary reversal of a long-term trend toward smaller families.

And so what?

In the '70s and '80s, Canada's senior population increased dramatically. As a whole, the senior population rose by about 80%. The increase was even greater among those aged 75 and over. This group increased by 90%, while the group aged 55-75 grew by 75%.

How will our aging society affect medicare, social services and government finances in years to come? Will a growing senior population be a burden that today's young people will have to shoulder or will they be an asset to them? Questions like these are being hotly debated by ordinary citizens, as well as by policy makers and service providers.

Table IV – Median Age and Proportion of the Population 0-14 and 65 and Over, Canada, 1851-2036

Year	Median Age		Proportion 0 - 14		Proportion 65+	
1851	17.2		44.9		2.7	
1861	18.2		42.5		3.0	
1871	18.8		41.6		3.7	
1881	20.1		38.7		4.1	
1891	21.4		36.3		4.6	
1901	22.7		34.4		5.0	
1911	23.8		32.9		4.7	
1921	24.0		34.4		4.8	
1931	24.8		31.6		5.6	
1941	27.1		27.8		6.7	
1951	27.7		30.3		7.8	
1956	27.2		32.5		7.7	
1961	26.3		34.0		7.6	
1966	25.5		32.9		7.7	
1971	26.2		29.6		8.1	
1976	28.1		25.6		8.7	
1981	29.6		22.5		9.7	
1986	31.6		21.3		10.6	
	High	Low	High	Low	High	Low
1991	33.5	33.6	20.7	20.7	11.8	11.8
1996	35.5	35.6	19.8	19.8	12.8	12.8
2001	37.5	37.7	18.6	18.6	13.5	13.7
2006	39.2	39.6	17.4	17.3	14.2	14.4
2011	40.6	41.1	16.6	16.3	15.5	15.8
2016	41.6	42.3	16.2	15.9	17.6	18.1
2021	42.6	44.0	15.9	15.6	19.8	20.4
2026	43.4	44.2	15.6	15.3	22.0	22.9
2031	44.2	45.0	15.2	14.9	23.8	24.9
2036	44.8	45.7	14.9	14.5	24.5	25.7

Note: Projections use total fertility rate of 1.67 and immigration of 200,000 (high) and 140,000 (low).

Rodrick Beaujot[73]

Move over, motherhood
Canadian women increasingly postpone marriage and child rearing

34. Average Age of Mother for 1st and 2nd Births

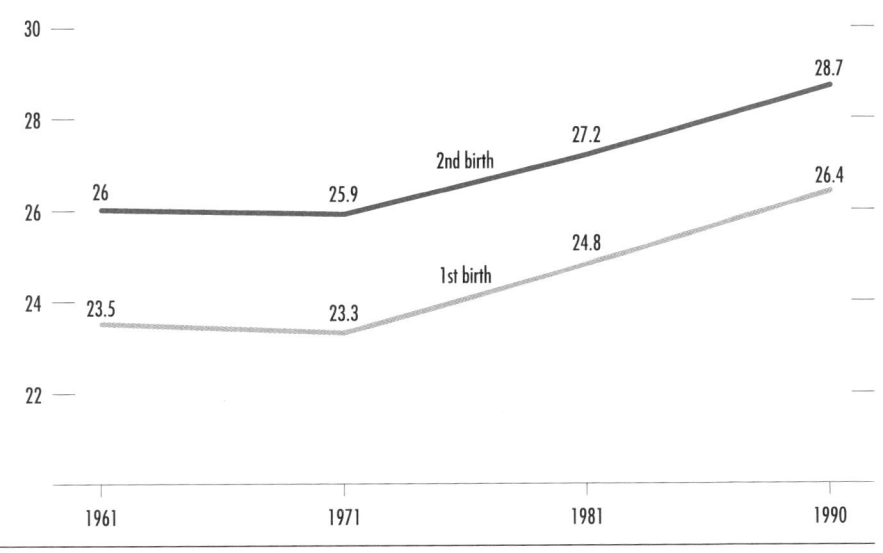

Year	1st birth	2nd birth
1961	23.5	26
1971	23.3	25.9
1981	24.8	27.2
1990	26.4	28.7

Prepared by the Centre for International Statistics

Women are waiting about three years longer to marry and to start their families than they did 20 years ago. The average age of mothers at the births of their first and second babies has increased along with the increase in the average age of women at their first marriages. On average, the first child comes along soon after marriage, followed, two and a half years later, by the second child.

And so what?

The implications of postponing children are many – decreased fertility rates, smaller family sizes, and an increase in "only child" families. These trends, in turn, are affecting every aspect of family life. Having children later means that parents may be better established in their careers, but it also may mean that they have less time and energy for their children. Having fewer siblings means that children need to look elsewhere for playmates when they are young, and for family ties as they age.

As children of such families age, other implications emerge. Parents may become elderly and in need of support themselves before their children become financially secure adults. "Such parents may be faced with reduced resources and heightened needs before their children can help them and when they still have need for parental assistance."[74]

The Vanier Institute of the Family

Whatever her intentions, the older a women gets the less likely she is to have many children...
John Kettle[75]

Women's age at first birth is a critical predictor of subsequent life events. In particular, early childbirth is a strong predictor of divorce.
Charles Jones,
Lorna Marsden,
Lorne Tepperman[76]

...whereas in earlier generations women typically bore their children over a period of ten to fifteen years, today they do so in five years or less. With this 'compression' of the childbearing period, the number of years when one or more children are present in the home has dropped from thirty to twenty years. This, together with increasing longevity, means that instead of spending almost no time alone with a spouse in the 'empty nest', present wives can expect to average twenty or thirty years in that state.
Charles Jones,
Lorna Marsden,
Lorne Tepperman[77]

Hanging up the shotgun
Births to not-married women on the increase

35. Births to Not-married Women as a Percentage of Total Births

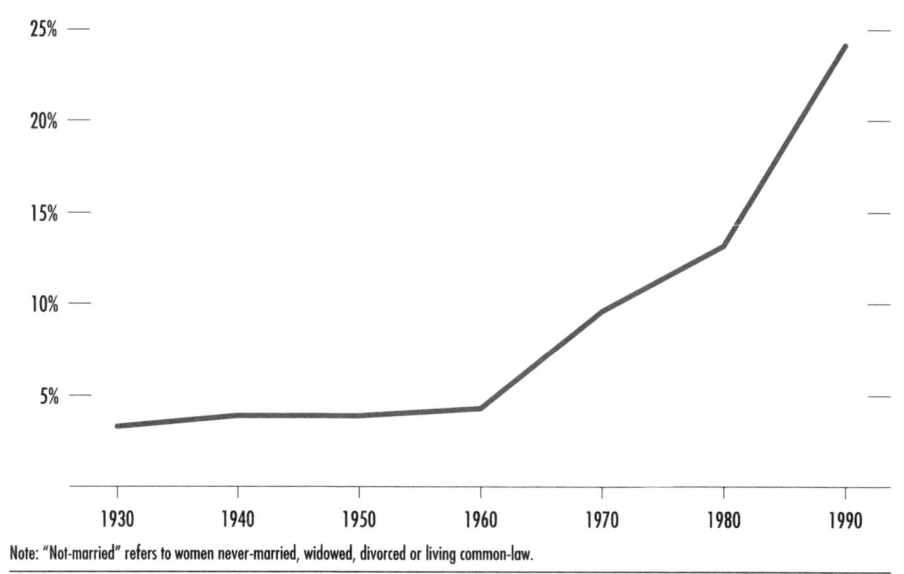

Note: "Not-married" refers to women never-married, widowed, divorced or living common-law.

Prepared by the Centre for International Statistics

36. Births to Not-married Women by Age
(1990)

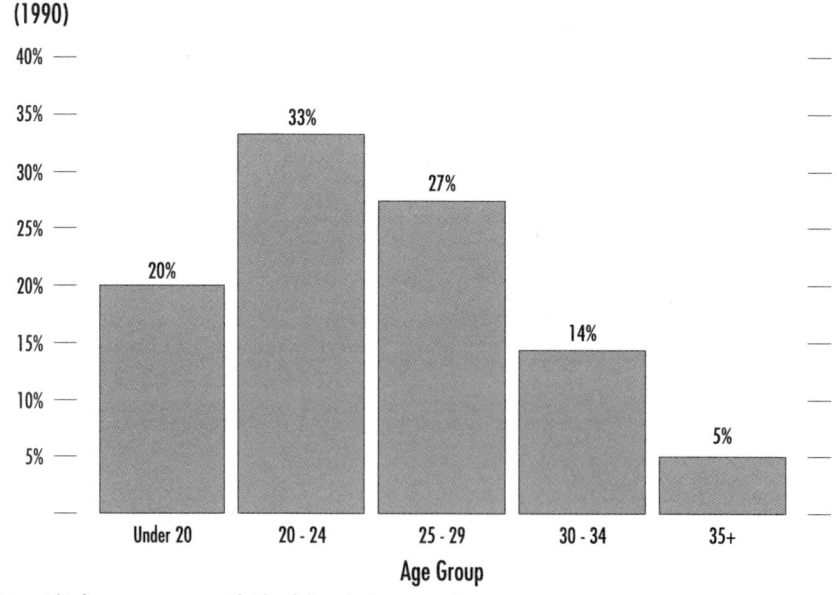

Age Group	Percentage
Under 20	20%
20 - 24	33%
25 - 29	27%
30 - 34	14%
35+	5%

Note: "Not-married" refers to women never-married, widowed, divorced or living common-law.

Prepared by the Centre for International Statistics

In the last thirty years, there has been a huge increase in the number and proportion of all babies born to women who are not currently married. In 1990, 24% of all live births were to women who were not married, compared with only 4% in 1960. These include women who were widowed, divorced, or living common-law, as well as single women. Many factors account for this increase, including the growth of common-law relationships, desertion by would-be fathers, the increasing social and economic independence of women choosing to bear and raise children alone, and the growing acceptability of out-of-wedlock births.

Teenage pregnancy is out of control – Not

Contrary to popular opinion, the majority of out-of-wedlock babies are not born to teenage women. In fact, in 1990, 60% of the unmarried women who gave birth were between the ages of 20 and 29. Furthermore, both the number of teenage pregnancies and the number of births to teenagers has declined dramatically over the past thirty years. In 1971, there were 40,000 births to teenagers. The number dropped to less than 23,000 by 1989.

And so what?

A generation ago, having a baby out of wedlock was a family disgrace. Today it is more and more accepted as part of modern life. In fact, that acceptance has resulted in a doubling of the percentage of such births in the past decade.

It may surprise many people that, unlike the U.S., Canada has no epidemic of "children having children." Yet the number of births to unmarried women of all ages is rising. And despite the increased societal tolerance that lone mothers enjoy, they still must contend with the economic disadvantages of bearing sole financial responsibility for their families.

The statistics give the lie to the popular assumption that teen pregnancy is out of control. At the same time, it is worth asking why so many women in their twenties are having babies out of wedlock. While many of them are separated, divorced, widowed, or living in common-law marriages, there is also a strong element here of choice. Many unmarried women are having babies deliberately, because they want to and feel they can handle the joys and responsibilities of parenthood on their own.

The Vanier Institute of the Family

Almost as many children are born into two-parent families today as in the past, even though those parents are now more likely to be involved in a common-law marriage.
Nicole Marcil-Gratton[78]

The typical adoptive applicant is Caucasian, married, Protestant, between 31 and 35 years of age, infertile, with at least high school education and no prior parenting experience. Applicants who pursue adoption in the private sphere are older and better educated.
The Vanier Institute of the Family[79]

The emphasis has become one of providing families for children, rather than children for families.
Terri Spronk[80]

Where once love was deemed enough, it is now being acknowledged that families need ongoing supports after an adoption, to assist them in meeting the needs of older children who've been left emotionally scarred and damaged by their past.
Terri Spronk[81]

Adoption
More applicants, fewer kids

37. Domestic Adoptions: Public and Private

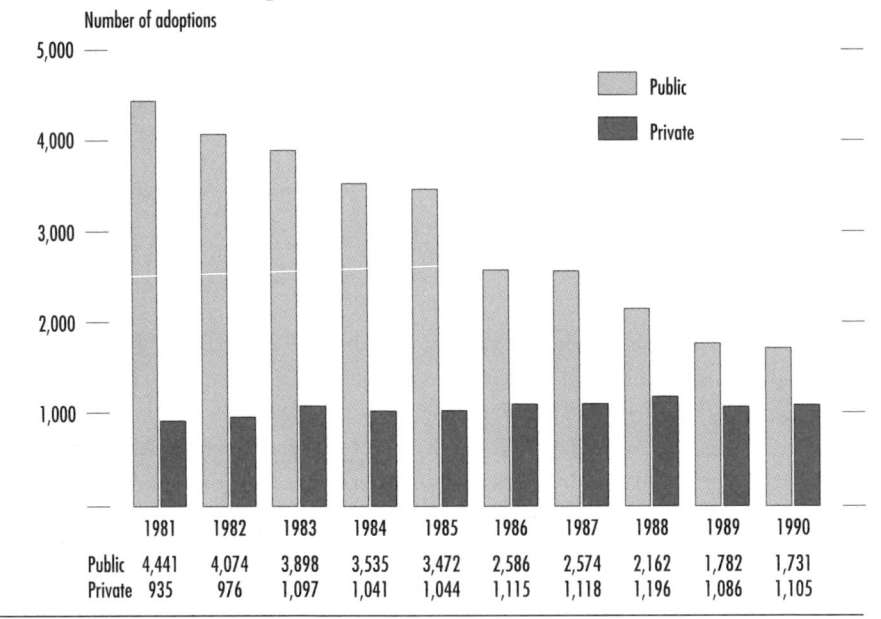

	1981	1982	1983	1984	1985	1986	1987	1988	1989	1990
Public	4,441	4,074	3,898	3,535	3,472	2,586	2,574	2,162	1,782	1,731
Private	935	976	1,097	1,041	1,044	1,115	1,118	1,196	1,086	1,105

Prepared by the Centre for International Statistics

There were only about half as many children adopted in 1990 (2,836) as there were just a decade earlier (5,376). The number of private adoptions rose while the number of public adoptions dropped dramatically over the decade. There were three applicants (about 5,000) for each public adoption and almost as many applying for private adoptions.

In addition, various estimates suggest that 2,000 to 5,000 Canadians are actively pursuing international adoption. This does not include children who are brought to Canada from other countries and then adopted. Such cases are recorded as domestic, rather than international, adoptions. A common form of international adoption occurs when children are adopted in their home country and then brought to Canada. Records regarding the number of children adopted in other countries are not always accurate, however, and it was not until late in 1991 that Canada began to collect data on these adoptions.

And so what?

The demand for adoptive children – especially healthy, white babies – appears to be growing while the supply of babies shrinks due to the legal availability of abortions and the increased acceptability of lone parenting and birth out of wedlock.

The trend away from public adoptions and toward private adoptions has several implications: Private adoptions are more costly than public ones, so adoption is increasingly becoming an option for wealthy families only. In the case of private adoptions, the public has less control of the process. This can, in some cases, lead to abuses of all parties involved – the children, the birth mother and the adoptive parents. The relative increase in private adoptions makes it harder for public agencies to keep accurate adoption records.

Given the small numbers of children available for adoption, more parents are adopting children with troubled backgrounds. These can include international adoptees, transracial adoptees, and older children who have been hard to place due to health or behaviour problems. These adoptive parents often need special supports to help them meet the challenges that are unique to adoptive families.

Mine, yours and ours
Big families are often blended families

38. Blended and Non-blended Families by Number of Children

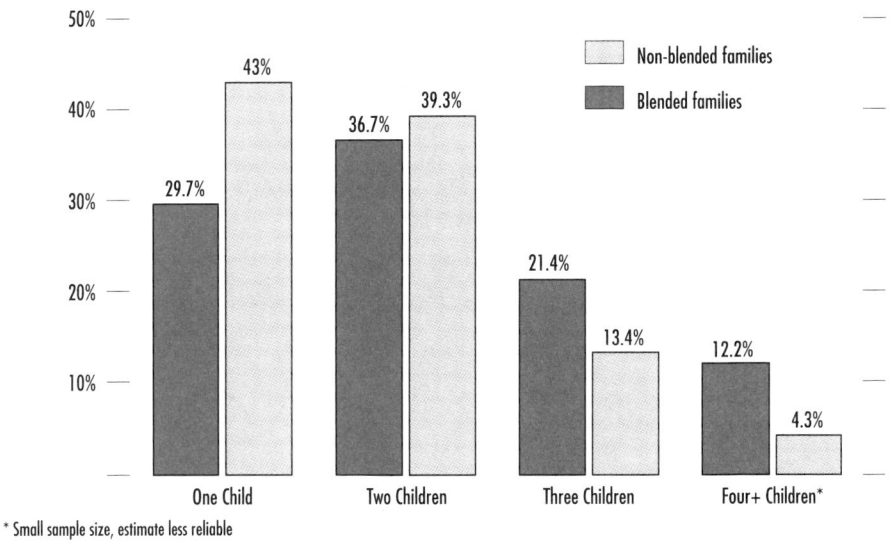

Number of Children	Blended families	Non-blended families
One Child	29.7%	43%
Two Children	36.7%	39.3%
Three Children	21.4%	13.4%
Four+ Children*	12.2%	4.3%

* Small sample size, estimate less reliable

Calculated by the Centre for International Statistics

"Blended families" – married or common-law couples with at least one step-child – become increasingly common as divorce and remarriage rates go up. In 1990 there were 343,400 blended families – representing about 7% of all families raising children.

This number underestimates the actual number of step-families because many stepchildren have grown up in blended families but are no longer living at home. Moreover, given the likelihood that divorce and remarriage rates will remain high, the number of blended families can be expected to increase significantly in years to come.

Blended families tend to be larger than non-blended families. Just three in ten blended families had only one child. In comparison, 43% of non-blended families – half again as high a proportion – had just one child. And more than two in ten blended families (21.4%) had three children. The percentage for non-blended families: 13.4.

And so what?

A principal reason for larger family sizes in blended families is the uniting of children from previous relationships. At least three children are needed to have a "mine, yours and ours" family, in which each spouse brings one or more children from previous relationships, and the couple has at least one child together.

It used to be common to ask parents how many children they had. Today, one asks children how many parents they have.

The Vanier Institute of the Family

Many thousands of people cohabit without benefit of marriage in homes where there are children by their partner's [former] marriage. Though they may look and act like parents, there is no name for this species. In real terms they are unparents or unstepparents.
Elizabeth Mehren[82]

Classified Ad: Yard Sale: Recently married couple is combining household. All duplicates will be sold, except children.[83]

...despite the traditionally low status involved in being a stepmother, the odds of becoming one are great. If you have three daughters in your household today, chances are that one will eventually become a stepmother.
Airdrie Thompson-Guppy[84]

CANADIAN FAMILIES
MAKING ENDS MEET
...OR NOT

The Vanier Institute of the Family

No one home during the day

39. Labour Force Participation Rates, Males & Females Age 15 and Over

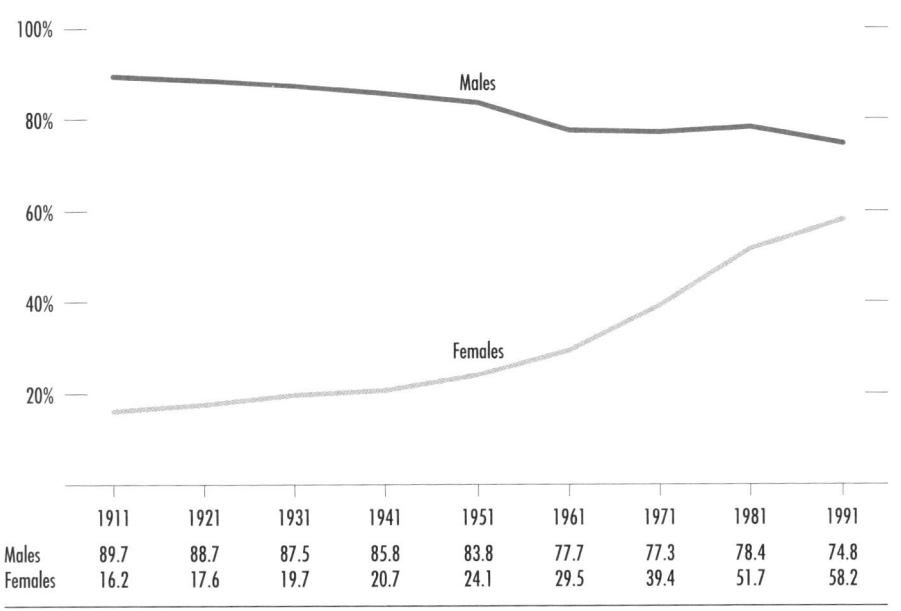

	1911	1921	1931	1941	1951	1961	1971	1981	1991
Males	89.7	88.7	87.5	85.8	83.8	77.7	77.3	78.4	74.8
Females	16.2	17.6	19.7	20.7	24.1	29.5	39.4	51.7	58.2

Prepared by the Centre for International Statistics

Between 1911 and 1991, male labour force participation rates have gradually dropped while rates for women have soared. In 1911, nine of ten men (89.7%) were in the labour force. In 1991, it was three in four (74.8%). During the same period, rates for women jumped from 16.2 to 58.2%, with the sharpest increase occurring during the 1970s and 1980s.

While women's participation in the paid labour force has grown enormously in the post-war period, the recent recession has – at least temporarily – slowed this trend. In 1992, the female labour force participation rate stood at 57.6%, following the third consecutive year of decline. The male participation rate also declined during this period to 73.8% in 1992.

More than half of Canada's young people are also in the labour market, a higher percentage than in 1970. The growth in the labour force participation rates for youth between the ages of 15 and 19 reflects the rapid growth in the service sector. Retail and fast food outlets rely heavily on youth labour.

Though there has been an overall upward trend in youth employment levels, young people may be particularly vulnerable to the effects of recession. They tend to have little or no seniority or job security and are more likely than other workers to hold part-time jobs. As the supply of "good" jobs diminishes, many young people find themselves in competition with older, more experienced workers for the part-time, low-wage, unskilled jobs that have traditionally been the domain of younger workers. Labour force participation rates for teens dipped during the recession of the early 1980s and recovered to reach a high in 1989. Since 1989, the rate has dropped from 61% to 53% for males and from 57% to 51% for females.

The Vanier Institute of the Family

The family has changed significantly in recent years, but these changes reflect basic, long-term changes in our society, changes going back at least to the last century. In a traditional, agriculturally based society, most activities, including work activities, take place in the household. In a modern urban society, most activities, especially work, are carried on outside the household. A major part of men's activities has been moving out of the household for more than a century. Women have been making the same shift, although with a delay of several decades compared to men. Finally, household size has been declining in parallel with its loss of economic functions, from an average of 5.2 in the late 19th century to 2.8 today.
The Demographic Review[85]

The majority of working-age women are now participating in the labour force despite the burdens traditionally imposed by the nature of household work and the responsibilities that it entails. This transformation has taken place along with important changes in educational attainment, marital patterns, family composition and work schedules.
Statistics Canada[86]

And so what?

Women's labour force participation has mirrored Canada's shift from a rural, agricultural society to an urban, industrial one. While the big jump in the 1970s and '80s participation rates for women reflects the women's movement and the shift toward smaller families, it is part of a trend dating back to the beginning of this century. Although many believe that women returned home from the workplace after the war, the statistics show that women have sought work outside the home in ever-increasing numbers since 1941. This long-term trend is, it seems, irreversible.

The impacts of this trend are many, varied and pervasive. From stay-pressed fabrics to TV dinners, many of the time-saving conveniences and services available today were developed, at least in part, to meet the needs of families that at one point might have depended on the full-time work of a homemaker. From school nurses to city planners to telephone installers, anyone who deals with the public should realize that in most households, there is no one at home during the day. And for young people, a balance needs to be struck between too much employment and too little. For young men, intensive work involvement appears to substantially increase the risk of dropping out of school. Among young women, however, *lack* of employment is associated with the highest risk of dropping out.

Most women have two careers
At home and on the job

40. Labour Force Participation Rates, Men and Women by Marital Status

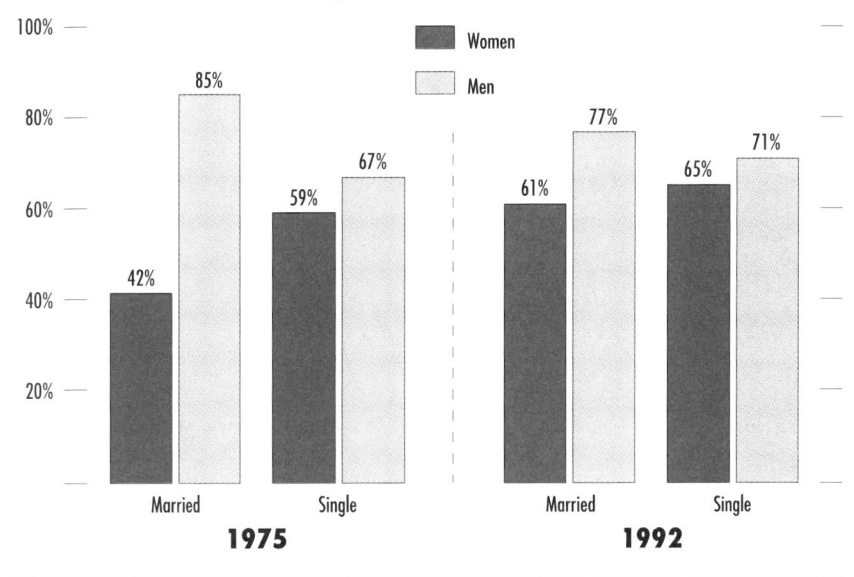

	Married (1975)	Single (1975)	Married (1992)	Single (1992)
Women	42%	59%	61%	65%
Men	85%	67%	77%	71%

Prepared by the Centre for International Statistics

Labour force participation rates are higher for married men than for single men, and lower for married women than for single women. Married men are the most likely to be in the labour force followed, in descending order, by single men, single women and married women. But the gap between married women's and married men's participation in the labour force is narrower than ever before. In the past, women tended to hold jobs only until they married. Most, by the age of 25, had married and left the paid labour force to raise families. Today, most women, like most men, remain in the labour force before, during and after marriage. Although married women have always worked, they have flocked to the *paid* labour force in the last 20 years, bringing their participation rate up to 61% in 1992 from 42% in 1975. During the same period, the labour force participation rate of married men declined from 85% to 77%.

Men are more likely than women to have employment income. Marital status evidently has some bearing on employment, but its effect differs according to gender. While a higher proportion of divorced women than married women have employment income, the reverse holds true for men. Divorced men are *less* likely to have employment income than married men. Married men have the highest employment rates, followed by divorced men, divorced women and married women.

The Vanier Institute of the Family

Twenty-year-old Canadian women can now expect to have 37 years of working life – only five years less than comparable men.
Charles Jones, Lorna Marsden, Lorne Tepperman[87]

Employment is the central foundation for the quality of life and financial preparedness for most families (Kilty & Behling, 1986).
Barbara H. Settles[88]

Now, for the largest proportion of families, both mom and dad are in the labour force, young children often are looked after outside the home, more of the food comes from McDonald's and more of the dishes are washed by machine.
Pat Armstrong and Hugh Armstrong[89]

The proportions of men and women who work full-time, full-year, follow the same pattern. Married men are the most likely to work full-time, full-year, followed by divorced men, divorced women and married women. Not surprisingly, married men also have the highest average earnings, followed in the same order by the other groups. The differences in average earnings between groups cannot be accounted for, however, by the differences in their labour force participation. The earning pattern remains consistent even for full-time, full-year workers: married men have the highest average earnings, followed by divorced men, divorced women and married women. Among full-time, full-year workers, married men averaged approximately $3,000 more than divorced men, who averaged about $9,000 more than divorced women, who, in turn, averaged about $3,000 more than married women.

And so what?

As more and more women enter the work force, the family dynamic changes. The majority of women are no longer at home on a full-time basis. As a consequence, responsibilities for food preparation, laundry, cleaning and home maintenance, not to mention child care and elder care, must be shared differently.

Women on the job
A steady climb since 1941

41. Female Labour Force Participation Rates by Marital Status

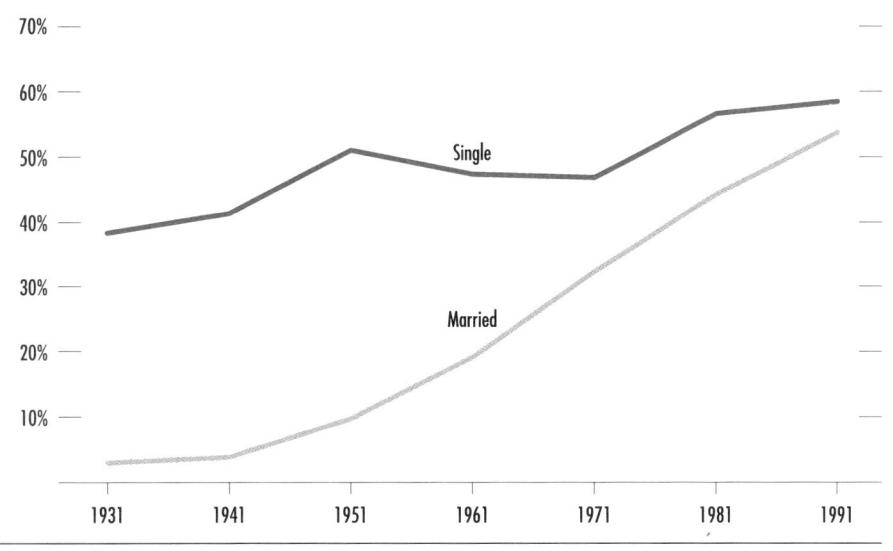

Prepared by the Centre for International Statistics

Married women joined the paid work force in increased numbers during World War II and have never looked back. During the 50-year period between 1941 and 1991, the labour force participation rate of married women increased steeply and steadily from 5% to 61%. The rate of growth of single women's labour force participation was less consistent, decreasing during the post-war period, but showing an overall increase from 47% to 67% over the 50-year period.

And so what?

Feminism was hardly born in the 1960s with the "women's liberation" movement. One of the historical roots of that movement is certainly the sharp and steady growth in the participation of married women in the labour force. Since 1941, married women, as a group, have shown little sign of reversing that trend.

The Vanier Institute of the Family

What we can say is that economic activity is central to the situation of women in any society, whatever form it takes.
Charles Jones, Lorna Marsden, Lorne Tepperman[90]

The transformation that the labour market has undergone in the past two decades has shattered any myth regarding women's role as 'marginal' workers, having only a temporary hold on employment and easily displaced from the labour force due to household responsibilities.
Statistics Canada[91]

Between 1971 and 1986, about 4% of farm operators were women. In 1991, the proportion jumped to 25%.
Chris O'Toole and Marc Prud'homme[92]

Children keep us working

42. Labour Force Participation Rates, Adults 15 - 64
(1991)

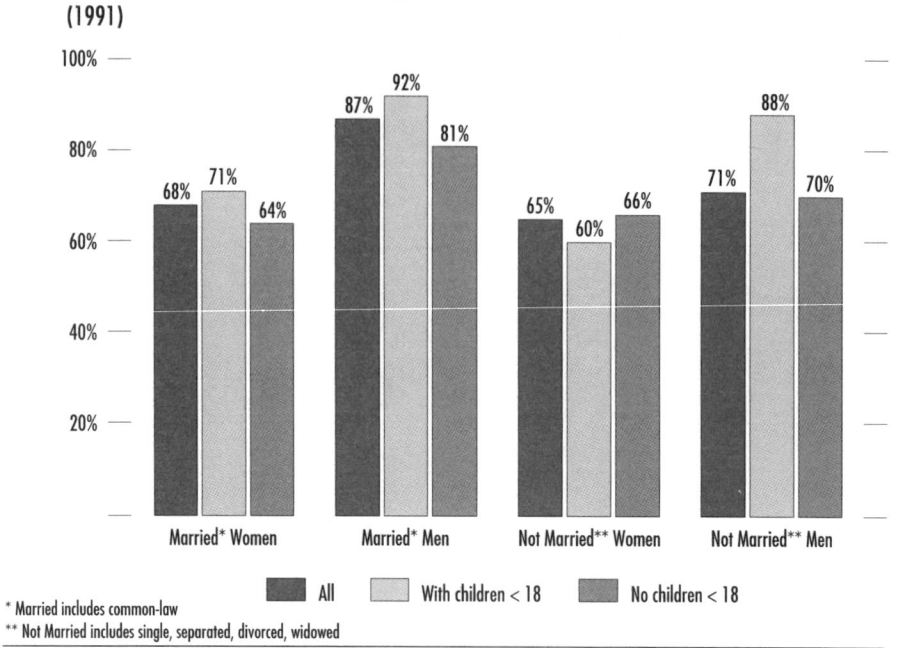

Category	All	With children < 18	No children < 18
Married* Women	68%	71%	64%
Married* Men	87%	92%	81%
Not Married** Women	65%	60%	66%
Not Married** Men	71%	88%	70%

* Married includes common-law
** Not Married includes single, separated, divorced, widowed

Calculated by the Centre for International Statistics

Male or female, Canadians are generally more likely to participate in the labour force if they have children at home. While 68% of all married women are in the labour force, 71% of those with children under 18 participate, compared with just 64% without children under 18. The split is even greater for men. Among married men, 92% of those with children under 18 participate, compared with 81% for those without. For not-married men, the difference is even greater: 88% with children under 18 versus 70% without. Only among not-married women is there a lower rate of participation among those with children under 18 (60% versus 66%).

And so what?

Raising children is expensive, so most parents today need jobs. Seven out of ten married women with children are in the labour force, as are roughly nine out of ten married and unmarried men with children. Six in ten lone mothers are in the work force as well. Their lower participation rate is due, in part, to the lower wages that women tend to earn as compared with men's, as well as the lack of affordable child care and the direct employment costs they would incur for transportation, clothing, taxes and so on. Their income potential is often so low that it makes more financial sense for many of them to stay home and scrape by on social assistance, alimony or other sources of subsistence income.

...families meet the cost of raising children in many ways, including increasing their incomes, increasing the amount of time spent in household work, reallocating income from other expenditures to child goods, or decreasing their savings... Families with children spent less on food away from home, tobacco and alcohol, parental clothing, and recreation than families without children in all regions.
Robin A. Douthitt and Joanne Fedyk[93]

The Vanier Institute of the Family

How times change!
Both parents employed in 7 of 10 families, up from 3 in 10 twenty years ago

43. Employment Status of Husbands and Wives With Children Under 19 Years of Age
(1990)

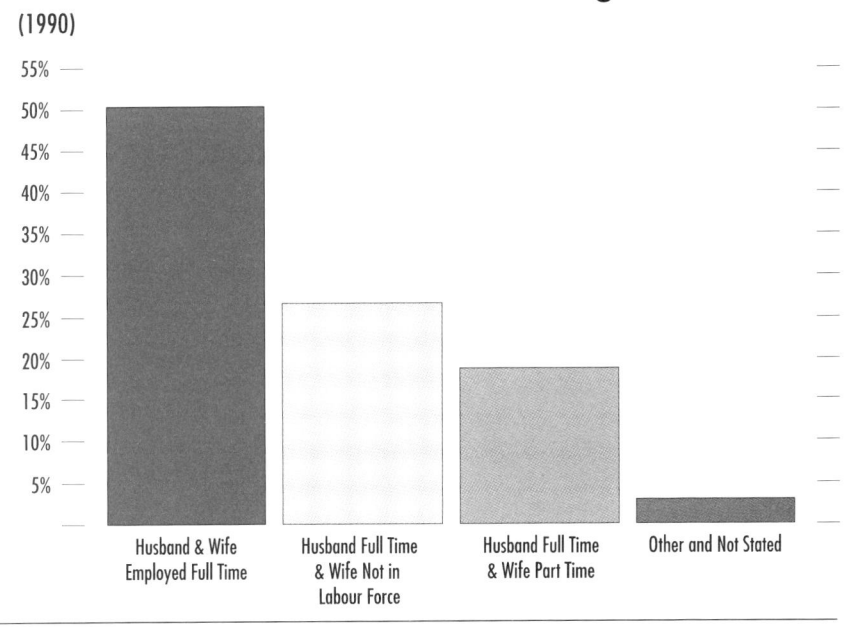

[Bar chart showing:
- Husband & Wife Employed Full Time: ~50%
- Husband Full Time & Wife Not in Labour Force: ~27%
- Husband Full Time & Wife Part Time: ~19%
- Other and Not Stated: ~3%]

Prepared by The Vanier Institute of the Family

Both parents work outside the home in most families. In 1990, seven out of ten couples with children under 19 years of age were dual-earner families. This is the reverse of twenty years ago, when only 30% of such families were dual-earner.[94] Both parents were full-time employees in 51% of families with children under 19. Just 27% of families with dependent children living at home followed the traditional male-breadwinner model in which the husband was employed full-time and the wife worked at home.

And so what?

In a very short time, the norms have changed for Canadian families. Dual-earner families now constitute the large majority of families. Not everyone in society, however, has caught up with these changes. From work schedules to business hours to procedures for dealing with sick children at school, many rules and operating procedures seem still to be based on the idea of a full-time homemaker available at home in every household. To the extent that such rules and procedures fail to recognize the realities of today's families, they will continue to cause stress for family members of all ages.

The Vanier Institute of the Family

Several characteristics of dual-earner families set them apart from couples in which the husband alone has an earned income. Spouses in dual-earner families are relatively young. They tend to have more formal education than other couples, and as a result, a higher proportion are employed in managerial or professional occupations. They are also less likely than traditional families to have children at home.
Maureen Moore[95]

Who's minding the kids?

The Vanier Institute of the Family

While women, like men, now face a lifetime in the labour force and can survive without a family, unlike men, women take on two jobs, have babies and more frequently experience poverty if they end up parenting alone. Historical analysis clearly demonstrates that if women and men are to share equally in family life, they must also share equally in work in and out of the labour force.
Pat Armstrong and Hugh Armstrong[96]

44. Female Labour Force Participation Rates by Age of Youngest Child

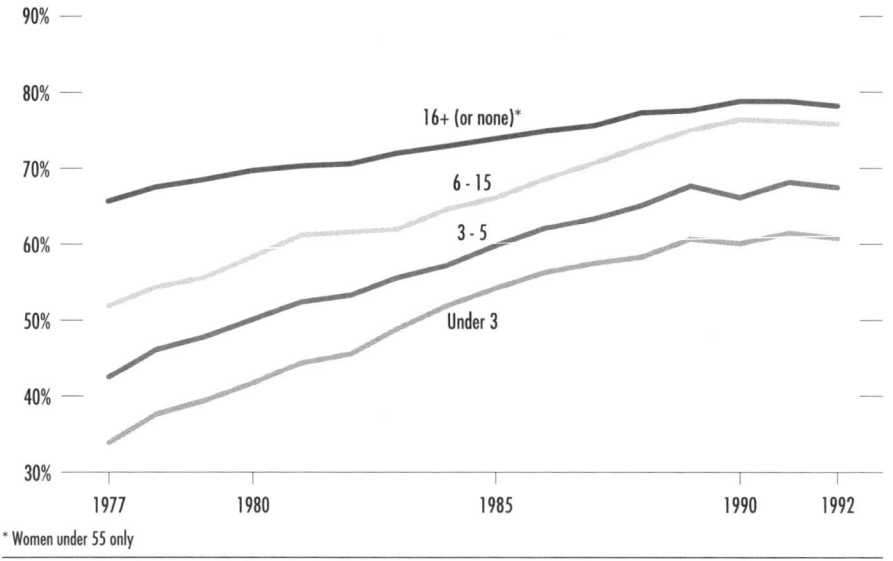

[Line graph showing participation rates from 1977 to 1992 for four groups: 16+ (or none)*, 6-15, 3-5, and Under 3. Rates rise from approximately 65%, 52%, 42%, and 33% in 1977 to approximately 78%, 76%, 67%, and 61% in 1992.]

*Women under 55 only

Prepared by the Centre for International Statistics

45. Labour Force Characteristics of Women by Age of Youngest Child
(1991)

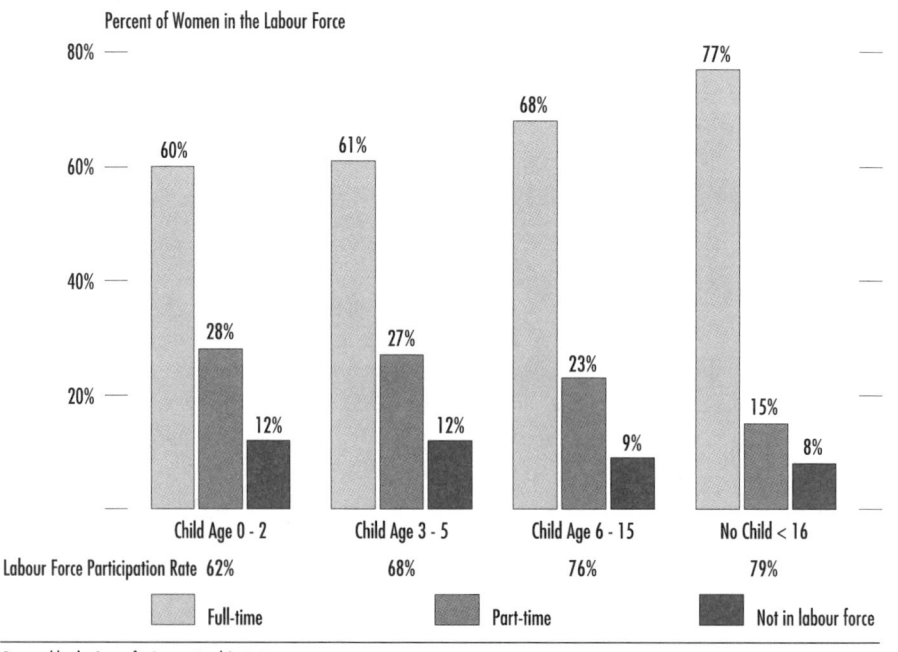

Percent of Women in the Labour Force

	Child Age 0-2	Child Age 3-5	Child Age 6-15	No Child < 16
Full-time	60%	61%	68%	77%
Part-time	28%	27%	23%	15%
Not in labour force	12%	12%	9%	8%
Labour Force Participation Rate	62%	68%	76%	79%

Prepared by the Centre for International Statistics

The vast majority of Canadian mothers are part of the paid labour force. This is true regardless of the age of the children. Even among those mothers with children under the age of three, the labour force participation rate is over 60%. Almost 70% of mothers whose youngest child is between 3 and 5 years old are in the labour force, as are over 75% of mothers of school-age children.

These high labour force participation rates are new for mothers of young children. In 1977 only 38% of mothers with children under the age of 6 were in the labour force. Just 15 years later, in 1992, 63% were labour force participants. Mothers of children between the ages of 3 and 5 now participate in the work force at a greater rate (68%) than did women in 1977 who had no children or children over the age of 16 (66%).

Among lone mothers, labour force participation is consistently lower. Lone mothers with children under the age of three had a participation rate of 41%, in 1991, increasing to 60% for those whose youngest child is age 3-5, and to 62% for those with children between the ages of 6 and 15.

Women with young children are more likely to have part-time employment than women with school-age children.

And so what?

Women still assume primary responsibility for child rearing, particularly for preschool children. As a result, women with children under six years of age continue to have a lower labour force participation rate than women with older children. Nevertheless, the majority of women with preschool children are either employed or looking for paid employment.

Women often take unpaid leave from paid employment in order to raise children, either by choice or necessity (i.e. unavailability of affordable child care). The implications of this can be far-reaching, and may include losing ground in their careers as technological advances outpace them, reduced contributions to pension plans, or part-time employment which may offer fewer benefits.

Employers who overlook the special child care needs of these mothers of young children do so at their own risk. Without flexible work options, these women are prone to incur higher rates of absenteeism, job turnover and performance problems. Family-sensitive personnel policies can help to alleviate some of these stressful and costly problems.

The Vanier Institute of the Family

...we do know that most mothers are now remaining in the labour force after the births of their children. Others, who do elect to stay at home with young children for a period of time, now return to the labour force much more quickly than their own mothers did. It is also evident that the shift to this pattern of parenting shows no sign of slowing down.
Status of Women Canada[97]

The Vanier Institute of the Family

The typical Canadian family is increasingly becoming a 'workaholic' unit. There are more double-income families, a growing percentage of single youth still living at home are in the labour force, and other relatives living in the same household are now participating in the labour market.

The family is now made up of busy people who increasingly view the home as a place to rest and relax between work periods.
Roger Sauvé[98]

A legacy of the slowing growth of productivity during the late 1970s and 1980s has been the stagnation of real wages. Indeed, if families with heads aged less than 65 had had to depend solely on the husband's earnings, there would have been virtually no growth at all in real family income.

The result was that between the years 1973 and 1986, the average real income of families in their working years increased by 13%. This reflected a 5% decline in the contribution of the husband to the family's real earnings and a whopping 46% increase in that of other members of the family.
The Economic Council of Canada[99]

Bringing home the bacon... together

46. Earners in Husband-Wife Families
(1990)

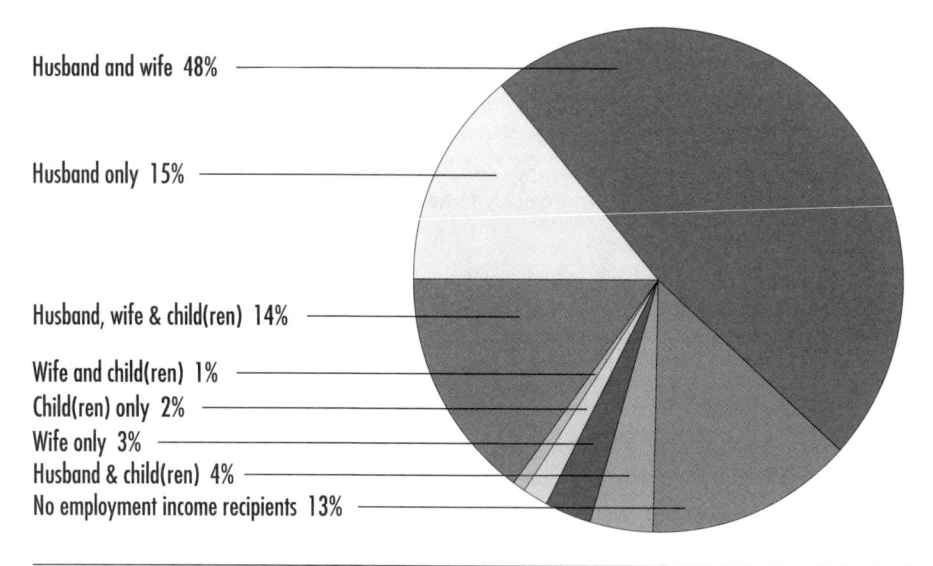

- Husband and wife 48%
- Husband only 15%
- Husband, wife & child(ren) 14%
- Wife and child(ren) 1%
- Child(ren) only 2%
- Wife only 3%
- Husband & child(ren) 4%
- No employment income recipients 13%

Prepared by the Centre for International Statistics

The traditional male "breadwinner" family is no longer the norm. Only 15% of husband-wife families receive employment income from the husband only. Both husband and wife have employment income in 62% of husband-wife families, up from an estimated 34% in 1967. In addition, children receive employment income in 21% of husband-wife families.

Dual-earner couples tend to be younger, possess a higher level of educational attainment, occupy more professional positions and have few or no children.

And so what?

In most families today, both husbands and wives work. Many people, however, have a hard time accepting this reality for a variety of reasons. Some feel families should be like the ones in which they were raised. Some believe that married women are working simply to obtain "frills" or "luxuries" for their families. The reality is, however, that most families need the monetary contributions of both spouses in order to cover essential costs – to pay the mortgage, write the rent cheque, buy the groceries and clothe the children. Moreover, it is not just individual families that now depend on two wages. Indeed, the Canadian economy as a whole depends on the capacity of families to adapt to new economic realities. The health of the private sector is sustained, in large measure, by the expenditures families make in the marketplace and the public sector services on which Canadians count are paid for with the taxes contributed by both men and women.

More than "pin money" but...

47. Contribution of Wife's Earnings to Overall Family Income
(1991)

Wives without earnings 34%

Wives with earnings 66%

Wife's earnings as % of total family income

50% or more	=	16%
40 - 49%	=	16%
30 - 39%	=	18%
20 - 29%	=	18%
10 - 19%	=	17%
< 10%	=	15%

Of the 4.1 million employed wives, 16% had earnings that amounted to 50% or more of total family income.

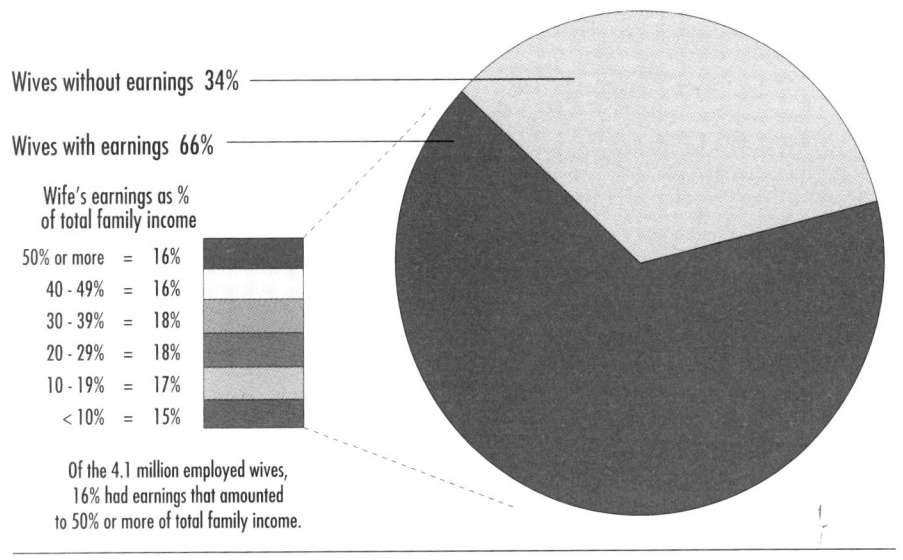

Calculated by the Centre for International Statistics

Two thirds of all married women in 1991 had employment earnings. In almost one third of dual-earner couples, wives' earnings contributed close to or more than one half of the family's total income. However, relatively few (16%) of them had earnings that amounted to 50% or more of the total family income. And in fact, most working wives' earnings amounted to less than one third of the family income. Though women have made progress over the years in closing the earnings gap, they still earn only 70 cents for every dollar earned by men*. As well, a higher proportion of women than men work part-time. Although many women earn less than men, their earnings are often necessary to provide an adequate standard of living for their families.

* Refers only to full-time, full-year workers

And so what?

Family incomes have increased over the past two decades, but by far the largest increases have gone to dual-earner families. During the 1970s, the real incomes of single-earner families increased modestly. During the 1980s, the real incomes of such families actually *fell*, while the incomes of dual-earner couples rose slightly. The lesson for most families is clear: to get ahead, having both spouses in the work force is not an option – it's a necessity.

The Vanier Institute of the Family

Any increase in family buying power can be attributed almost entirely to the fact of women working, since we know that between 1980 and 1988 there have been no real gains in the earnings of single-income families. More than a third of families where both spouses work would be below the poverty line if they had to live on one income.
Jeanne Morazain[100]

The historical shift of women into the workplace has been going on for a century, but did not reach a critical mass until the 1970s. The long-term impact of post-industrialism on family life was magnified by the effects of inflation. The shift in the economy was reducing the number of high-paying blue-collar jobs for auto and steel workers, and creating a demand for the low-paying pink-collar jobs like typist and file clerk. Also, since the mid-1960s, the costs of food, housing, education, and other goods and services have risen faster than the average male breadwinner's income. Despite their lower pay, married women's contributions to the family income became critical to maintaining living standards in both middle- and working-class families.
Arlene Skolnick[101]

In the last recession in 1979, families had to be extremely flexible, and we saw women entering the labour force in record numbers. When the next recession hit in 1989, they had to start working twice as hard to stay in exactly the same place. Four years later, working harder isn't enough. They've got to start cutting back.
Alan Mirabelli[102]

The Vanier Institute of the Family

....the diminishing income prospects since the '70s are being generated by more family earners than ever before (although in some cases it may stretch further because there are fewer children in families). Even more important is what is not represented in the income figures: the extra costs associated with acquiring the income. There are direct employment costs such as commuting, purchases of clothing and equipment, taxes, training expenses; there are indirect costs associated with child or elder care; and there are all the costs resulting from the loss of domestic production such as home maintenance, food preparation, cleaning and laundering and so on. Looking at income alone gives a false representation of how much better off families are.

When the comprehensive costs of obtaining extra income are calculated and offset, the real income gains are much smaller.
— David P. Ross and Clarence Lochhead[103]

Working more for less?
After big gains in the '70s, family incomes flatten off despite more earners per family

48. Trends in Average Family Income* and Average Family Size

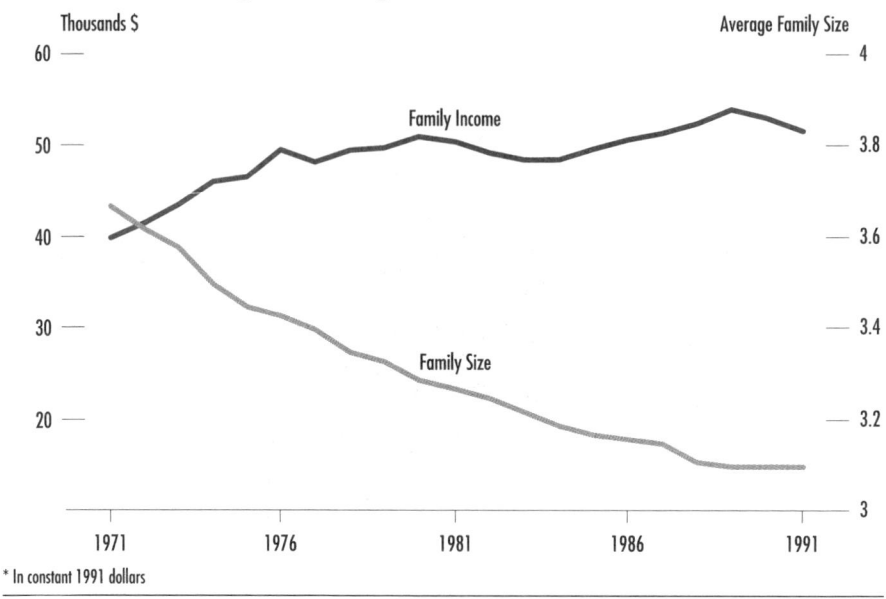

* In constant 1991 dollars

Prepared by the Centre for International Statistics

Between 1971 and 1991, average family income increased 29% while average family size decreased 16%. On average, families in 1971 had an income of $40,045 (in constant 1991 dollars) and 3.67 family members. By 1991, average family income had increased to $51,856. At the same time, family size decreased to 3.1 persons. As a result, average income per family member jumped by 53%, from $10,911 in 1971 to $16,728 in 1991.

Most of the increase in family income occurred during the 1970s. One reason for this was that more family members – women, in particular – joined the work force. Average family income rose $11,168 between 1971 and 1980. Yet between 1980 and 1991, it only rose by $643.

The impact of the recession of the early 1980s on family income was formidable. Average family income slid for several years during the recession, and then took several more years to climb back to its pre-recessionary level. It rose above that level for only two more years before succumbing to the next recession.

And so what?

Canadian families are working more for less gain. When women entered the work force in large numbers in the 1970s, family incomes rose sharply. The gains through the '80s, though, were painfully slow – despite the labour force participation of most women. As a result, most families now find it necessary to have more than one member earning an income.

Family incomes going nowhere fast

Table V – Average Family Income* by Family Type

	1980 ($)	1989 ($)	1991 ($)	% Change 1980 - 91
Families	51,213	54,215	51,856	+1.3
Elderly families	35,174	40,154	38,558	+9.6
Non-elderly families	53,417	56,515	54,094	+1.3
Couples, no children	53,100	52,809	52,436	-1.3
one earner	44,079	45,054	40,829	-7.4
two earners	59,105	58,531	59,800	+1.2
Two-parent with children	55,224	60,087	57,678	+4.4
one earner	42,486	46,234	42,237	-0.6
two earners	57,605	59,862	59,412	+3.1
3 or more earners	73,007	76,599	72,839	-0.2
Lone-parent males	34,649	43,651	36,470	+5.3
Lone-parent females	21,930	24,110	21,712	-1.0
no earners	9,600	12,381	12,926	+34.6
one earner	21,871	24,648	23,730	+8.5

* Income before tax, in constant 1991 dollars
Prepared by the Centre for International Statistics[104]

Despite gains in the '80s, most families are making no more money now than they did 12 years ago. During the 1980s, average family income (in constant 1991 dollars) increased for most family types. However, between 1989 and 1991 the recession largely offset these gains. By 1991, the average income of some family types – particularly single-earner families – was actually lower than in 1980.

Between 1980 and 1991, non-elderly single-earner couples with no children living at home experienced a 7.4% decrease. Two-parent, single-earner families with children at home also experienced a decline. The most drastic decline was in the latter few years of that period. Only the so-called DINKS (Dual Income couples with No Kids) and lone, unemployed mothers saw their incomes go up between 1989 and 1991. The average family income for single-mother families with no earners increased during that period by 4.4%, and over the decade by one third. This sounds like a lot, but these families had such low incomes to begin with that the increase had virtually no effect on their poverty rates – 95% of them lived below the poverty line in 1991.

And so what?

The modest increase in gross family income recorded over the last two decades does not take into account the heavier burden of taxation assumed by Canadians. In 1990, after-tax family income declined by 2.2% from the year before. A reduction in after-tax family income of this magnitude had not been seen since the recession of the early '80s. It has been estimated (Patrick Grady, *Globe and Mail*, November 5, 1992) that the average Canadian family paid $1,894 more in federal taxes in 1990 than it would have in 1984. Moreover, this increase reflects only changes at the federal level and not those at the provincial or municipal level. By 1990, income taxes consumed almost 20% of family income, up from approximately 15% in 1980.

The Vanier Institute of the Family

Middle-income families, particularly those with children, have borne the brunt of the tax increase since 1984. High-income families have faced less than proportionate tax increases, and the lowest-income families will have even enjoyed tax cuts or transfer increases.
Patrick Grady[105]

If we compare the real average family earnings of younger families in 1973 with the average earnings of an older generation of families, aged 30-64, they stood at 82%. But by 1990 this proportion had fallen to 71%.

Restated in dollar terms, young families fell $8,093 short of the average family income of the previous generation of families in 1973, and this shortfall almost doubled to $15,042 in 1990, as measured in inflation-adjusted dollars.
David P. Ross and Clarence Lochhead[106]

As for the financial strain on the solo-parent families, especially those headed by women, there can be little doubt. Also under stress are two-parent families headed by younger men with little education or few marketable skills, and many retired couples. Nor is there any doubt that a disproportionate number of persons not living in a domestic family experience considerable financial deprivation.
Emily M. Nett[107]

Middle class not dead yet
Most Canadian families are "middle-income"

49. Percentage Distribution of Families by Level of Family Income
(1991)

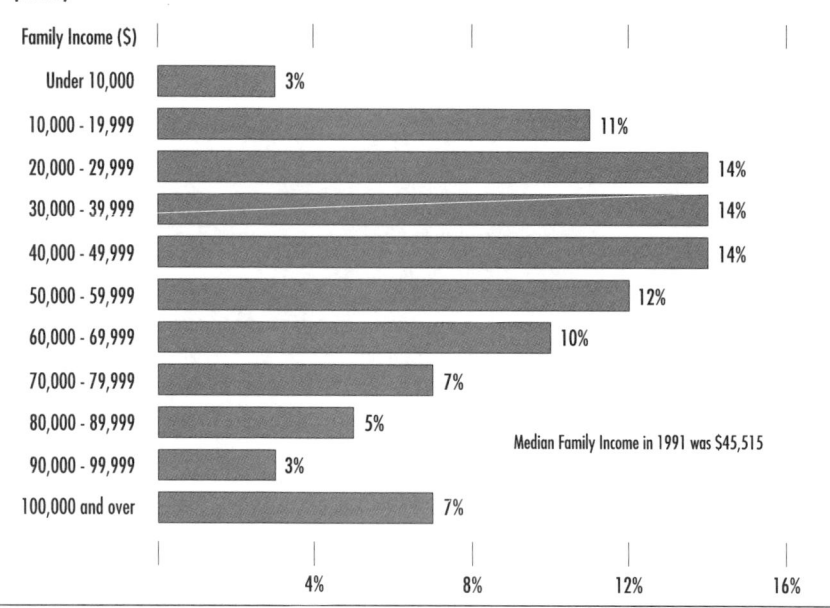

Family Income ($)	%
Under 10,000	3%
10,000 - 19,999	11%
20,000 - 29,999	14%
30,000 - 39,999	14%
40,000 - 49,999	14%
50,000 - 59,999	12%
60,000 - 69,999	10%
70,000 - 79,999	7%
80,000 - 89,999	5%
90,000 - 99,999	3%
100,000 and over	7%

Median Family Income in 1991 was $45,515

Prepared by the Centre for International Statistics

In 1991, 28% of Canadian families had family incomes of less than $30,000, while 32% had family incomes of $60,000 or more. The remaining 40% of families fell into the $30,000 to $60,000 range. At the extreme ends of the scale, 3% of families had less than $10,000, while 7% had more than $100,000. Median family income – the level at which half of Canadian families make more and half make less – was $45,515.

And so what?

These statistics on family income are rather encouraging, but they date back to 1990. That was just at the onset of the current recession. The recession has caused – or been triggered by – economic restructuring and wholesale job loss. Because so many of the jobs that have been lost were those of older, highly-paid workers, the proportion of middle-income families may be somewhat lower in 1994 than in 1990.

Communities and governments tend to thrive when their families enjoy comfortable incomes. Low family incomes can be ruinous. They may result in health and social problems; higher demand for services like training, counselling and social assistance; and lowered government revenues to pay for these expenses.

There is evidence that middle-level, middle-income jobs are taking a declining share of the job pie with employment growth primarily in high-income or low-income, low-skill positions.
The Economic Council of Canada[108]

Family incomes vary from sea to sea to sea

Table VI – Average Family Income in Constant (1990) Dollars, Canada, Provinces and Territories,
(1985 and 1990)

	1985 ($)	1990 ($)	Average Annual Change (%)
Canada	47,087	51,342	1.8
Newfoundland	35,950	40,942	2.8
Prince Edward Island	37,905	43,295	2.8
Nova Scotia	41,002	44,001	1.5
New Brunswick	38,000	42,148	2.2
Quebec	43,048	46,593	1.6
Ontario	51,898	57,227	2.0
Manitoba	44,173	46,091	0.9
Saskatchewan	43,153	44,174	0.5
Alberta	50,713	52,346	0.6
British Columbia	46,873	52,403	2.4
Yukon Territory	50,114	56,034	2.4
Northwest Territories	49,757	55,795	2.4

Prepared by the Centre for International Statistics[109]

In 1990, the average family income was $51,342. That's up from $47,087 (in constant 1990 dollars) in 1985 – an average annual increase of 1.8%. In general, average family incomes were lower in the East and higher in the West, but Ontario had the highest average annual income in both 1985 and 1990. Newfoundland and Prince Edward Island had the lowest average family incomes in 1985, but experienced the greatest increases between 1985 and 1990, at 2.8% annually. Nevertheless, Newfoundland still has the lowest average family income in Canada at $40,942.

Within these averages there are significant differences across the country. For example, the Northwest Territories had the highest proportion of families with incomes of $100,000 or more in both 1985 (8.3%) and 1990 (13.9%). This is probably the result of the isolation pay and bonuses many employees receive there. The Northwest Territories also showed the greatest proportional growth in such families over the five-year period.

On the other hand, the Atlantic provinces, which had the highest proportion of families with incomes of less than $30,000, also had the lowest proportion of families with incomes in excess of $100,000 (3-4%).

The Vanier Institute of the Family

As men and women age, the income gap grows

Table VII – Number of Married Men and Women by Age, Showing Proportion with Employment Income and Average Earnings, 1990

	Married Persons With Employment Income			Employed Full-time Full-year*	
	Number	% of all Married	Average Earnings	% of all Married	Average Earnings
Married Men**	5,284,430	80	35,956	55	41,282
By Age					
15 - 24	166,235	90	18,782	42	24,273
25 - 34	1,399,290	95	31,000	65	35,408
35 - 44	1,635,390	95	39,507	70	43,678
45 - 54	1,152,425	94	41,938	68	46,235
55 - 64	728,435	75	35,417	50	42,105
65 & over	202,650	20	23,525	6	33,723
Married Women**	4,287,690	65	18,966	31	26,047
By Age					
15 - 24	291,610	80	12,227	30	18,312
25 - 34	1,355,710	79	18,269	37	25,290
35 - 44	1,366,115	80	20,991	40	27,978
45 - 54	836,635	73	20,493	38	26,883
55 - 64	371,605	43	16,944	18	24,065
65 & over	66,020	9	13,175	2	20,462

* Individuals who worked 30 or more hours per week for at least 49 weeks in 1990
** Includes common-law, excludes married but separated.
Prepared by the Centre for International Statistics[110]

Among married (including common-law) persons with employment income, the average earnings of men in 1990 were almost double those of women. In every age group, the average earnings of married men were higher than those of married women.

Among those who were employed full-time, full-year, average earnings for married men, at $41,282, were substantially higher than average earnings for married women ($26,047). Married women who were employed full-time, full-year earned only 63% of what their male counterparts earned in 1990.

The gap between the average earnings of married men and married women is narrowest in the younger age groups, widening with every age group except among retired people. For example, among married people aged 15-24 who work full-time and full-year, women average 75% of men's earnings, decreasing to 71% in the 25-34 age group, and 64% in the 35-44 age group. In the 55-64 age group, women average only 57% of men's earnings.

Average earnings for married men increase with every age group until peaking in the 45-54 age group. Earnings for married women follow a similar pattern, although they peak earlier (in the 35-44 age group) and much lower. Married men in their late forties and early fifties are earning, on average, approximately $20,000 more per year than their female counterparts.

And so what?

Some say that the face of poverty is old and female. It's no wonder. If men lead women in income, and that gap widens as they age, the income prospects for older women are poor indeed. The implications for older women are chilling – to be poorest at a time when one needs more support and is less capable of fully independent living.

Divorce a good career move for women?

Table VIII – Number of Divorced Men and Women by Age, Showing Proportion With Employment Income and Average Earnings, 1990

	Divorced Persons with Employment Income			Employed Full-time Full-year*	
	Number	% of all Divorced	Average Earnings	% of all Divorced	Average Earnings
Divorced Men**	268,615	74	31,172	44	38,129
By Age					
15 - 24	1,895	82	16,354	30	25,030
25 - 34	47,065	89	27,407	53	33,595
35 - 44	99,375	85	31,831	53	38,017
45 - 54	76,120	82	34,561	50	41,419
55 - 64	36,950	61	29,585	32	38,059
65 & over	7,215	19	22,926	6	33,532
Divorced Women**	376,435	69	23,014	40	29,020
By Age					
15 - 24	3,825	67	12,436	22	19,442
25 - 34	64,795	74	19,452	39	25,635
35 - 44	142,220	81	24,199	49	29,909
45 - 54	107,545	79	25,128	49	30,497
55 - 64	50,110	59	21,726	33	27,704
65 & over	7,925	14	15,425	4	24,382

* Individuals who worked 49 to 52 weeks, mostly full-time.
** Excludes individuals who are separated only.
Prepared by the Centre for International Statistics[111]

Divorced women with employment income have higher average earnings than married women, but still lag far behind married or divorced men. Among those who work full-time, full-year, divorced women are considerably closer in average earnings to divorced men than married women are to married men. Married women working full-year, full-time average 63% of married men's earnings, while divorced women working full-year, full-time average 76% of divorced men's earnings.

Interestingly, divorced women have higher average earnings than married women, whereas divorced men have lower average earnings than married men.

Single mothers are struggling

50. Percentage Distribution of Male and Female Lone-parent Families by Level of Family Income
(1990)

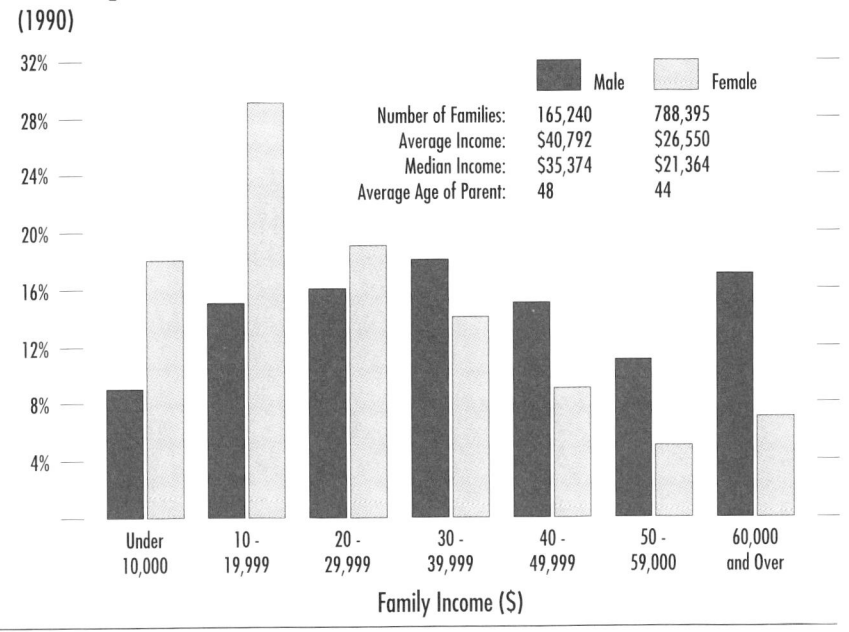

	Male	Female
Number of Families:	165,240	788,395
Average Income:	$40,792	$26,550
Median Income:	$35,374	$21,364
Average Age of Parent:	48	44

Family Income ($): Under 10,000; 10 - 19,999; 20 - 29,999; 30 - 39,999; 40 - 49,999; 50 - 59,999; 60,000 and Over

Prepared by the Centre for International Statistics

There were almost one million lone parents in Canada in 1990, and the vast majority of them (83%) were female. One of the most fundamental differences between male and female lone parents is their very different economic circumstances. The average family income of female lone-parent families in 1990 was $26,550 which is only 65% of the male lone-parent average family income of $40,792. Almost half (47%) of female lone-parent families and one-quarter (24%) of male lone-parent families had family incomes under $20,000 in 1990.

There are many reasons for the economic differences between male and female lone parents. On average, women earn less than men. In addition, lone fathers tend to be older and better-educated, have more labour force experience, and have older children. Their careers are often established before they become lone parents and their children are often already school-aged.

Finally, low levels of child support awarded by the courts and the high numbers of men who do not, in fact, comply with the court orders are a significant cause of the financial hardship experienced by many lone mothers and their children.

And so what?

Most single mothers and their children have much lower family incomes than other families. Children of poor families are more at-risk in almost every way. They tend to have more health problems, fare worse at school than others, and develop more behavioural problems than other children. Their problems, in turn, affect us all. Thus the low incomes of the growing number of families headed by lone mothers should be of real concern.

The Vanier Institute of the Family

...the proportion of men below the poverty line after paying support was 18% in 1986 and 16% in 1988. However, approximately two thirds of women and children have total incomes below the 1988 poverty lines with support included. Where support is excluded (e.g. support may not be paid), approximately three quarters of women and children live below the poverty line following divorce.

In some cases the family's resources are simply insufficient to provide adequate child support. In these situations the problems of low child support awards is part of the larger problem of poverty in Canada, which is intensified by the onset of divorce. However, in other families the resources are available but they are simply not being shared in a manner that would allow all family members to benefit from similar standards of living following divorce. This is confirmed by the fact that such a large proportion of women and children live in poverty following divorce.
        Federal/Provincial/
        Territorial Family Law
        Committee[112]

The short end of the stick
Women much worse off than men after separation and divorce

51. Child Support and Alimony as a Percentage of Recipient's Total Income by Recipient's Family Type
(1990)

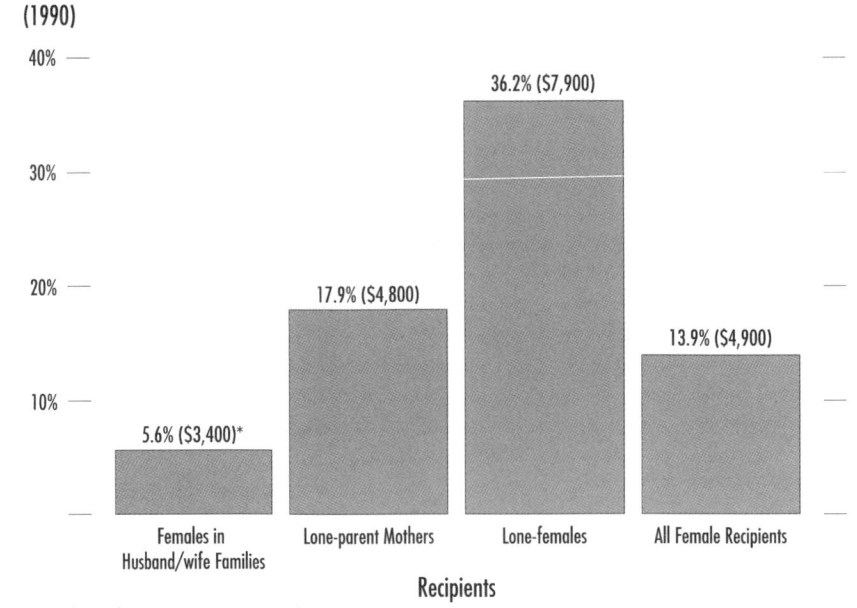

Recipients	Percentage (Average Payment)
Females in Husband/wife Families	5.6% ($3,400)*
Lone-parent Mothers	17.9% ($4,800)
Lone-females	36.2% ($7,900)
All Female Recipients	13.9% ($4,900)

* Number in parenthesis indicates average payment received

Prepared by the Centre for International Statistics

The vast majority (98%) of alimony recipients are women.* According to tax data, in 1990, 265,000 reported receiving alimony. On average, these women received $4,900 in alimony payments, representing 14% of their total family income, which averaged $33,500. For the men who paid alimony, this amounted to an average of 9% of *their* total incomes, which averaged $55,400.

Of those women who received alimony, two in three (64%) were lone mothers. One in four (27%) were in husband-wife families, and one in ten (9%) were lone persons with no spouse or dependent children. On the other hand, almost half (47%) of the men who paid alimony were lone persons, while 46% were in husband-wife families.

Among those lone mothers who received alimony, those payments amounted to nearly one fifth (17.9%) of their total income. However, many women who have been granted child support by the courts never receive anything from their ex-spouses. In Ontario alone it is estimated that there are 90,000 delinquent payers.

*Revenue Canada, the only reliable source of information on this topic, lumps alimony and child support payments under the heading "alimony."

And so what?

For most women, separation or divorce results in drastic reductions in income and a decline in living standards. They feel the financial effects of divorce much more harshly than men do. But divorced women, of course, are not alone in their discomfort. Their children usually accompany them on their slide into poverty. So while the children of these families represent just 3% of all Canadians, they constitute more than one quarter of all persons in low-income families.

Despite legislative attempts to improve the disadvantaged position of divorced women and their children, things have not gotten much better for them. Two groups are particularly affected: middle-aged women who were not in the work force when married, and women in their thirties and forties who assume custody of their children. Even without counting the many who do not receive court-ordered support payments, our high rates of separation and divorce and the paltry nature of most support payments consign many Canadian women and children to poverty.

As the Federal/Provincial Territorial Family Law Committee notes: "Any method of determining child support should include or take into account the following principles:

#1 Parents have legal responsibilities for the financial support of their children.
#2 Child support legislation should not distinguish between the parents or children on the basis of sex.
#3 The determination of child support should be made without regard to the marital status of the parents.
#4 Responsibility for the financial support of children should be in proportion to the means of each parent.
#5 In determining the means of each parent, his or her minimum needs should be taken into consideration.
#6 Levels of child support should be established in relation to parental means.
#7 While each child of a parent has an equal right to support, in multiple family situations the interests of all children should be considered.
#8 The development of any new approach to the determination of child support should minimize collateral effects (e.g. disincentive to remarriage, joint or extended custody arrangements and voluntary unemployment or underemployment) to the extent compatible with the obligation to pay child support."[113]

Many teens working too

Table IX – Employment and Average Earnings of Teenagers (Aged 14 - 17) Living With Parents, 1993

Age	Total Number of Youth (Age 14 - 17) Living in Parents' Household	Percentage with Employment Income	Average Earnings of Those with Employment Income
14 - 15	725,000	21%	$2,293
16 - 17	715,400	69%	$3,667
All (14 - 17)	1,440,400	45%	$3,346

Calculations by the Centre for International Statistics[114]

In 1993 there were almost a million and a half teenagers between the ages of 14 and 17 who lived with their parents. Of these, approximately 648,200 (45%) had employment income. Two out of ten of the younger teens and seven out of ten of the older teens had employment income. Average earnings were approximately 60% higher for the older teens than for the younger teens, at least partly as a result of working more hours. Teenagers between the ages of 14 and 17 who lived at home and had employment income in 1993 earned, on average, $3,346 each. Collectively, they earned over two billion dollars.

And so what?

While most discussions about family incomes focus on the incomes of marriage partners, teenage children also account for significant earnings. Adolescent employment can contribute to the development of good work habits and discipline, as well as contributing to the teen's budget for personal expenses. As well, many families need money from their children to help make ends meet. Yet teenage employment has both advantages and drawbacks. Studies have shown that for males, the lowest risk of dropping out of school is for those who work between one and 20 hours a week. Those working more than 20 hours per week have the highest risk. For females, the highest risk of dropping out is for those with no job at all. Some teenage Canadians, it seems, are becoming as overburdened with school, work and family commitments as adults. Along with the overwork come some similar side effects – stress, reduced performance, and lack of personal or family time.

...senior high school students give the following reasons for wanting to work (in descending order of importance): to develop a feeling of independence and a sense of responsibility (16.7%); to buy clothes (16%); and to be independent of parents (10.9%). Among junior high school students (including those in special streams) the reasons were: to buy more clothes (20.2%); to develop a feeling of independence and a sense of responsibility (11.9%); and to buy a car or a motor-bike (10.1%).
Bernard Fortin[115]

On an immediate personal level, Canadian young people have four dominant concerns: the pressure to do well at school, the feeling of never having enough time, lack of money, and wondering what they will do when they graduate.
Reginald W. Bibby and Donald C. Posterski[116]

Family poverty
Seniors escaping, single moms sinking

52. Poverty Rates Among Canadian Families
(1981 & 1991)

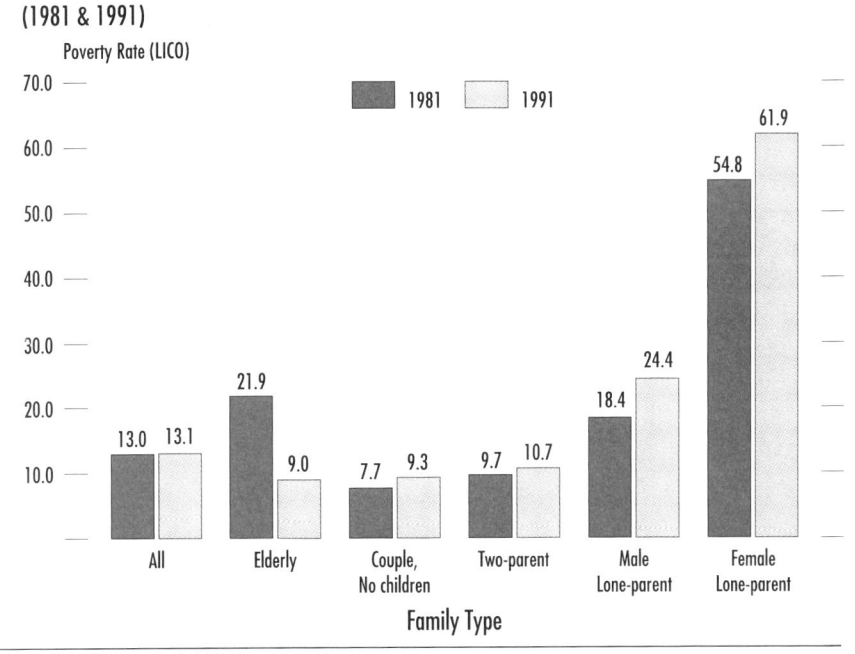

Poverty Rate (LICO)

Family Type	1981	1991
All	13.0	13.1
Elderly	21.9	9.0
Couple, No children	7.7	9.3
Two-parent	9.7	10.7
Male Lone-parent	18.4	24.4
Female Lone-parent	54.8	61.9

Prepared by the Centre for International Statistics

When Canadians refer to the poverty line, what they usually mean is Statistics Canada's Low Income Cut-Offs (LICOs, pronounced "like-oze"). LICOs vary according to size of community and size of family. They attempt to gauge the amount of money families need in order to live adequately. While not an official measure of poverty, LICOs are popularly interpreted and used as such.

Overall, the poverty rate among Canadian families was 13.1% in 1991, almost unchanged from a decade earlier.

However, the data indicated that certain family types are far more vulnerable to poverty than are other family types. Roughly one in ten two-parent families was below the poverty line in 1991, compared with six in ten female lone-parent families. Poverty rates among single-parent families have worsened substantially since 1981.

The family poverty rate for almost all family types increased between 1981 and 1991, some more dramatically than others. The only exception was elderly families, which experienced a plunging poverty rate, from 21.9% in 1981 to 9% in 1991. The change came about because governments made it a priority to reduce poverty among seniors.

"Working" families with children are not immune to poverty. In 1991, earned incomes were reported by 84% of poor couples with children and by 47% of lone mothers.[117]

Since 1982, more and more Canadians have had to turn to social assistance (welfare). In the early '90s the recession contributed heavily to steep increases in welfare rolls. High unemployment, combined with cutbacks to Unemployment Insurance (shorter eligibility periods, lower benefits) have hastened the descent from employment to unemployment to welfare for many Canadian families. In no province do welfare payments come close to keeping families above the poverty line.

In March 1993 approximately 2,975,000 persons – about one in nine Canadians – were receiving social assistance.

The Vanier Institute of the Family

Although many believe that poor families are poor largely because of their lack of work effort, it is clear that poverty can persist even with a high degree of labour force participation. The inability of many families to escape poverty even when they expand their work effort reflects the growth of part-time, low-paying, unstable jobs in which the poor are caught.
  Child Poverty Action Group and the Social Planning Council of Metropolitan Toronto[118]

And so what?

Incredibly, three out of every ten poor families lived more than $10,000 below the poverty line in 1991. The average poor family had $7,429 less.

Ironically, most of Canada's poor would feel well-off if their incomes even came close to the poverty line. It would represent a substantial improvement in their standard of living, in some cases doubling or tripling their actual incomes.

The poverty line in 1991 ranged from $13,799 for a family of two in a rural community to $37,833 for a family of seven in a large city like Toronto. Almost 30% of Canada's 949,000 poor families lived more than $10,000 below the poverty line. That means there were 276,000 families struggling along on the equivalent of $3,799 for the rural family of two – $316 *per month* – or $27,833 for the big-city family of seven.

53. How Poor is Poor?
Depth of poverty shown as $ below "poverty line"
(1991)

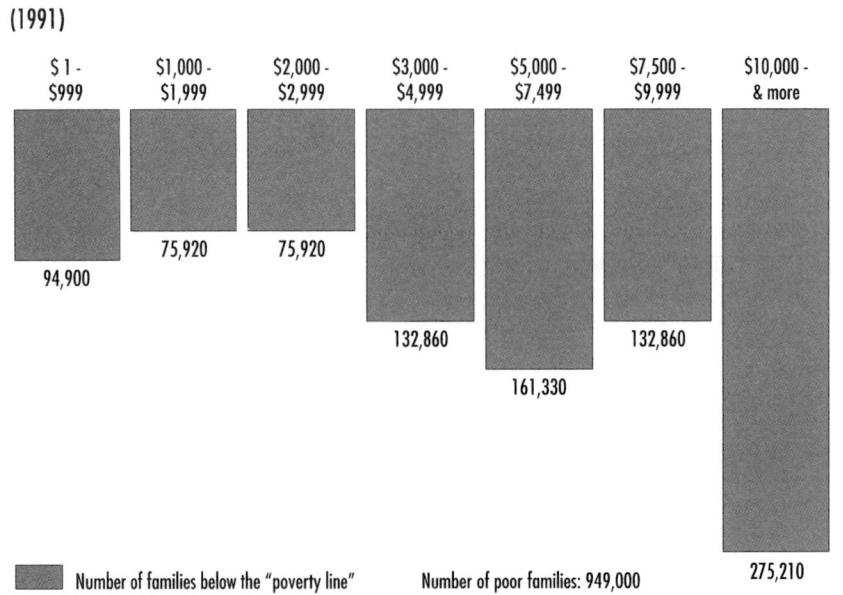

$1 - $999	$1,000 - $1,999	$2,000 - $2,999	$3,000 - $4,999	$5,000 - $7,499	$7,500 - $9,999	$10,000 - & more
94,900	75,920	75,920	132,860	161,330	132,860	275,210

Number of families below the "poverty line"   Number of poor families: 949,000

Prepared by the Centre for International Statistics

The good news is that Canadians have proven that poverty can be beaten. The major drop in poverty rates for senior families proves that when governments get serious, poverty can be alleviated.

...families with children ran a greater risk of poverty. Compared with childless couples, families with one or two children were twice as likely to be poor, while families with three children or more were almost three times as likely to be poor.
Canadian Child Welfare Association, et al.[119]

No progress on child poverty

54. Child Poverty Rates by Family Type

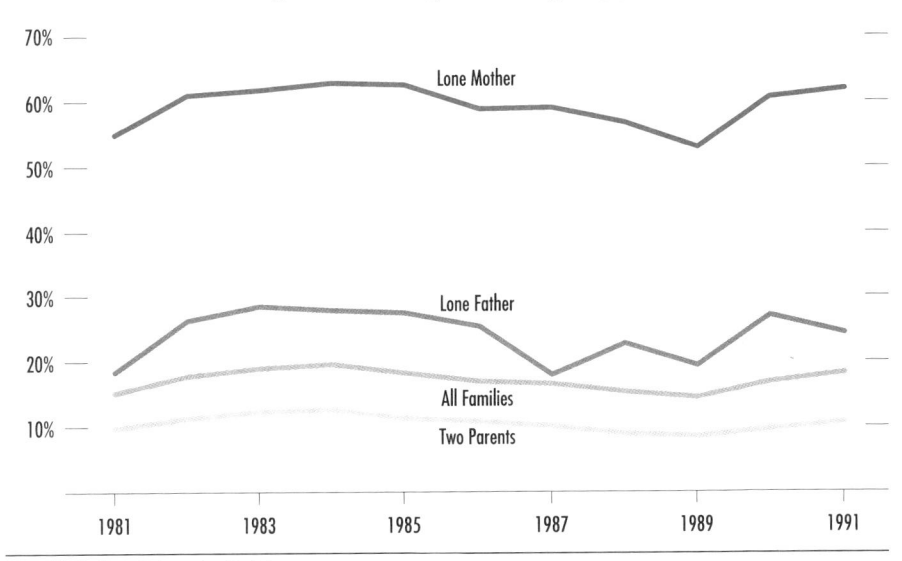

Chart showing child poverty rates from 1981 to 1991 for Lone Mother (around 55-63%), Lone Father (around 18-28%), All Families (around 15-20%), and Two Parents (around 10-12%).

Prepared by the Centre for International Statistics

The child poverty rate fell dramatically throughout the 1970s. In part, this was due to more women entering the paid labour force, which boosted family incomes. The recession of the early 1980s ended the downward trend in child poverty, however. The rate climbed steadily throughout the first half of the 1980s. In 1985, the rate began to drop again, until the next recession in the early 1990s.

In effect, there was little overall progress against child poverty in the 1980s. While the children in two-parent families fared slightly better, this was largely offset by increases in poverty among the children of single-parent mothers. In 1991, as the recession deepened, there were 1,210,000 children (18.3%) under the age of 18 who were living in poverty, compared with 998,000 children (15.2%) ten years earlier.

And so what?

With widespread unemployment and economic restructuring over the past decade, it should not be surprising that so many children are living with their parents in poverty.

Child poverty is costly to society as a whole. Poor children have more health and social problems, and many grow up to become adults with problems that are expensive for society to resolve. Child poverty is resistant to quick fixes. Periods of slow economic growth and high unemployment deprive governments of the resources to alleviate child poverty. Yet as the experience with senior families has illustrated, governments can substantially reduce poverty when they are determined to do so.

Canadians are currently experiencing many of the conditions under which poverty thrives: a slow economy, high divorce rates, high unemployment, inadequate education, lack of sufficient child care options, low wages (especially for women), and cutbacks to social programs.

The Vanier Institute of the Family

Younger families are falling behind the previous generation's average income, and not gaining. Given that the majority of dependent children are being raised in these younger families it does not auger well for the future welfare of Canada's children. It helps explain why Canada's child poverty rate has stubbornly resisted any downward movement.
— David P. Ross and Clarence Lochhead[120]

Only about one in five lone-parent families headed by women receive spousal and child support.
The Vanier Institute of the Family[121]

Most poor children live in two-parent families

55. Who Do Poor Children Live With?

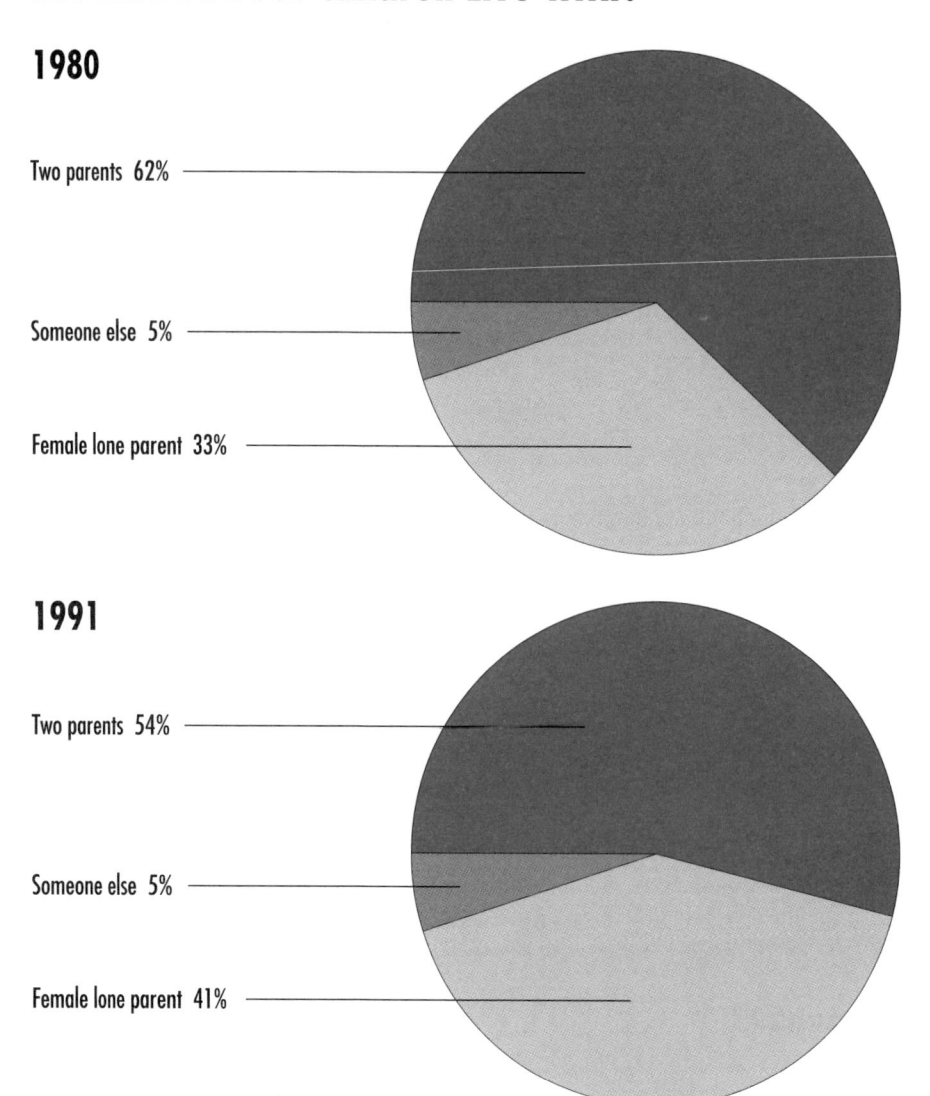

1980

Two parents 62%
Someone else 5%
Female lone parent 33%

1991

Two parents 54%
Someone else 5%
Female lone parent 41%

Prepared by the Centre for International Statistics

Most children living in single-parent families are poor. *Most poor children, however, live in two-parent families.* In 1991, 54% of Canada's poor children lived in two-parent families (657,000 children); 41% lived in single-mother families (496,000 children); and the remaining 5% lived either in single-father families or in other circumstances. Among children in two-parent families, the poverty rate was 11.7%, in sharp contrast to that among children in single-mother families, at 65.8%. Two out of every three children in single-mother families lived below the poverty line!

And so what?

In 1992, the families of approximately 900,000 children had to count on food banks at various times during the year.

Before the recession of the early 1980s, food banks didn't even exist in Canada. Today, there are 436 operating across the country, a grim reminder that poverty and hunger are serious problems even in a relatively wealthy country like Canada.

The Vanier Institute of the Family

Social and economic commentators frequently warn that Canada cannot continue to compete and prosper in the global arena if approximately one-sixth of our children continue to grow up poor, and under circumstances that seriously jeopardize their chances of becoming happy and productive citizens.
    Senate Committee on Social Affairs, Science and Technology[122]

To be born poor is to face a greater likelihood of ill health – in infancy, in childhood and throughout your adult life. To be born poor is to face a lesser likelihood that you will finish high school; lesser still that you will attend university. To be born poor is to face a greater likelihood that you will be judged a delinquent in adolescence and, if so, a greater likelihood that you will be sent to a 'correctional institution'. To be born poor is to have the deck stacked against you at birth, to find life an uphill struggle ever after. To be born poor is unfair to kids.
    The National Council of Welfare[123]

Making ends meet

Table X – Average Expenditure of Urban Canadian Households* on Selected Goods and Services

	Average Expenditure ($)	Percentage of Income (%)
Housing	8,304	14.5
Groceries	4,995	8.7
Clothing	3,049	5.3
Income taxes	12,577	21.9
Property taxes	1,724	3.0
Homeowner insurance	380	0.7
Life insurance	714	1.2
Savings**	6,439	11.2
Recreation	2,880	5.0

* The households contained in the above table include at least one census family.

** Savings include voluntary savings, annual contributions to government and trusteed pension plans, and contributions to life insurance annuities and life insurance premiums.

Note: Average urban households consisted of approximately three people and had an average income of $57,443 in 1990.

Prepared by the Centre for International Statistics[124]

What do Canadian families spend, and on what? The average urban Canadian household spent approximately one seventh of its income on housing, one fifth on income taxes, one tenth on groceries, and one twentieth on clothing. This is only a limited list of the average Canadian expenditures. It does not include what Canadians spend on: basic pharmaceutical necessities such as toothpaste and shampoo; dentist bills; occasional meals in restaurants; or the daily newspaper. Caution must be used when analyzing the above figures since over half (53%) of these households were married couples with single children and only one in ten were single-parent families. These three-person families in general were more prosperous than many other groupings. Larger families spend more on housing, groceries and clothing, while the single-parent families had, generally, lower incomes so they saved less, spent less on recreation, and spent a greater proportion of their income on the necessities.

The Vanier Institute of the Family

Statistics Canada's SURVEY OF FAMILY EXPENDITURES for 1992 ...showed Canadians are spending a smaller proportion of their take-home pay on food, clothing, furniture, appliances and alcohol, and more on shelter and transportation costs and in-home entertainment.

Spending on food, for instance, accounts for 16% of the average family's take-home pay, down from 22% in 1969. Likewise, spending on clothing is down to 6% of take-home pay, compared to 10% in 1969. Spending on alcohol has dropped by almost a quarter since 1986. Car purchases have also decreased 13% since 1986, whereas families are spending 30% more on maintenance and repair of their older cars.

The Ottawa Citizen[125]

Baby needs new shoes
Couples with children lead family spending race, lone parents left in the dust

56. Average Yearly Expenditure by Family Type
(1990)

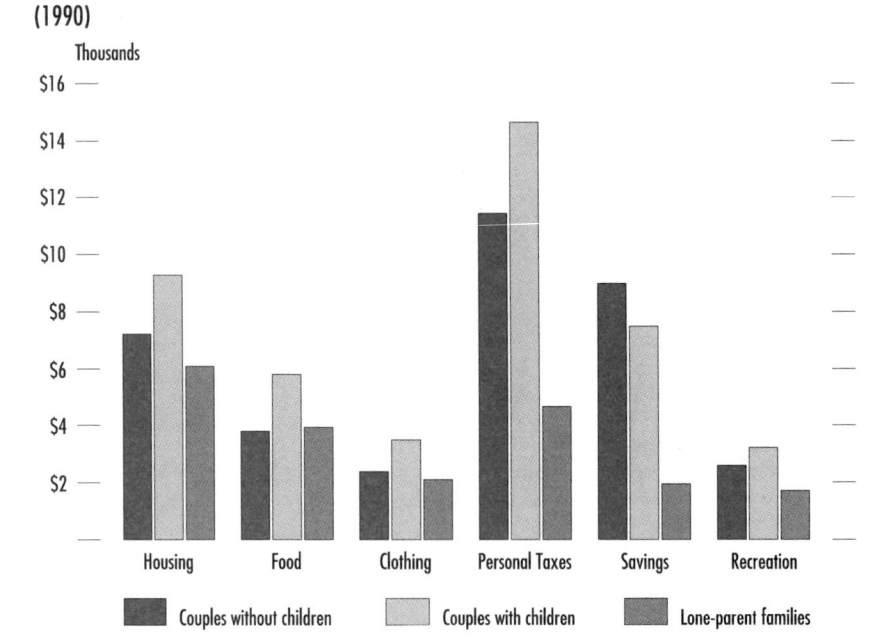

■ Couples without children   □ Couples with children   ■ Lone-parent families

Note: Chart uses 1990 Family Expenditure Survey. Sample is restricted to persons living in private households in 17 largest CMAs (Census Metropolitan Areas) in Canada, therefore expenditures are likely to be higher than those found for Canada as a whole.

Prepared by the Centre for International Statistics

Some families earn a lot more than others, and their spending patterns reflect this. In 1991, average incomes for lone-parent families were less than half what married couples with children averaged who in turn earned just a little more than childless married couples. In every category except savings*, in which childless couples led, married couples with children spent the most.

More mouths to feed means more spending on the necessities: food, clothing, housing and health care. Married couples with children averaged nearly 4 people per family. Lone-parent families averaged 2.6 people. Married couples with children also paid the most in personal taxes followed by childless married couples. Lone-parent families paid less than a third of what married couples with children paid in personal taxes, but their incomes averaged less than half those of married couples with children. Lone parents spent least on basic necessities and personal taxes, and they saved least.

*Includes voluntary savings; annual contributions to government and trusteed pension plans; and contributions to life insurance annuities and premiums.

How come we've got no money left?

Table XI – Where Did the Money Go?*

Purchases	Married Couples	Married Couples With Children	Lone-parent Families
Average Family Income	$ 52,231	$ 64,705	$ 29,917
Average Number of Persons/Family	2	3.8	2.6
Food from store	3,809	5,792	3,949
Restaurants	1,835	1,960	1,196
Principal accommodation	7,215	9,276	6,073
Reading materials	299	312	198
Education	654	991	702
Tuition	711	1,022	767
Clothing	2,394	3,506	2,111
Drycleaning	160	140	127
Health	851	1,035	660
Health care insurance	434	578	398
Recreation	2,598	3,234	1,711
Lottery tickets	179	173	106
Personal taxes	11,432	14,633	4,664

* This is only a partial list of family expenditures and does not include, among other things, costs of transportation, charitable donations, household maintenance and capital expenditures such as furniture and appliances.
Prepared by the Centre for International Statistics[126]

Although the average incomes of lone-parent families are much lower than those of other families, many of their expenses, particularly for the necessities, are nearly as high. In 1990 in Canada's biggest metropolitan areas, they spent 91%, on average, of what childless couples did on groceries, although they spent much less in restaurants. They spent 84% of what childless couples did on housing. With more people to house, though, this suggests that their accommodations were substantially lower in quality than other families'. Married couples with children averaged half again as much ($9,276) for housing as lone-parent families ($6,073). On clothing, lone-parent families spent almost as much ($2,111) as childless couples ($2,394) and 60% of what married couples with children spent ($3,506).

And so what?

In the early years of marriage, young couples have lower earning potential and lower expenses. As they age, couples, on average, increase their earning power, but their expenses grow as they add children to their families. The basics are expensive for all families.

A family can shave only so much from its budget. On basic necessities, it is very difficult to cut spending beyond a certain point. The breakdown of spending by family types shows that despite their low incomes, the spending of lone-parent families on essential items was similar to that of other families. Looking beyond these rough figures, it becomes clear that just getting by is a lot tougher for some families than for others.

The Vanier Institute of the Family

Economists expecting consumer spending to lead us out of recession might look at family incomes and then place their hopes elsewhere.

Between 1973 and 1990, real gross family income per earner for the population aged 15-64 grew by 11%, and for the younger families 15-29 it grew by 3%.
David P. Ross and Clarence Lochhead[127]

Couples who fight about money argue more often about how it is to be spent than about how much they have.
Phillip Blumstein and Pepper Schwartz[128]

About 9% of an average Canadian family's expenditure could be classified as going toward the purchase of durable goods, 5% of which is attributable to vehicle purchase.
Robin A. Douthitt and Joanne Fedyk[129]

The Vanier Institute of the Family

It's become a risky, thankless task, this business of raising children and building families. Risky in that divorce can quickly destroy a lifetime of investment in family, leaving a displaced homemaker teetering on the edge of poverty, struggling to earn a living in a labor market that exacts large penalties for career interruptions. Thankless in that we no longer seem to value these activities. The story told by our public policies is that almost any endeavor is more worthy of support than child raising.
Sylvia Ann Hewlett[131]

Children are big-ticket items

Table XII – The Cost of Raising a Child

Boy

Age	Food	Clothes	Health Care	Personal Care	Recreation/ School	Transportation	Child Care	Shelter	Total
Infant	1,411	1,654	182	0	0	0	3,961	1,800	9,008
1	903	403	182	78	307	0	5,825	1,949	9,647
2	973	431	182	78	307	0	4,850	1,925	8,746
3	973	431	243	78	307	0	4,850	1,902	8,784
4	1,326	430	243	78	307	0	4,850	1,902	9,137
5	1,326	430	243	78	388	31	4,850	1,902	9,249
6	1,326	633	243	78	499	31	3,453	1,902	8,165
7	1,436	633	243	75	707	31	3,453	1,902	8,480
8	1,436	633	243	75	707	31	3,453	1,902	8,480
9	1,436	659	243	75	707	31	3,453	1,902	8,507
10	1,618	659	243	75	707	31	3,453	1,902	8,689
11	1,618	659	243	75	707	31	3,453	1,902	8,689
12	1,618	986	243	133	723	276	0	1,902	5,881
13	1,764	986	243	133	723	276	0	1,902	6,026
14	1,764	986	243	133	815	276	0	1,902	6,118
15	1,764	957	243	267	973	276	0	1,902	6,381
16	2,068	957	243	267	973	276	0	1,902	6,685
17	2,068	957	243	267	973	276	0	1,902	6,685
18	2,068	957	243	267	813	276	0	1,902	6,525

Girl

Age	Food	Clothes	Health Care	Personal Care	Recreation/ School	Transportation	Child Care	Shelter	Total
Infant	1,411	1,654	182	0	0	0	3,961	1,800	9,008
1	903	434	182	78	307	0	5,825	1,949	9,679
2	973	449	182	78	307	0	4,850	1,925	8,765
3	973	449	243	78	307	0	4,850	1,902	8,802
4	1,326	448	243	78	307	0	4,850	1,902	9,154
5	1,326	448	243	78	388	31	4,850	1,902	9,266
6	1,326	648	243	78	499	31	3,453	1,902	8,180
7	1,355	648	243	75	707	31	3,453	1,902	8,414
8	1,355	648	243	75	707	31	3,453	1,902	8,414
9	1,355	651	243	75	707	31	3,453	1,902	8,417
10	1,436	651	243	75	707	31	3,453	1,902	8,499
11	1,436	651	243	75	707	31	3,453	1,902	8,499
12	1,436	1,002	243	236	723	276	0	1,902	5,818
13	1,550	1,002	243	236	723	276	0	1,902	5,931
14	1,550	1,002	243	236	815	276	0	1,902	6,023
15	1,550	1,047	243	293	973	276	0	1,902	6,284
16	1,555	1,047	243	293	973	276	0	1,902	6,289
17	1,555	1,047	243	293	973	276	0	1,902	6,289
18	1,555	1,047	243	293	813	276	0	1,902	6,129

Financial Post[130]

It can cost $150,000 or more to raise a child to age 18. That's what Manitoba's Agriculture Ministry figures show, based on average prices for consumer goods and day care in Winnipeg in 1992. That's probably close to the Canadian average, since Winnipeg prices are lower than in bigger cities and possibly higher than in some smaller centres.

By far the biggest cost for children under 12 is child care. The cost of licensed care ranged from about $3,500 per year for older children to $5,825 for one-year olds. The next most expensive items were food, which steadily increases as children grow, shelter and clothing. Boys tend to eat more, while girls tend to cost more to clothe.

And so what?

Children may be priceless but any parent knows they're not cheap. The average one-child, middle-income family that owns its own home and that has both parents in the work force spends about 15% of everything the parents earn to feed, clothe, house, educate and care for their son or daughter. If that family has two children, they will spend almost a quarter of their gross family income on their children, and those families with three or more children invest almost a third of their before-tax income in their children. While the costs of a newborn tend to be high, costs in subsequent years tend to remain fairly consistent until the teen years.

How do adults adjust to the increased demands on their finances when they become parents? First, they can devote more time to their jobs in order to bring home bigger pay cheques. They don't eat out as much, and mothers and fathers tend to spend less on themselves than they did before they "started a family". Savings is one category of expenditure that takes a back seat to the immediate costs of raising children.

The generally high cost of child care, as a proportion of family income, is an important factor that parents take into account when deciding whether both parents should work outside the home. This is particularly true in the case of those families with low or modest incomes with more than one child. The break-even point, where it becomes more economical for the wife – or husband – to stay home probably comes somewhere between two and four children, at least – for those parents in lower-paying jobs.

The Vanier Institute of the Family

Place roof over four walls
Add love and/or children

57. Percentage of Family Households* Owning Their Home
(1991)

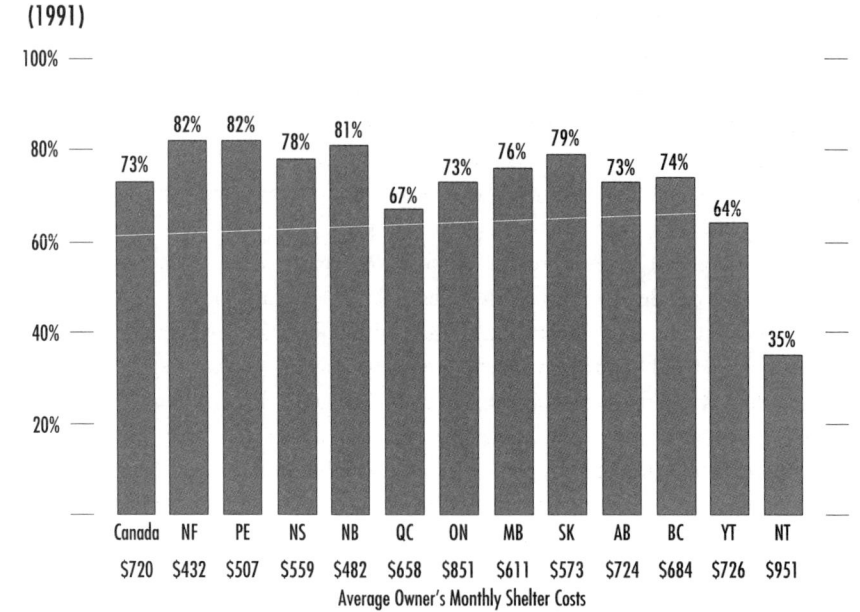

	Canada	NF	PE	NS	NB	QC	ON	MB	SK	AB	BC	YT	NT
%	73%	82%	82%	78%	81%	67%	73%	76%	79%	73%	74%	64%	35%
Avg. Monthly Shelter Cost	$720	$432	$507	$559	$482	$658	$851	$611	$573	$724	$684	$726	$951

Average Owner's Monthly Shelter Costs

* Private households, containing at least one census family includes farm & reserve dwellings

Prepared by the Centre for International Statistics

58. Percentage of Family Households* Renting Their Home
(1991)

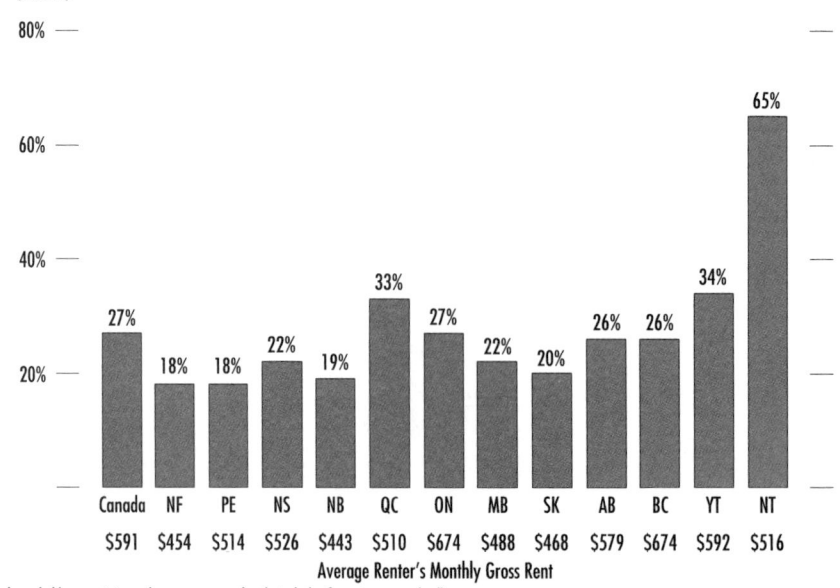

	Canada	NF	PE	NS	NB	QC	ON	MB	SK	AB	BC	YT	NT
%	27%	18%	18%	22%	19%	33%	27%	22%	20%	26%	26%	34%	65%
Avg. Monthly Gross Rent	$591	$454	$514	$526	$443	$510	$674	$488	$468	$579	$674	$592	$516

Average Renter's Monthly Gross Rent

* Private households, containing at least one census family includes farm & reserve dwellings

Prepared by the Centre for International Statistics

In 1991 the average monthly shelter cost for Canadian home owners was $720. (Shelter costs include mortgage payments, property taxes, utilities, and, where applicable, condominium fees.) The average cost for renters was $591 a month. Despite the higher monthly costs, almost three-quarters (73%) of family households owned their own homes.

Average monthly rental costs varied less across the country than did home ownership costs. Average rents ranged from $443 in New Brunswick to $674 in Ontario and British Columbia. Average home ownership costs ranged from $432 in Newfoundland, to $951 in the Northwest Territories.

Home ownership costs appear to have considerable influence on a family's decision to buy or rent, more so than average rental costs. In the Northwest Territories, where the average shelter cost for homeowners is $231 above the national average, only 35% of residents own their own homes. In Newfoundland, Prince Edward Island, and New Brunswick, on the other hand, where average monthly ownership costs were about $500 or less, more than 80% of families owned their own homes. Of course, other factors may be at play as well. People who move often, or know they will settle only temporarily in a location, may be less inclined to purchase. Those in rural areas may be more able to construct their own homes and thereby reduce costs.

And so what?

Those who rent pay a bit less, but they receive a lot less. Homes are the greatest assets most families own. They provide economic security, equity, and "a place to call your own."

Where home prices are high or incomes are low or uncertain, families are less likely to buy homes. Today's tough economic climate, along with high home prices, makes it hard for young families to establish themselves by buying that first home. Others find it hard to *keep* their family homes: the laid-off older worker, the divorced woman and her children, the older woman living on a widow's pension.

And for some, the decision to rent or own is entirely academic, as an increasing number of families have found themselves homeless in recent years. One of the most effective pro-family policies could be to help ensure that families can own their own homes and keep them.

Shelter, whether a house or apartment, owned or rented, is the single largest dollar expenditure that Ontario families make over a life course. Shelter costs are the highest day-to-day living expenditures that most families incur. What an individual family can afford influences the quality both of the housing and of the surrounding neighbourhood that will be accessible to it. Simply stated, and with relatively few exceptions, poor families are more likely than others to live in poor housing in a poor neighbourhood. They are also far less likely to own their homes and more likely to remain renters throughout their lives.
Christine Kluck Davis[132]

Ours and the bank's
One third of Canada's families have mortgages, another quarter of them rent

59. Family Households* by Tenure
(1991)
6.3 Million Family Households

Owners with mortgage 39.5%
23% of those with mortgages have shelter costs totalling 30% or more of their household income**

Renters 27.7%
29% of renters have gross rental costs totalling 30% or more of their household incomes**

Owners without mortgage 32.8%

* Private one-family households in tenant or owner occupied non-farm, non-reserve dwellings
** 1990 household income

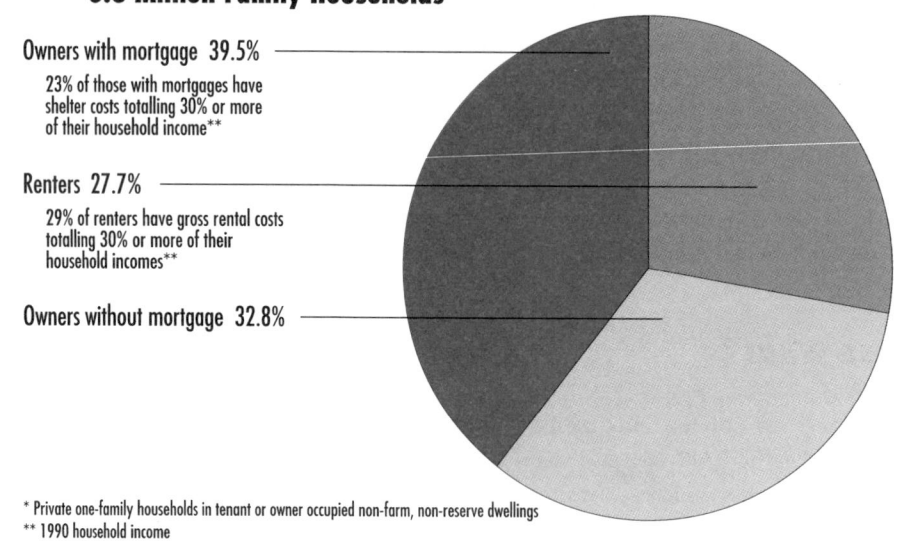

Prepared by the Centre for International Statistics

There are 6.3 million one-family households in Canada (excluding those on reserves or farms). Out of every fifteen, five of the residences are owned outright by their occupants, another six are owned but mortgaged, and the other four are rented.

Of the 4.5 million families that owned their own homes in 1991, 55% of them had mortgages. Almost one quarter (23%) of the mortgaged households had total shelter costs amounting to 30% or more of their total 1990 family income. Most government agencies consider that level of spending to indicate "core housing need." Still, homeowners were much less likely than renters to spend high proportions of their income on shelter. Twenty-nine percent of the 1.7 million families who rented housing spent 30% or more of their income on shelter costs.

And so what?

To quote Aron N. Spector and Fran Klodawsky: "The majority of urban Canadian adults are assumed to move from the family home to a series of rental accommodations, then to a single family owner-occupied home designed for child rearing, and possibly back to a condominium or rental unit (Social Planning Council of Metropolitan Toronto, 1979). The design of much of the Canadian urban housing product is predicated on the assumption that during the full extent of the life cycle, each household unit is occupied by either a single unattached individual or a single nuclear family, headed by a husband and wife. Extended family households, containing multiple unit families, are becoming far less common. In addition, older children have, within the last two decades, more frequently left the family home while older adults have joined separate communities away from younger adults raising children. An impact of all of these trends has been an increasing demand for separate housing units each occupied by a smaller number of people."[133]

The Vanier Institute of the Family

80% of families headed by a senior own their own homes, 72% of them mortgage-free.

In 1987, 75% of older Canadians said they would prefer to stay in their own homes as long as possible. 20% indicated that they would consider cashing in home equity to pay for in-home care to eliminate or postpone the need to be institutionalized.
  The National Advisory Council on Aging[134]

The single parent lives as one adult in a world designed for nuclear families. Housing options must be both supportive and maintainable. Housing for single-parent families must be designed to provide secure, safe, and appropriate housing, and adequate facilities for child rearing.
  Aron N. Spector and Fran Klodawsky[135]

Canadians plugged in to bare necessities

Table XIII – The Luxury Goods Canadian Families Own (1990)

	Number of Families	% of Families
Telephone lines		
one	6,539,398	91.9
two or more	530,983	7.5
Colour TV	7,026,600	98.7
Microwave oven	5,909,341	83.0
VCR	5,848,094	82.2
Cable TV	5,170,762	72.6
Gas barbeque	4,385,823	61.6
Dishwasher	3,752,208	52.7
2 or more vehicles	3,719,189	52.2
CD player	2,063,846	29.0
Home computer	1,690,397	23.7
Call waiting	1,559,730	21.9
Video camcorder	908,001	12.8
Swimming pool	562,062	7.9
Snowmobile	547,769	7.7
Vacation homes (in Canada)	504,126	7.1
Travel trailer	364,979	5.1

Calculations by the Centre for International Statistics[136]

A colour television and at least one telephone line have become staples in almost every Canadian household. Almost 100% of Canadian families have these items. But not as many families have the accessories. Seventy-two percent rent cable TV service. Microwave ovens and VCRs are becoming common acquisitions. Most Canadian households have both. The luxury goods that many Canadian families still do not have are the big-ticket items associated with recreation: vacation homes, travel trailers, swimming pools, and snowmobiles. Less than 10% of families own these items. Interestingly enough, automobiles are not categorized in this survey among the so-called luxury items. In fact, about eight of ten Canadian households own a private vehicle.

And so what?

Judging by the luxuries we own, Canadians look quite prosperous. There are some luxury items that most Canadians have, regardless of income. We are fairly sparsely populated, so it isn't surprising that we spend a lot on communications – phones, TVs and accessories. Even among the poorest one-fifth of Canadian households, 94.5% owned a colour TV in 1992. However, fewer than half (47.9%) of these same poor households owned VCRs, compared with 78.8% of middle-income households and 91.5% of the wealthiest households.

The Vanier Institute of the Family

In the period between the two wars (1920-1940), the 'consumer society' was born, and families were made aware by the new advertising industry of the increased numbers of necessities which were available to them for a more comfortable life. Between 1931 and 1951, the percentage of families with a refrigerator, for example, increased from 21% to 48%. Thus, the sole-wage-earner family came to be viewed more and more in terms of its economic role as a consumer, rather than as a producer, with the task of consumption being assigned to the wife.

Emily M. Nett[137]

Over the years, outstanding consumer credit has increased, and along with it consumer bankruptcies. Hira's study of personal bankruptcies in Winnipeg shows that the average age for those filing was 32 years (much younger than the average age of the Canadian population, 43). Most were married men with families, and most (three out of four) were employed. Car loans were a major reason for filing; the car debt is one of the most expensive for a couple. In over half of the cases the reason given for the action was lack of prudent financial management. Bankruptcy has been found in other research to increase the risk of separation and divorce.

Emily M. Nett[138]

The more things change...
Despite changed attitudes, women still do the lion's share of household work

60. Percentage of Women and Men Who Particpate Daily in Selected Household Chores*

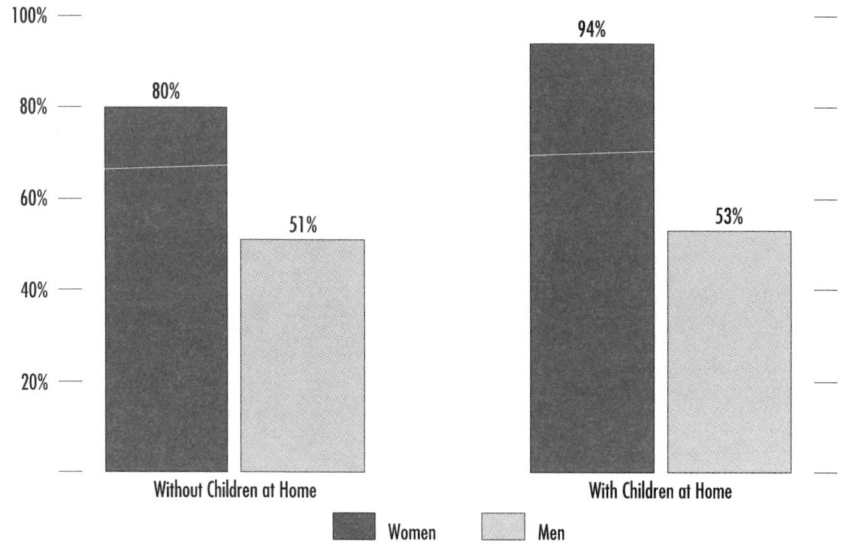

	Women	Men
Without Children at Home	80%	51%
With Children at Home	94%	53%

* Household chores, as defined by Statistics Canada in the General Social Survey, include meal preparation and clean-up, indoor and outdoor cleaning, laundry, home repairs and maintenance, gardening, pet care, bill-paying, and traveling to and from these household chores.

Prepared by the Centre for International Statistics

Most Canadian adults in 1986 did household chores on a daily basis. Women, however, were doing substantially more of them than men. Four in five women without children at home and fully 94% of women with children at home participated in daily chores. For men, the presence of children had little effect. Their daily participation rate for household chores was only two percentage points higher (53% compared with 51%) with children than without them.

Not only do more women than men participate in daily household chores (which includes housework), they tend to spend considerably more time each day on them. On average, women with children spent 3 hours and 22 minutes and women without children spent 2 hours and 39 minutes. Among the men who participated daily, those with children averaged 2 hours and 1 minute, and those without children averaged 1 hour and 49 minutes. This indicates that the presence of children in the household has a profound effect on the amount of daily chores performed by women, and a comparatively mild effect on the amount performed by men. In turn, it is likely that having children would also mean very different things for men and women in terms of time available for personal and leisure pursuits.

In many specific job categories, on any given day in Canada, women did overwhelmingly more than men. Two and one-half times as many women as men prepared meals (77% compared to 29%), and they averaged 30 minutes more daily on this (1 1/4 hours against 3/4). Almost four times as many women as men (54% to 15%) cleaned up after meals and 4.5 times as many (45% to 10%) did indoor housekeeping.

For employed women and men, the spread is even bigger. Eighty-nine percent of married, employed women did housework every day. This compares with 51% for men.

Have things changed since 1986? Although wives' responsibility for housework declined as their work force involvement increased, husbands, in general, did not take up the slack. In full-time, dual-earner families in 1992, women spent about 1.2 hours more on unpaid work than did their male partners. Men in these families also enjoyed, on average, 50 minutes more free time per day than did their spouses. In fact, women in general, devoted an average of 1.2 hours per day on cooking and meal clean up compared to 22 minutes for men. Similarly, women spent an average of 1.1 hour per day on housecleaning and laundry in comparison to men's 13 minutes.

Only in the areas of household maintenance and repair did men spend more time than women, 19 minutes per day for men compared to 4 minutes for women.

And so what?

Suggestions of the appearance of a "new-age man" or a "new model of fathering" may be premature. Although there has been a slight change among younger and better-educated couples, most marriage partners appear to be following traditional patterns of household work allocation. This works well for most men, but women, understandably, are less satisfied. As employment for married women becomes more common, we can expect to see a harsh impact on these women. Since they work so much at home, it should not be surprising if many employed, married women are constantly exhausted. And it should not be surprising to see more marriages suffer from tensions created by the unequal division of household work.

...89% of wives who were not in the labour force were solely responsible for meal preparation; this compared with 86% of wives employed part-time and 72% of those employed full-time.

The majority (52%) of wives employed full-time had all of the responsibility for daily housework, while 28% had most of this responsibility. Only 10% of dual-earning couples shared responsibility for housework equally; in the remaining 10% of couples, the husband had all or most of the responsibility.
Katherine Marshall[139]

A woman's work is never... valued

The Vanier Institute of the Family

...without the hidden contribution of women as wives, mothers and homemakers, the industrial economy would not have been possible. Owners and workers alike depended on wives and daughters to bake, grow gardens, process food, cook, sew, look after children and sick persons, and manage the household finances. As middle- and upper-class women's work became increasingly hidden in the household, the myth was born that wives did not work, and eventually the norm was established that wives at every social level should stay at home. To enter the labour force was to be remiss in one's duties to husband, children, and society. The family pattern representative of this norm came to be called the 'breadwinner family'...
— Emily M. Nett[141]

61. Average Value of Household Work*: Men and Women
(1986)

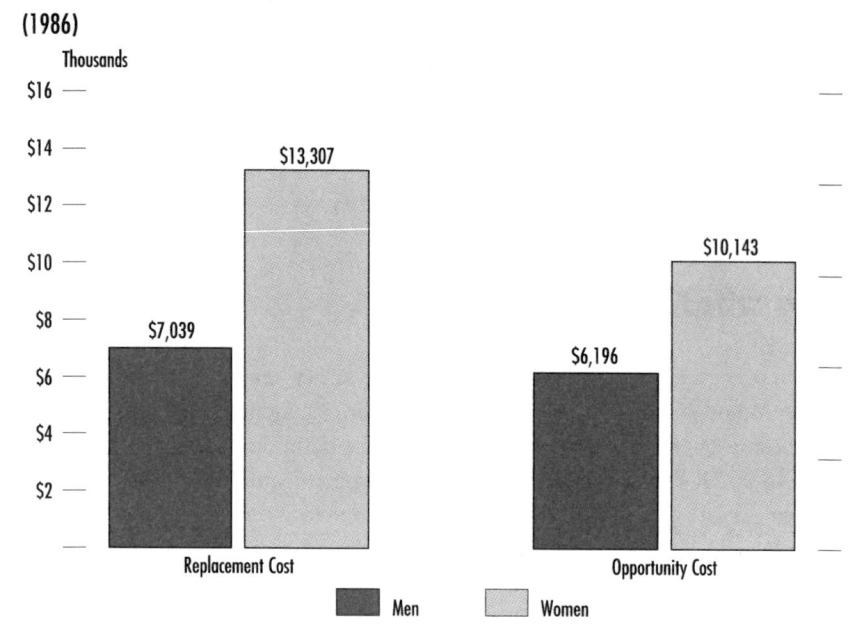

Thousands

	Men	Women
Replacement Cost	$7,039	$13,307
Opportunity Cost	$6,196	$10,143

* Included in "household work" are: food prepartation, cleaning, clothing care, reapairs/maintenance, gardening, pet care, shopping and child care.

Prepared by the Centre for International Statistics

It is hard to calculate the exact worth of unpaid household work.

There are two established methods of assessing its value. The first is to calculate the opportunity cost of household work. That's the value of other work not done while doing household work. The second is to calculate the replacement cost – what it would cost to hire others to perform each household task. For example, if you wash and iron a shirt, what would it cost to send it to the cleaner?

Either method can be deceiving. Since men, on average, earn more than women, their missed opportunity costs will generally exceed women's. Men's household work will, therefore, have a higher value, in theory. At the same time, men generally do more outside work and home repairs, while women typically cook and clean more. Wages for "men's" work are generally higher than wages for "women's" jobs, resulting in higher replacement costs for the jobs that men tend to do at home. Either way, comparisons of equal amounts of work performed by men and women will tend to result in higher values for men than for women.

Despite all this, and using either method, the dollar value of the household work performed by women is far higher than that performed by men. That's because women as a group and on average contribute far more of their time to such work.

The dollar value of household work is enormous. The replacement cost value of household work in 1986 was nearly $200 billion – nearly 40% of Canada's gross domestic product (GDP).[140]

And so what?

When most families had a breadwinner husband and a wife at home, the value of household work was less of a real issue. Today, many families find they must pay for things their parents might have done for themselves, from daycare to disposable diapers to microwave dinners. The high rate of marriage and separation is also forcing couples to think more about what their time and labour is worth. Who does what is a real issue for married couples – and what it's worth is an even bigger issue for divorcing couples. And what of older women who had been wives at home and are now widows on pensions? There is a very high rate of poverty among this group in Canada. Many older women would be better off if their pensions were computed on the basis of the true value of the unpaid household work they did throughout their unpaid work lives.

The Vanier Institute of the Family

How easily we could turn the tables on the economists if we all decided that from tomorrow morning, the work of the domestic economy should be paid for. Instead of cooking dinner for her own lot, each housewife would feed her neighbours at regular restaurant rates; then they'd cook for her family and get their money back. We'd do each other's housework and gardening at award rates. Big money would change hands when we fixed each other's tap washers and electric plugs at the plumbers' and electricians' rates. Without a scrap of extra work the gross national product would go up by a third overnight. We would increase that to half if the children rented each others' backyards and paid each other as play supervisors, and we could double it if we all went to bed next door at regular massage parlour rates. Our economists would immediately be eager to find out what line of investment was showing such fabulous growth in capital/output ratio. They'd find that housing was bettered only by double beds and they'd recommend a massive switch of investment into both.

Hugh Stretton[142]

The Vanier Institute of the Family

Volunteers come from a variety of occupations and backgrounds and volunteering provides an outlet for talents not used, or appreciated, on the job or in the home. A chief executive plies carpentry skills to build items for sale at church bazaars, a doctor acts in the local theatre, a childless electrician is also a Big Brother, a farm housewife from Saskatchewan attends board meetings in Toronto twice a year, a public servant in the transport ministry writes briefs on child welfare, an accountant teaches swimming to children with disabilities, and a local merchant coaches baseball. These are the kinds of mutually beneficial pairings provided by voluntary activity.
The National Voluntary Organization[143]

Doing our bit
Volunteering in Canada on the rise despite increase in dual-earner families

62. Where Do People Volunteer?

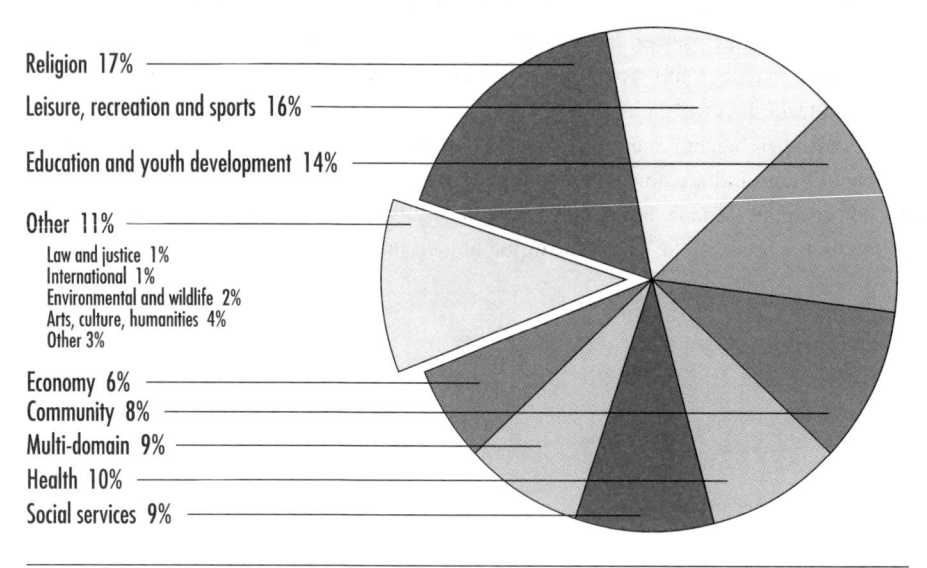

Religion 17%
Leisure, recreation and sports 16%
Education and youth development 14%
Other 11%
- Law and justice 1%
- International 1%
- Environmental and wildlife 2%
- Arts, culture, humanities 4%
- Other 3%

Economy 6%
Community 8%
Multi-domain 9%
Health 10%
Social services 9%

Prepared by the Centre for International Statistics

Despite all the demands on family time, the number of people who participate in volunteer work is still high. In 1987 there were 5.3 million people aged 15 and older who formally volunteered in 9.2 million volunteer positions. This accounted for over a quarter (26.8%) of all Canadians in that age group. The number of volunteers has nearly doubled since 1980, when there were 2.7 million volunteers, 15% of the over-fifteen population. Voluntary participation peaked in the 35-44 year-old age bracket.

Married people volunteer at a greater rate than single people. Employed married women had the highest participation rate. Employed persons of both sexes tend to have higher participation rates than those who are unemployed or not in the labour force.

Collectively, the 5.3 million volunteers contributed over 1 billion hours of their time within a 12-month span. This is equivalent to 615,000 full-time full-year positions. In addition to their time, volunteers spent $842 million in out-of-pocket expenses directly related to their volunteer activities.

The majority – 56% – of Canada's volunteers are women, and almost 30% of women volunteer. The participation rate for men is 24%.

And so what?

We tend to undervalue the things we do not pay for. Until recently, at least, that was our attitude toward housework. And that attitude still persists with volunteer work. Yet volunteers contribute an enormous amount to society, often performing highly skilled jobs for free. Much of their work consists of personal service to some of the most vulnerable members of society: the elderly, the infirm and the disabled. Who would do this work, if volunteers were not available to do it? Will women, the traditional backbone of the voluntary sector, be able to continue this role, despite the double burden of increased hours of employment and predominant responsibility for housework that most carry? And, as society ages, will the number of available volunteers taper off?

Volunteer work makes our communities healthy and human. Who will do this vital work tomorrow?

CANADIAN FAMILY LIFE TODAY
HOW IT FEELS

The Vanier Institute of the Family

Canadian Family Life Today
How it feels

The Vanier Institute of the Family

No two families are exactly alike. They vary in so many ways – structure, ages, cultural backgrounds, numbers of children, economic status…Yet most families do more or less the same things in life. They support themselves. They help and care for one another. They bring up young people.

Few of them do things in exactly the same ways, but most muddle through a very similar agenda of tasks, obligations and responsibilities.

A day in the life

Consider the typical routine of the now-typical young, dual wage-earning family. The particular family's circumstances may vary, but the routine is probably familiar:

Up early in the morning to get the kids dressed, (hoping that no one is showing signs of a stomach ache), breakfasts eaten, lunches made, animals fed, kids delivered to daycare or school, and in to work on time. And heaven help them if there's a snowstorm that day.

Then a harried workday – meetings, phone calls, clients, and memos, or maybe a production line, a pushy boss, demanding customers or simply an endless pile of work. Through the day, the parents hope that no major work crisis will require overtime or even a small delay because the baby-sitter is waiting and will quit if they're late again. Or maybe the school-age child is at home alone and may have friends over that the parents don't feel good about.

Then the commute home – stressful enough, even without traffic jams or remembering to buy milk – pick up the little ones from daycare, prepare a reasonably nutritious meal while juggling phone calls, the latest mechanical calamity, and the children's problems. Pray that no one is showing signs of getting a cold because the sitter won't accept children who have anything infectious. If things go well, the kids will watch TV quietly so the parents can get the meal on the table as quickly as possible.

And then a leisurely evening at home? Hardly. Instead, it's baths, homework, a quick load of laundry because someone needs that special shirt the next day. Or maybe it's hockey practice, ballet or music lessons, or 4-H Club for the kids or a community college course in dataprocessing or business administration for their parents to upgrade career prospects. And don't forget the parent-teacher meeting, or the community daycare meeting. And that exercise class to try and get the body in shape to keep up with this ridiculous pace! And that one evening a week to spend some time with an elderly parent. Then home in time for a scheduled amount of "inter-spousal" relating before falling asleep in front of the tube.

The weekends provide slight relief. On Saturday morning, they're dragging the kids out to shop for paint for the living room. That job will occupy at least Saturday (after four loads of laundry) and part of Sunday, the rest of which might be split between church, yard work, fixing that bicycle, and cleaning up and getting ready for friends to drop by for supper. Finally, they flop into bed Sunday night in order to be well rested to get up early in the morning in time to get the kids dressed, lunches made etc. etc.

It only gets tougher if there's only one parent – an infirm relative – not enough money to purchase time-saving conveniences – 80 cows to milk – a long commute – lots of overtime – or any number of other complications.

With infinite variations, families do pretty much the same things. Their members carry out responsibilities that flow from their relationships with one another. And they pack all these chores in within the limitations of time. It would seem that all too often today's families must live on the left-overs of human energy and time.

Parents say that they are constantly looking for ways to 'make time' with their children. Some try to stretch the day at both ends, waking up earlier and sending them to bed later than teachers or pediatricians might like. They also shave time off one routine in order to make time for another: skipping a shampoo may leave a few more minutes for a bedtime story; grabbing a drive-in dinner frees up time for the soccer game; postponing a dentist's appointment makes time to visit a friend's house. They also give up time with each other as a couple. They may work different shifts. They may try to do some of their work at home.
Barbara Dafoe Whitehead[145]

The time crunch

How severe is the "time crunch" that families face? It depends on which member of the family you ask.

Statistics Canada asked a representative sample of Canadians (aged 15 and over) ten questions about how they felt about their personal time. Roughly one-third of them felt their lives were busier than they would have liked, with insufficient time to meet the demands placed on them. Women, in general, felt the pressures of the time crunch more than men. Almost one-third more of them wanted to spend more time alone.

Table XIV – Percentage of the Respondents Agreeing With Statements on Perceptions of Time

	Male %	Female %	Total %
I plan to slow down in the coming year	19	22	21
I consider myself a workaholic	26	25	25
When I need more time, I tend to cut back on my sleep	45	43	44
At the end of the day, I often feel that I have not accomplished what I had set out to do	44	48	46
I worry that I don't spend enough time with my family or friends	33	32	32
I feel that I'm constantly under stress trying to accomplish more than I can handle	31	35	33
I feel trapped in a daily routine	32	37	34
I feel that I just don't have time for fun any more	25	31	28
I often feel under stress when I don't have enough time	41	48	45
I would like to spend more time alone	19	26	22

Prepared by the Centre for International Statistics[144]

Fully a quarter of those asked consider themselves to be workaholics – a term only invented a few years ago. If the sample fairly represents the rest of us, more than four out of ten of us are skipping sleep in order to get through our obligations. Close to half of us often feel we're not getting things done that we have to do. One-third of us don't feel we're getting enough family time. That we're constantly under stress. That we're trapped in a rut. Fully three out of ten Canadians feel they don't have time for fun anymore. If families appear to be under pressure, we need look no further than the stressed-out members of those families to see why.

Some, of course, feel the time crunch more than others. Retired people, couples without children, and singles have more time to call their own. Men, in general, feel less time pressure than women. People with children report that they feel very pressured. Employed women with young children feel exceptionally pressed. Full-time employment and the addition of children to the family increase the pressure, especially for women.

Employed women get small slice of time-use pie

Most Canadians split their time between a great many obligations and commitments. If we look at individual time as a pie, many of us get very small slices for our own personal use. For employed women, especially mothers, the size of the slice is very small indeed.

63. Average Weekly Time Use: Employed Women

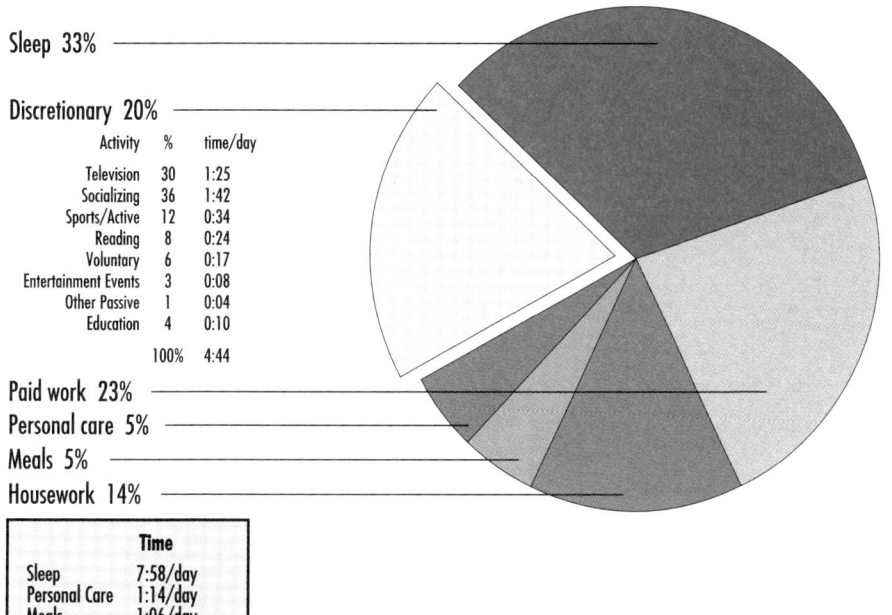

Sleep 33%

Discretionary 20%

Activity	%	time/day
Television	30	1:25
Socializing	36	1:42
Sports/Active	12	0:34
Reading	8	0:24
Voluntary	6	0:17
Entertainment Events	3	0:08
Other Passive	1	0:04
Education	4	0:10
	100%	4:44

Paid work 23%
Personal care 5%
Meals 5%
Housework 14%

	Time
Sleep	7:58/day
Personal Care	1:14/day
Meals	1:06/day
Housework	3:15/day
Paid Work	39:54/week
Discretionary	33:08/week

Note: Paid Work includes commuting and other activities related to employment. This chart pertains to women whose main activity is paid employment.

Prepared by the Centre for International Statistics

Over the course of a seven-day week, employed women in 1992 claimed an average of 20% of their time for their own. This figure doesn't tell the whole story, however. For one thing, it doesn't make any distinction between the work week and the somewhat more relaxed pace of the weekend. If employed women can claim 20% (about 4 3/4 hours a day) of their time for discretionary purposes overall, the proportion must drop sharply during the week. More significant, however, is the added pressure that employed mothers must feel. Parenting takes a lot of time. From dropping off children and picking them up at daycares and lessons, to caring for babies and sick children, supervising homework, extra laundry, and so much more, many parents feel that they never stop working. That 4 1/2 hours per day averaged over seven days for all employed women is quickly whittled down to little or nothing, especially on week days.

The Vanier Institute of the Family

...the average number of hours worked per week at home and in the work place by adults with families:
- *85 hours for a woman with husband and children*
- *65 hours for a husband with wife and children*
- *75 hours for a single mother*

Note: Husbands cause an extra ten hours work per week!

Dana Friedman[146]

109

64. Average Weekly Time Use: Employed Men

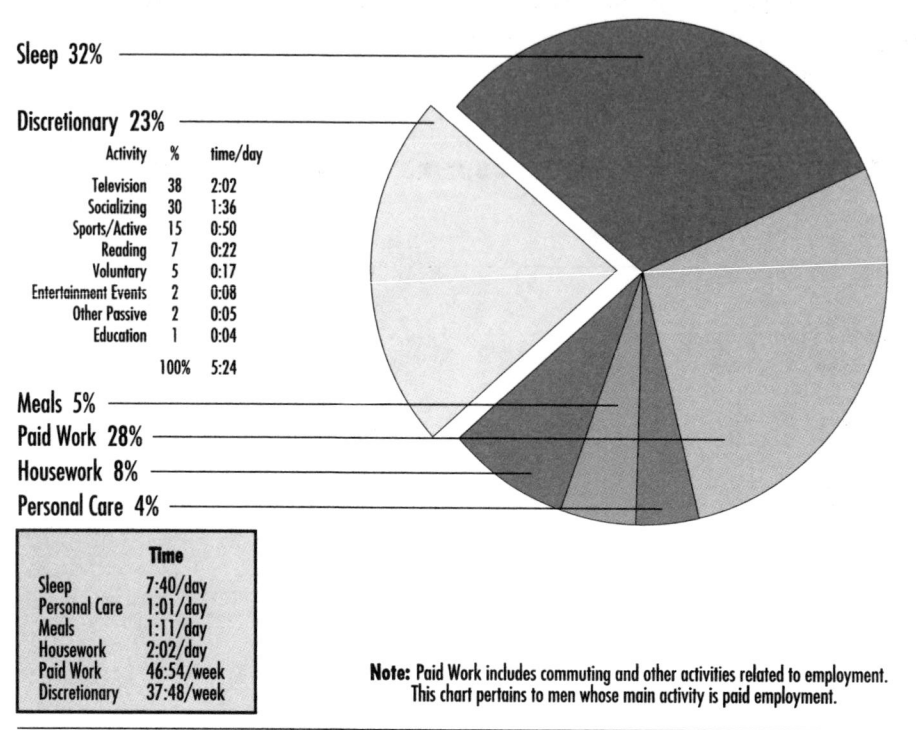

Sleep 32%

Discretionary 23%

Activity	%	time/day
Television	38	2:02
Socializing	30	1:36
Sports/Active	15	0:50
Reading	7	0:22
Voluntary	5	0:17
Entertainment Events	2	0:08
Other Passive	2	0:05
Education	1	0:04
	100%	5:24

Meals 5%
Paid Work 28%
Housework 8%
Personal Care 4%

	Time
Sleep	7:40/day
Personal Care	1:01/day
Meals	1:11/day
Housework	2:02/day
Paid Work	46:54/week
Discretionary	37:48/week

Note: Paid Work includes commuting and other activities related to employment. This chart pertains to men whose main activity is paid employment.

Prepared by the Centre for International Statistics

The picture for employed men is similar in some respects to that of employed women. In 1992 they had an average of 23% of their time (about 5 1/2 hours) for discretionary purposes. They did spend more time on paid work than women (28% as opposed to 24% of their time), but they also did less household work (9% against 14%). One half-hour difference in discretionary time between women and men may not seem like much. But when the difference between weekends and work days and the well-known difference between fathers' and mothers' contributions to child-rearing and household work are taken into account, the actual difference in time pressure for employed mothers and fathers is probably much greater. It is no wonder that in survey after survey, employed mothers report considerably more pressure from work and family commitments and more dissatisfaction with their lives and family arrangements.

65. Average Weekly Time Use: Female Homemakers

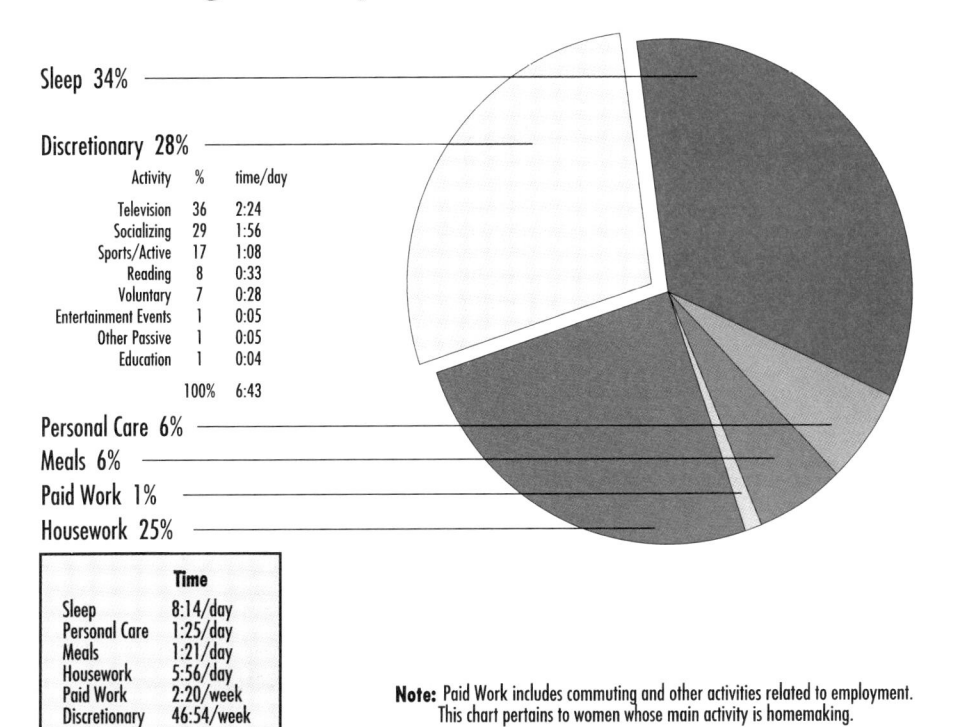

Sleep 34%

Discretionary 28%

Activity	%	time/day
Television	36	2:24
Socializing	29	1:56
Sports/Active	17	1:08
Reading	8	0:33
Voluntary	7	0:28
Entertainment Events	1	0:05
Other Passive	1	0:05
Education	1	0:04
	100%	6:43

Personal Care 6%
Meals 6%
Paid Work 1%
Housework 25%

	Time
Sleep	8:14/day
Personal Care	1:25/day
Meals	1:21/day
Housework	5:56/day
Paid Work	2:20/week
Discretionary	46:54/week

Note: Paid Work includes commuting and other activities related to employment. This chart pertains to women whose main activity is homemaking.

Prepared by the Centre for International Statistics

Averaged over seven days, full-time homemakers could lay claim in 1992 to 28% of their time (6 3/4 hours) for discretionary uses. Naturally enough, housework took a lot of their time (25%) – about the same amount of time that employed women devoted to paid work. In other respects, their use of time was very similar to that of their employed counterparts. While full-time homemakers do not experience the same kind of time crunch that employed people do, many experience other forms of stress. Many feel isolated and experience a lack of recognition for the contribution they make as homemakers. Young children, infirm or disabled family members who need special care, poverty, or geographical isolation can render homemaking a demanding task.

The Vanier Institute of the Family

While informal care by kin may seem to be cost-effective to governments, it can be very costly to caregivers who must rearrange their work and family lives to fit their caregiving duties. Caregiving is a lonely job, cutting a caretaker off from the rest of the world.
Teresa M. Cooney[147]

According to economist Victor Fuchs, children have lost ten to twelve hours of parental time per week since 1960. Parental time has been squeezed by the rapid shift of mothers into the labor force; by escalating divorce rates and abandonment of children by their fathers; and by an increase in the number of hours required on the job. Today the average worker puts in six hours more per week than in 1973.
Sylvia Ann Hewlett[148]

Daycare is just an abstract concept until you have a child. After you have a child, it is a gut-wrenching issue. And it is the issue that spills first from the lips of every working parent I talk to.
Wendy Dennis[149]

Who cares for the kids?

The 1988 Canadian National Child Care Study estimated that 2.7 million children needed child care while their parents worked outside the home. Six in ten (58%) of these children were below age 6, while the rest were aged 6-12. More than half of all infants (up to 17 months) and nearly two-thirds of all toddlers (18-35 months) were in non-parental care at least part of the week. And fully eight out of ten 3-5-year olds were in care. Among children 6-12 years of age, just under half were in non-parental care for part of the week.

Who cares for the kids and how is an overwhelming concern for most two-earner families with children. It can be hard to find care that is affordable and that fits the particular needs of children and their parents. Many never find a fit at all and have to get along with unsatisfactory solutions. For some, placing their children with strangers in uncertain settings can be a source of constant anxiety and guilt.

Child care arrangements differ depending on the age of children. It is necessary to consider preschool-age children (age 0-5) separately from school-age children. Preschool-age children are more likely to require full-time care, whereas school-age children require care only after school. Parents make different arrangements to accommodate these two age groups.

66. Primary* Child Care Arrangement for Children 0-5, Whose Parents are Employed

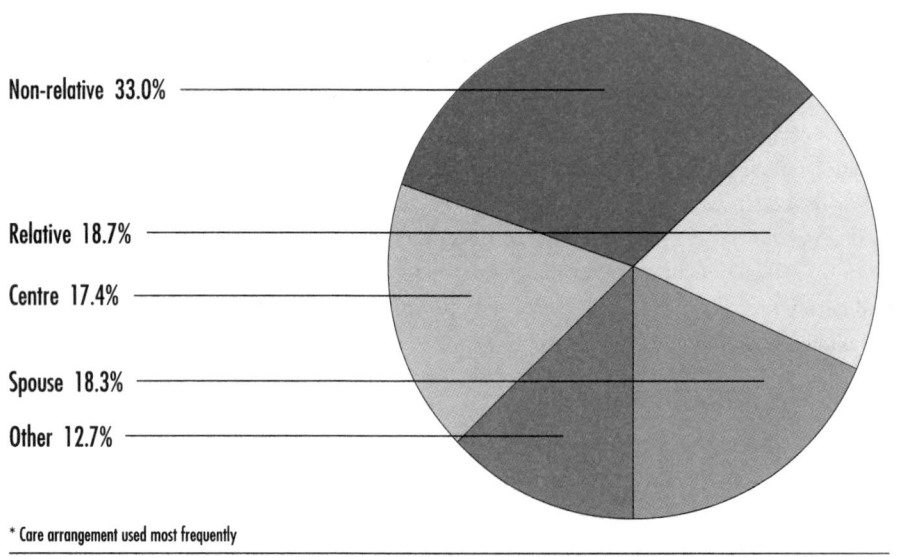

Non-relative 33.0%
Relative 18.7%
Centre 17.4%
Spouse 18.3%
Other 12.7%

* Care arrangement used most frequently
Calculated by the Centre for International Statistics

67. Primary* Child Care Arrangement for Children 6-12, Whose Parents are Employed

Spouse 26.6%
Relative 10.5%
Non-relative 14.2%
Self/Sibling 21.2%
Other 23.5%
Centre 4.0%

* Care arrangement used most frequently
Calculated by the Centre for International Statistics

In 1988, the most common care arrangement for children under 6 was care by a non-relative, either licensed or non-licensed. Nearly twice as many children were in these kinds of home care settings as were in the care of centres.

The situation is quite different for older children. Where more than half of all younger children were cared for in centres or by non-relatives, less than one-fifth of all children aged 6-12 received primary care from either of those sources. Spouses were the biggest source of care for this group, providing it to more than one quarter of all children. Another one fifth of these children were either in the care of a sibling or were taking care of themselves.

A great many families get along with a variety of makeshift care arrangements. This is what the category "other" refers to in the charts. It might include children whose parents take care of them while they work, children who shuttle between various caregivers over the course of the day, or school-age children enrolled in activities such as music lessons or Cub Scouts. Without doubt, many parents enroll their children in such activities primarily to help resolve their child care needs. With one eighth of all preschoolers and one quarter of all school-age children in "other" forms of care, it is evident that many parents have to make extraordinary arrangements to care for their children.

For many families, in-home, informal, and/or unlicensed care works well. For many others, it doesn't. Sometimes the consequences can be sensational, as in some highly publicized cases where caregivers have abused children. In most cases however, poorer-quality child care does not have such dramatic ill effects. There are still many possible sources of worry for parents with a child in care. The caregiver may not be trained or familiar with children. There may be too many children for the caregiver to handle, or they may not get enough individual attention. How's the food? Is there a clean place to sleep? Will the kids just be stuck in front of a TV or will there be active play?

The best child care plans can go off the rails when children get sick. Few daycare providers are equipped to handle sick children, so in most cases, the parents – usually the mother – must make special arrangements. This usually involves missing work. And women are much more likely than men to absent themselves from work in order to care for sick children. It is common practice for parents to use up their own sick leave benefits in order to stay home with their children.

There is also a sizable gap between the child care that parents want and that which they are able to obtain.

The Vanier Institute of the Family

Research from the '70s, the '80s and the '90s now seems to show it's the quality of the daycare experience that's important, not whether a child is in daycare. No evidence indicates that children in daycare have weaker attachments to their mothers, or stronger attachments to their other caregivers. The research shows that if children, especially infants, have consistent high-quality care, then there's no risk of emotional problems.

But it is hard to find consistent, high-quality care, especially for infants. There's a great demand and relatively few spaces. So parents solve the problem in a variety of ways – from job-sharing to flex time to using relatives or babysitters.
Hillel Goelman[150]

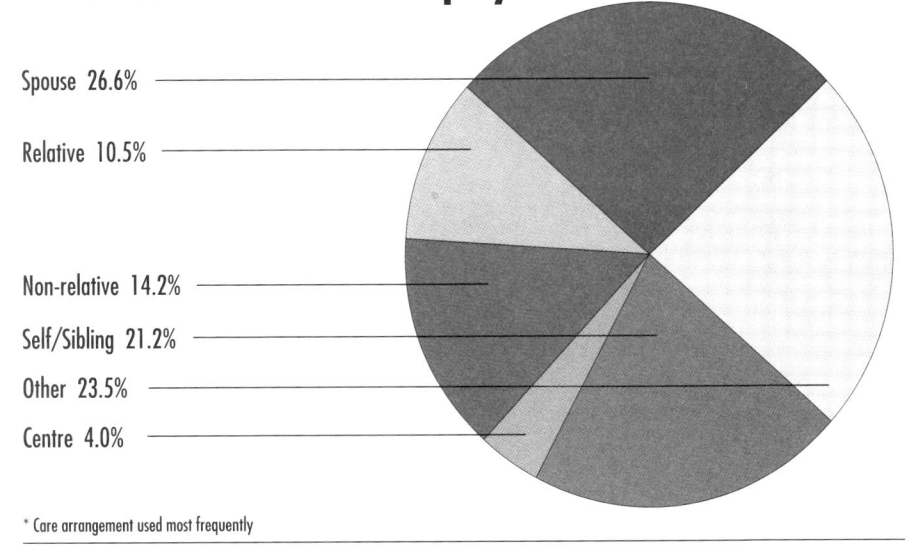

The Vanier Institute of the Family

...employers are always terrified that employees are going to march in and demand an on-site child care centre, and in the 12 companies in which we conducted focus groups, that was never the first choice. The first thing people wanted was to be able to stay at home when their children were sick. They say we lie about it now and do it anyway, but we really want to make it legitimate.
Ellen Galinsky[151]

Absenteeism for family reasons was particularly evident among parents (especially those with children 12 years of age and younger) and among employees with the dual responsibilities of child care and elder care.
Judith MacBride-King[152]

68. Parental Child Care Preferences* and Proportion Using Those Preferences

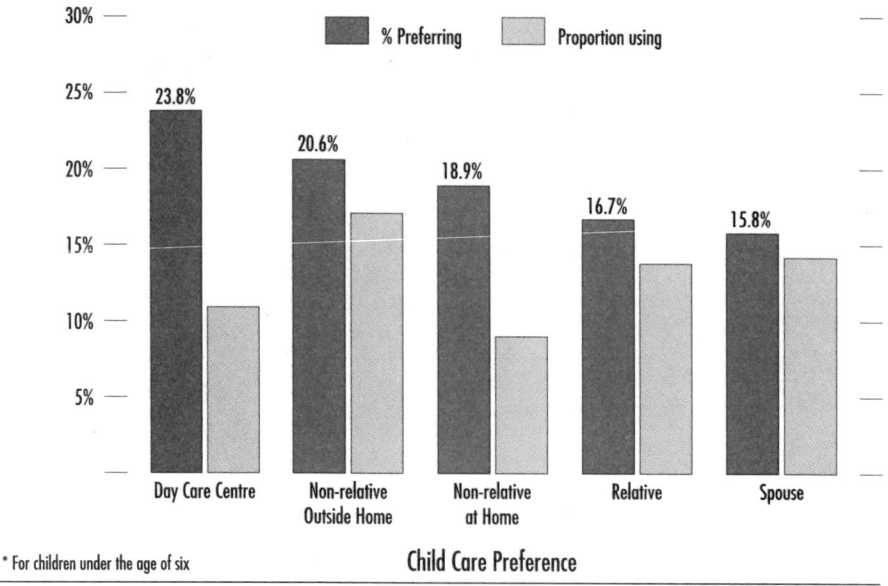

Child Care Preference	% Preferring	Proportion using
Day Care Centre	23.8%	~11%
Non-relative Outside Home	20.6%	~17%
Non-relative at Home	18.9%	~9%
Relative	16.7%	~14%
Spouse	15.8%	~14%

* For children under the age of six

Calculated by the Centre for International Statistics

Child care preference and usage are by no means synonymous. All kinds of reasons can prevent parents from using their preferred option for care. In 1988, one in four parents with children under the age of six would have preferred to place their children in day care centres while they are at their jobs.

Even that figure, however, may understate the actual number of parents who would like that option. Parents were not asked for their *ideal* form of care. Instead, they were asked to base their responses on what they could afford and on practicalities such as logistics and their work schedules. Spousal care for children, for example, is the least preferred arrangement for these parents. Few consider it to be ideal. Yet, while fewer than half of the children whose parents prefer daycare centres are actually in a centre, nearly all the children whose parents preferred spousal care were in such care. Working parents of young children learn that they must make compromises between what they feel are their family's best interests and what's available in real life.

This gap between what families want and what they end up with has a big impact on them. In dual-earner families where parents take turns caring for their young children, it can mean a hectic schedule based on "off-shifting". One parent comes off shift and takes on caregiving responsibilities, and the other hands them off and goes out to his or her place of employment. Their schedules rarely allow for much more than a brief exchange of information: "What am I supposed to make for supper?" "How are the kids?" "Is there anything I ought to know?" Over the long haul, this routine can result in chronic fatigue, stress, and considerable tension within the family.

In families that settle for other, non-preferred forms of child care, the impact can be just as troubling. Many live with constant anxiety, wondering whether their children are all right. And the inherent instability of informal care adds an extra element of stress to their daily lives.

Licensed care – Not much, not cheap

It isn't surprising that so few parents find licensed daycare spaces and that even fewer have their children in daycare centres. Canada ranks behind at least 16 other industrial democracies in the percentage of its children aged three to five in publicly funded child care. The need for affordable, accessible, high-quality child care far outstrips the supply of licensed care.

69. Number of Children with Mothers in the Labour Force and Number of Licensed* Child Care Spaces

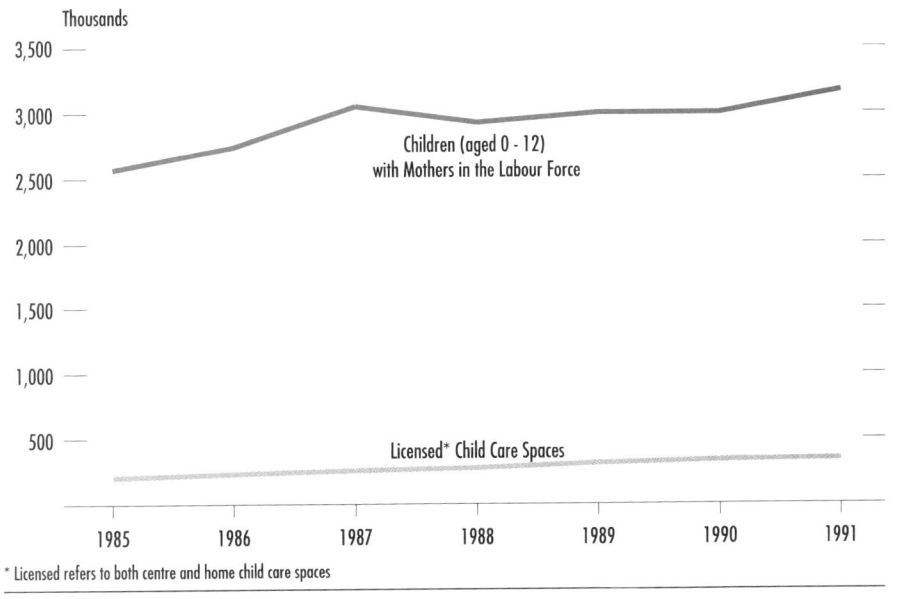

* Licensed refers to both centre and home child care spaces

Prepared by the Centre for International Statistics

In just six years (1985 - 1991), the number of children with mothers in the labour force jumped by almost one-quarter, from about 2,552,700 to 3,153,700. That is an increase of 602,000 children. During the same six years, the number of licensed child care spaces available increased by only 140,700 spaces. The gap between the number of mothers in the labour force and the number of licensed child care spaces has been large for quite a while. In recent years, it has grown.

The gap between supply and demand says a lot about the kind of hassle and improvisation with which families must contend. It is remarkable that despite this gap, so many mothers of young children remain in the labour force. Considering that "women's work" is dominated by lower-paying jobs in the service sector or in manufacturing, most of these women are probably not working outside the home merely for personal gratification. Most are in the labour force because they need the extra income to balance the family budget, despite the bother and expense of child care and other difficult aspects of combining work and family responsibilities.

And child care *is* expensive.

At work you think of the children you've left at home. At home, you think of the work you've left unfinished. Such a struggle is unleashed.
Golda Meir[153]

70. Average Monthly Day Care Fees* Licensed Centres

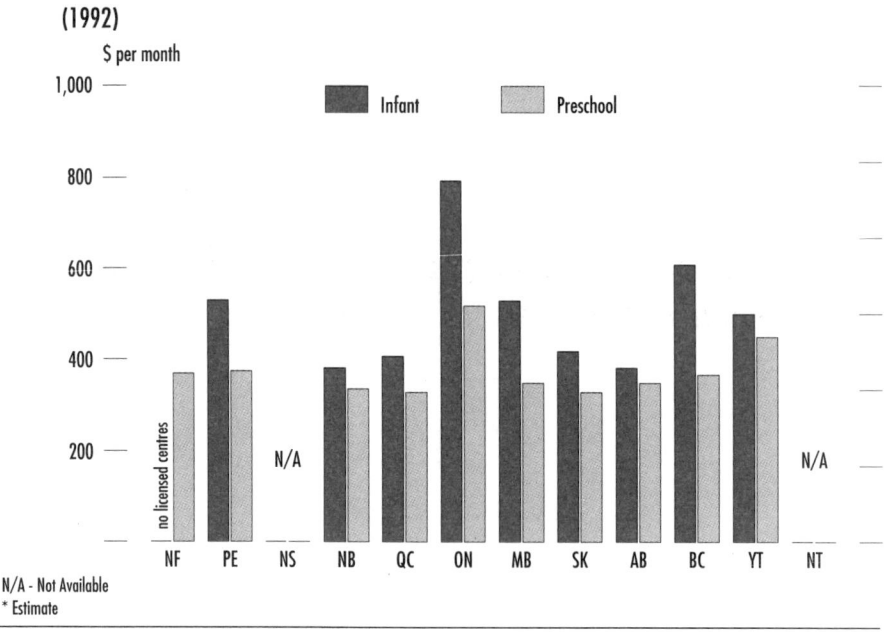

(1992)

N/A - Not Available
* Estimate

Prepared by the Centre for International Statistics

The average cost of a centre space for a preschool-age child is fairly consistent throughout the country ranging from approximately $330 to $450 per month. However the cost for infant care fluctuates greatly, from a low of approximately $380 to a high of $800. And the averages don't take into account the major variations within provinces, nor do they factor in the varying subsidies paid by provinces and municipalities. In the case of Ontario, for example, fees for a 3-5-year old can range from over $9,000 per year in Ottawa to as low as $5,500 in Western Ontario.

Even based on the lower averages for child care fees, it costs a lot to purchase supplementary child care. Consider, for example, a mother who earns $12 per hour or about $24,000 per year, which is high for much of the service sector in a low-wage area. If she has two young children in daycare, she pays $800 or more per month, or almost $10,000 per year. This amounts to half of her take-home pay or more. Once she pays for working expenses such as travel, clothing, and the conveniences she must purchase to fulfill her family obligations, she may be only a few thousand dollars per year better off for all the bother and stress of putting her children in daycare. But that few thousand dollars may make the difference between paying the monthly bills and family financial disaster.

For more than a decade, Canadians have debated child care as a public policy issue. For most Canadian families with young children, however, who cares for their children while they are on the job and how that care is provided is far more than a debating topic. It is a central reality that dominates their lives, their work and their consciousness.

One of the main sources of informal child care that often goes unnoticed is that provided by grandparents. Over 17% of Canada's seniors provide some kind of supplemental child care to their families. Is this an age-old solution to a current problem? Or, is it an unfair burden given the circumstances and needs of today's seniors?

A place for grandparents

In 1991, about 12% of Canada's total population were seniors aged 65 and over – twice as high a proportion as in 1961. Canada's senior population now stands at close to 3.2 million. With the aging of the baby boom, it is projected that by the year 2036, that number will climb to 8.7 million.

71. Living Arrangements of Seniors, 1991

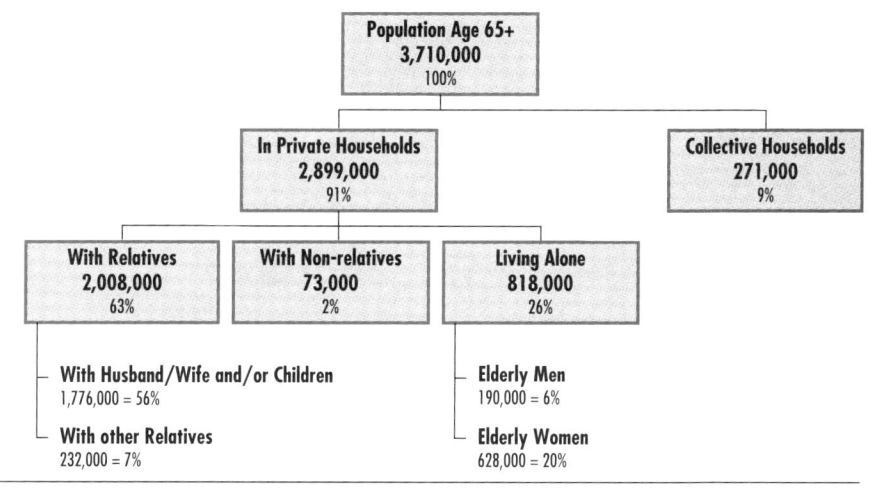

- **Population Age 65+**: 3,710,000 (100%)
  - **In Private Households**: 2,899,000 (91%)
    - **With Relatives**: 2,008,000 (63%)
      - With Husband/Wife and/or Children: 1,776,000 = 56%
      - With other Relatives: 232,000 = 7%
    - **With Non-relatives**: 73,000 (2%)
    - **Living Alone**: 818,000 (26%)
      - Elderly Men: 190,000 = 6%
      - Elderly Women: 628,000 = 20%
  - **Collective Households**: 271,000 (9%)

Notes: "In private households" refers to a person who occupies a private dwelling.
"Collective households" refers to a person who occupies a collective dwelling such as a home for the aged, nursing home, or hospital.

Prepared by the Centre for International Statistics

Most of Canada's seniors live independently in one way or another. Nearly two out of three seniors (63%) live in private households with other relatives, most often with their spouse or their children. One out of every four seniors (26%) lives alone. The remaining 9% live in collective households such as homes for the aged and nursing homes. Canada has one of the world's highest rates of institutional living for seniors.

Many Canadians fear that the rapid aging of Canada's population will mean an unbearable strain on the nation's economy and on our social safety net. This fear may be worse than the reality. People are not only living longer, they are healthier too. There is a continuing trend toward independent living. Over the past twenty years, the proportion of seniors maintaining their own households has increased, from 74.9% in 1971 to 83.5% in 1991. During the same period the proportion of seniors living in households maintained by someone else has dropped from one in four to just one in six.

The Vanier Institute of the Family

In contrast to caring for an adult child, the frail elders, usually thought to be frequent among those over 80 years of age, may have outlived both close friends and family. (Sanborn and Bould, 1991). These elderly people may also have outlived the plans and provisions they made which were quite adequate for the first decade or two of retirement. Survival and the quality of life in longer lifetimes have become major issues facing both individuals and the larger society...
Barbara H. Settles[154]

When the question of who is caring for the older citizens is posed and families are faulted for letting other institutions have a role in caregiving, the picture is of some young adult failing to respect their parents' needs....Nothing could be farther from the common situation. Although the parents of adolescents may be beginning to have elder care responsibilities, in health, housing, and retirement transitions, it is far more likely that an elder will need care from a 'child' who is also of retirement age....Many elders enter institutional care because their caregiver's health declines...
Barbara M. Settles[155]

> *It is estimated that today's woman will spend 17 years of adult life as a mother of a dependent child and 18 years more as daughter of an elderly parent.*
> — Teresa M. Cooney[156]

The big exception to this trend is in Newfoundland, where the proportion of older seniors living in other people's homes is 20%. This probably indicates the tighter family and community bonds of that isolated and traditionally-minded province, as well as its less affluent economy.

Living arrangements of seniors vary greatly by gender. Because women over the age of 75 tend to live longer than men the same age, most *older* seniors – 62% – are women, and two out of three of them (65%) are widowed. The exact same proportion (65%) of older senior *men* are married. Six out of ten older senior men (58%) live in their own homes with their spouses, a far higher percentage than for women (20%). While only 17% of older senior men live alone, four in ten (39%) older senior women do.

For these and other reasons, many of the oldest Canadian women are poor. Indeed, 70% of older senior women live alone on household incomes of less than $20,000, compared with just 50% of men in this age range. On the other hand, the growing number of older senior women who have a place of their own is also due to government income security programs that have been developed for seniors over the past decade or so. Thanks to theses programs, they can afford a place of their own.

"Sandwich generation" boxed in

No matter where senior family members may reside, they often must depend on younger family members for at least some support. This reality weighs heavily on many families. Parents who must care for both their young children and for one or more of their own parents have become known as the sandwich generation. These parents often feel stretched beyond the limit, caught between responsibilities to their loved ones.

Once again, the burden falls mainly to the women in these families. Women spend about twice as much time caring for elderly relatives as men do. As the intensity of that care and the seniors' needs increase, so do work conflicts for the caregivers. In one study, women giving care to older family members missed an average of 35 hours of work per year – nearly a full week – on that account. One in five of them had thought about quitting work entirely due to their caregiving responsibilities. In another study, one in three caregivers had either quit or adjusted their jobs to fit with their responsibilities for older family members.

Most people with disabilities live with their families

Many Canadians – one in seven – have disabilities. And the vast majority of them live with their families.

Studies indicate that approximately 5% of all children are disabled in some way and the proportion with disabilities increases with age. For more than one third of these children, their disabilities are severe enough to limit their participation in school, play and other normal activities. Parents who are raising and caring for children with disabilities experience increased stress and also a greater financial burden.

Of those Canadians aged 15 and over, approximately 14% have some form of disability. Most live with their families as husbands, wives, single parents, and so on. However, three in ten do not.

72. Distribution of Adults With Disabilities* by Family Status

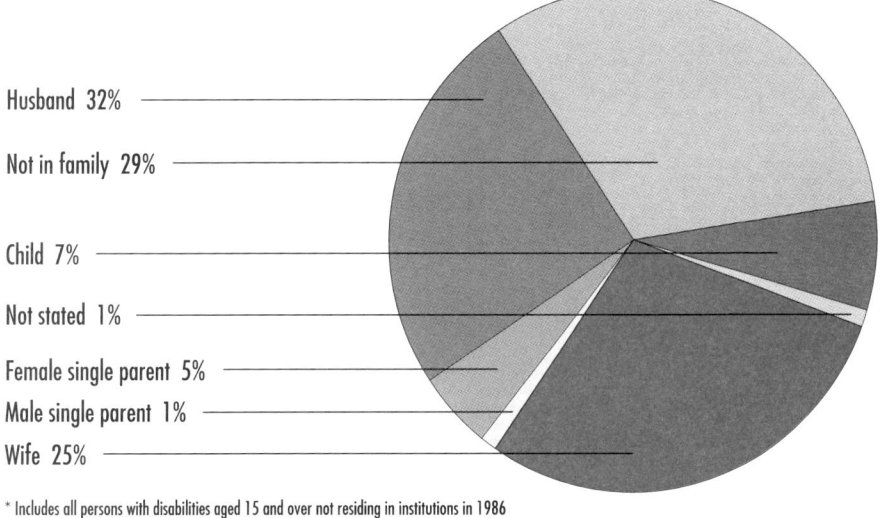

- Husband 32%
- Not in family 29%
- Child 7%
- Not stated 1%
- Female single parent 5%
- Male single parent 1%
- Wife 25%

* Includes all persons with disabilities aged 15 and over not residing in institutions in 1986

Prepared by the Centre for International Statistics

Some people believe that a great many disabled adults live with their parents. It isn't true. Of the adults with disabilities who live with their families, only one out of every fifteen (6.5%) are dependent children aged 15 and over. In fact, husbands represent about one third of all adults with disabilities who live in families.

Living with a disability can be hard, and the effects on families can be profound. The disabilities themselves and the lack of opportunities for disabled people tend to limit their prospects. The result is high rates of poverty and unemployment for people with disabilities and their families. In 1986, for example, over one third of the disabled population had only a primary school education. This compares with one sixth in the general population.

The Vanier Institute of the Family

Currently, about three-quarters of the years individuals live beyond age 76 are disability-free.
Teresa M. Cooney[157]

In Canada, about one child in 20 has a disability of some kind. Most children with disabilities live at home and are seldom institutionalized. This has led to the need for a continuum of services to be provided directly to families. Despite the range of services currently in place, the strain on the families of children whose needs are multiple and complex continues to be particularly acute.
Health Promotion Directorate[158]

In 1986, one quarter (25.4%) of the disabled population lived in poverty. Only 15.5% of the general population was poor. As with other groups in our society, young people and women with disabilities are particularly vulnerable. They have higher poverty rates than other persons with disabilities. And being poor carries a double burden for most people with disabilities because of the extra costs they face. Paying for medication, mobility aids and other special needs strains the budgets of most disabled people and their families. Calculations of poverty rates do not take into account any such additional costs.

If ordinary families find it a grind just to keep going, imagine the stress for families of disabled persons. In addition to the extra costs, most must make special arrangements to assist or take care of their disabled family members. Like employed parents of young children or the adult children of frail elderly people, families of disabled people often carry a difficult burden. It's always with them, and it affects every aspect of their lives.

With a little help from our friends... and family

For people with disabilities, for seniors, and, indeed, for nearly everyone, how well we get along depends on the support we obtain from those around us. Whether from family, friends, or the state, most of us draw on the help of others. As one analyst with Statistics Canada has written about the lifestyles of older seniors, "Most older seniors...had people in their lives they could rely on for support and perceived their lives as happy. Many older seniors also provided help to others."[159] In this respect, they are like most Canadians. While receiving help from others, they also return the favour and help others out.

73. Percent of Seniors Who Provide Unpaid Help* to Family Outside Their Household, by Type of Help Provided

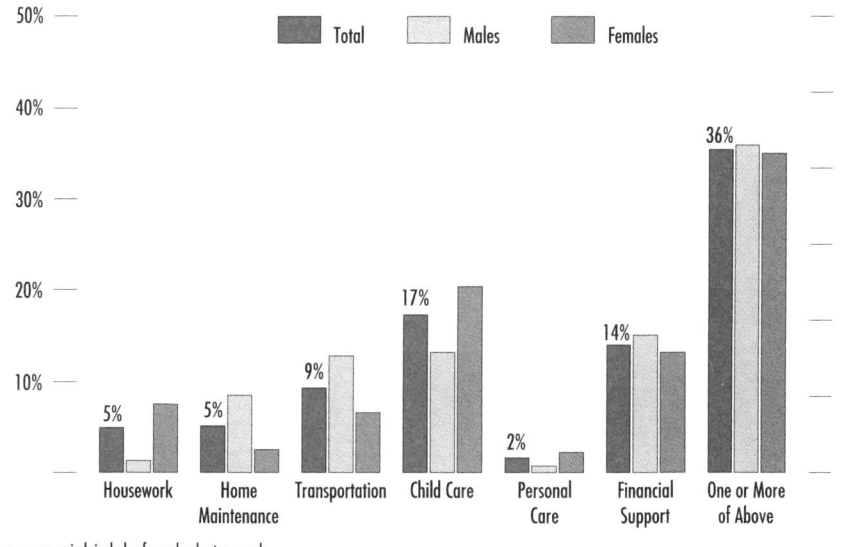

Type	Total	Males	Females
Housework	5%		
Home Maintenance	5%		
Transportation	9%		
Child Care	17%		
Personal Care	2%		
Financial Support	14%		
One or More of Above	36%		

* Over a one year period; includes formal volunteer work

Prepared by the Centre for International Statistics

Many of those who worry whether society can care for an increasingly older population often overlook the contributions that seniors themselves make to others. In 1990, one out of every two seniors (over 65) provided assistance to persons living outside of their household. Unpaid transportation, financial support and child care were the most common forms of help provided.

The Vanier Institute of the Family

Among the people who called (the Philadelphia Geriatric Center) for help in one typical day were: an exhausted, 70-year-old woman who could no longer go on caring for her disabled, 93-year-old mother; a recently-widowed 50-year-old who had just completed her education in preparation for a return to work, but found that her mother had Alzheimer's disease and could not be left alone; a couple in their late 60s with three frail parents between them; a divorcee of 57 who was caring for two disabled sons, a 6-year-old grandchild, and an 87-year-old wheelchair-bound mother; and a young couple in their early 30s, about to have their first child, who had taken two older people into their home – the wife's terminally-ill mother and the confused, incontinent grandmother for whom the mother had been caring.

Elaine Brody[160]

The Vanier Institute of the Family

Over one third (38%) of those aged 75 and over were limited in the kind or amount of activity in which they could participate because of a long-term illness, physical condition, or health problems....
Sandrine Prasil[161]

74. Percent of Seniors Who Provide Unpaid Help* to People Outside Their Household, by Type of Help Provided

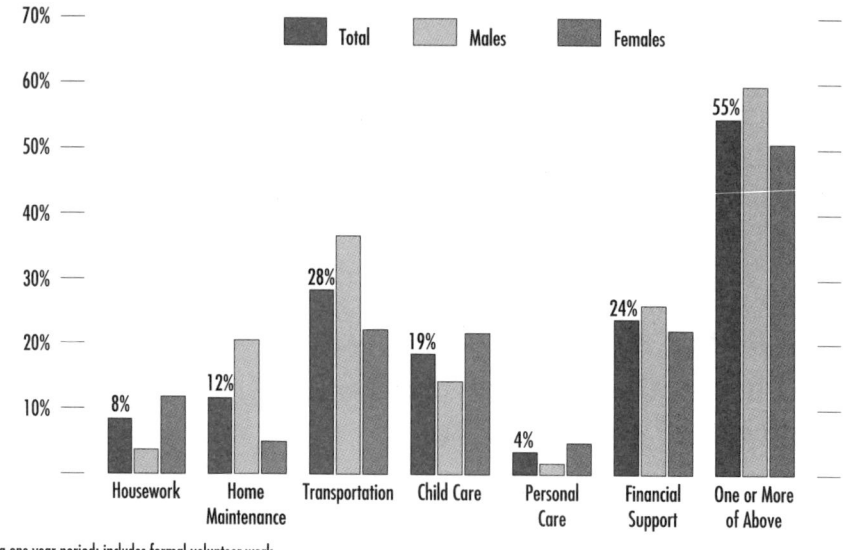

Legend: Total, Males, Females

- Housework: 8%
- Home Maintenance: 12%
- Transportation: 28%
- Child Care: 19%
- Personal Care: 4%
- Financial Support: 24%
- One or More of Above: 55%

* Over a one year period; includes formal volunteer work

Prepared by the Centre for International Statistics

Families helping families

The helpful efforts of seniors come as part of a lifelong pattern. Canadians of all ages provide unpaid social and economic support not only to those living within their households, but to family, friends and neighbours, and voluntary organizations. The types of support provided are many, ranging from help with cooking and cleaning, to home maintenance, transportation, child care and financial support.

75. Percent of Canadians Who Provide Unpaid Help* to People Outside Their Household, by Type of Help Provided

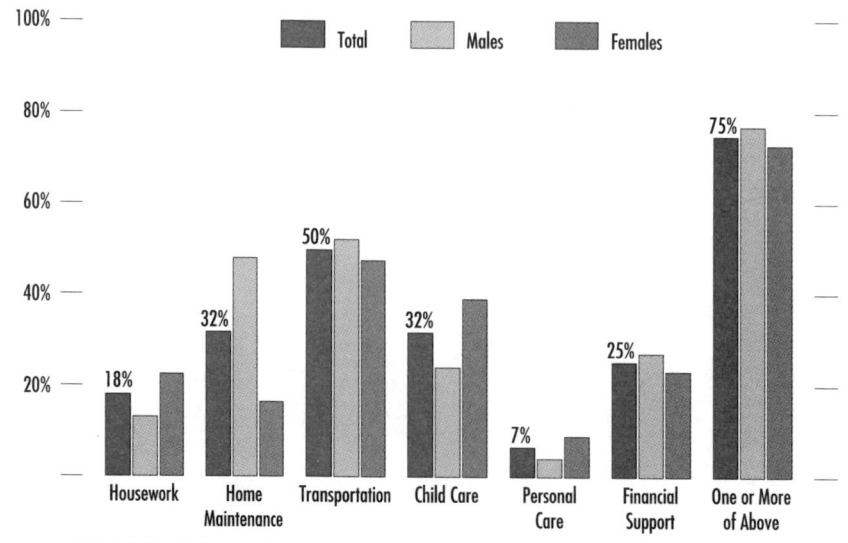

Legend: Total, Males, Females

- Housework: 18%
- Home Maintenance: 32%
- Transportation: 50%
- Child Care: 32%
- Personal Care: 7%
- Financial Support: 25%
- One or More of Above: 75%

* Over a one year period; includes formal volunteer work

Prepared by the Centre for International Statistics

In 1990, Statistics Canada found that three out of four Canadians aged 15 and over provided unpaid services to someone living outside of their own household. Among the types of help provided, transportation was the most common (50%), followed by child care and home maintenance (32% each). Of the latter two, women are more likely to provide help with child care and men more likely to provide help with home maintenance.

Canadians had a similar record of helping family members living outside their households.

76. Percent of Canadians Who Provide Unpaid Help* to Family Outside Their Household, by Type of Help Provided

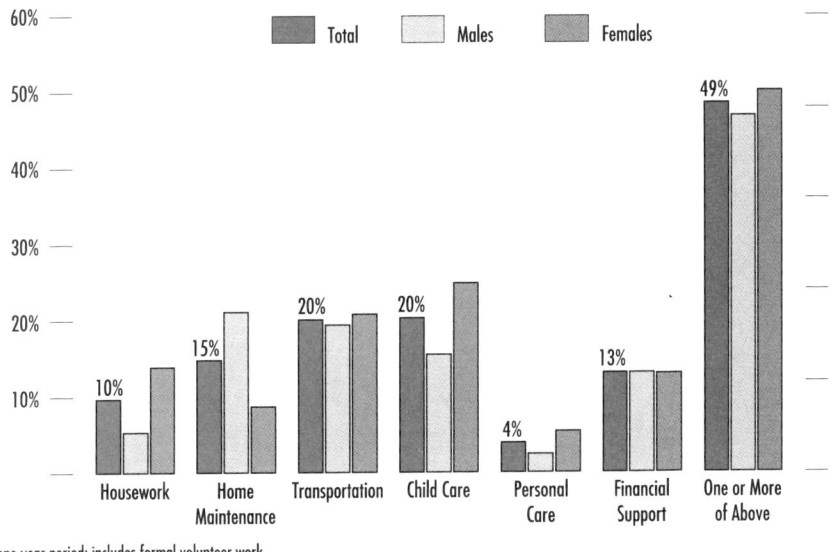

Type of Help	Total	Males	Females
Housework	10%		
Home Maintenance	15%		
Transportation	20%		
Child Care	20%		
Personal Care	4%		
Financial Support	13%		
One or More of Above	49%		

* Over a one year period; includes formal volunteer work

Prepared by the Centre for International Statistics

Thirty percent of women aged 75 and over received help from a daughter, compared with 19% of men that age. Help from sons was received by 22% of women and 21% of men. Among older seniors, 12% of women and 8% of men were helped by grandchildren, while other family members helped 19% of women and 10% of men.
— Sandrine Prasil[162]

The Vanier Institute of the Family

The Vanier Institute of the Family

Families in motion

The work of families goes on, regardless of where their members may live. It is often difficult, however, for families to care for their own because their members increasingly live at a distance from one another.

In 1989, for example, nearly one in five adults (18%) changed residences. Most of them, however, remained in the same region. Only 26% of all movers in 1989 moved more than 50 kilometers. More than half of all movers (54%) moved within 10 kilometers of their previous residence.

77. Mobility Status of Canadians

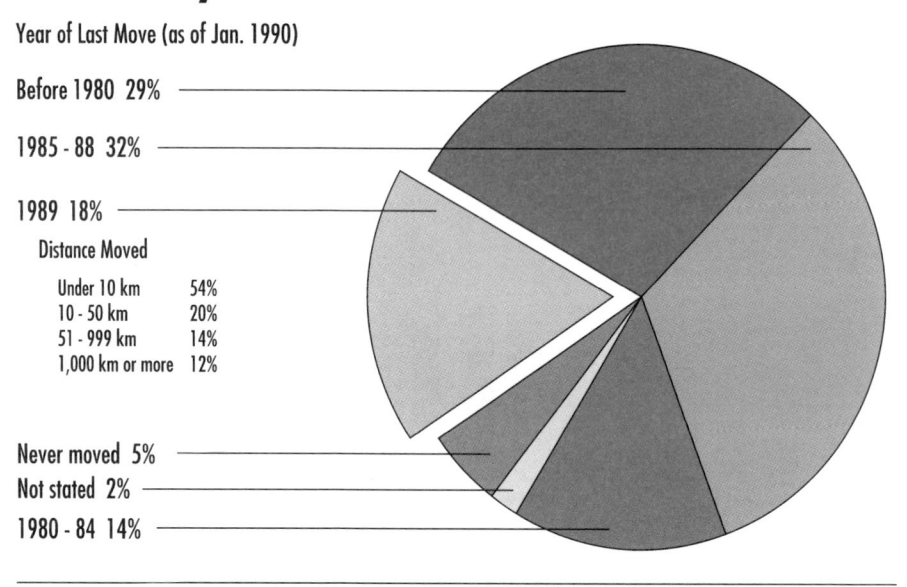

Year of Last Move (as of Jan. 1990)

Before 1980 29%
1985 - 88 32%
1989 18%

Distance Moved

Under 10 km	54%
10 - 50 km	20%
51 - 999 km	14%
1,000 km or more	12%

Never moved 5%
Not stated 2%
1980 - 84 14%

Prepared by the Centre for International Statistics

Why are Canadians on the move? Among those who moved the farthest (1,000 km or more), 44% cited their work or another family member's work as the reason. For those staying closer to home (moving 50 km or less), the primary reasons were needing a larger home (22%), followed by purchasing a home (16%). Overall, wanting a larger home motivated 17% of all moves, and employment-related reasons accounted for 16% of all moves.

While men and women were equally likely to move in 1989, women were much more likely to move because of a family member's employment than were men (7% and 1% respectively). Men were more likely to move for reasons related to their own employment than were women (16% and 9%). This is further evidence that although most women are now in the work force, the careers of their husbands continue to dominate family decision-making and economic life.

As people age, they tend to move less often. Canadians aged 15-34 were the most mobile (28% of them moved in 1989, compared to the national average of 18%), followed by those aged 35-44 (16%), 45-54 (8%), and 55 and over (6%).

Not surprisingly, renters moved more than homeowners (33% compared to 12% in 1989). University-educated persons were three times more likely to move than those with a Grade 9 education. This probably reflects their wider options and greater financial security.

Most Canadians get plenty of experience moving. Only one in three (35%) Canadian adults had lived in their residence for 10 years or more, and just one in twenty had never moved.

Canada has become a highly mobile society. Not only does this make it hard for families to remain in contact and support one another, it affects communities as a whole. As people increasingly move from an area in search of jobs and opportunities, they leave the important relationships that have been part of their lives. It takes time to re-establish these links in a new location. Most recognize how hard it is for children to establish themselves in a new school, but it can be just as hard for adults to get settled in a new neighbourhood. Little things can add up, like who feeds the cat when you go away, how to get to work if the car breaks down, or finding the best places to shop . Without the support of trusted friends, family, and neighbours, it is harder for most people to get along.

That long-distance feeling

Despite their mobility, about half of all Canadians live within 50 km of their parents. Adult children seem to live closer to their mothers than to their fathers. However, this differential is explained primarily by the fact that mothers tend to live longer than fathers. Also, with the higher rates of separation and divorce recorded in recent years, children who no longer live at home have maintained more regular and frequent contact with their mothers than their fathers. Over one third of children (35%) live within walking distance (10 km) of their mothers whereas only one quarter live within 10 km of their fathers. At the other extreme, the situation is reversed. Only one quarter of all Canadians (24%) live over 400 km from their mothers, yet one third (32%) live over 400 km from their fathers.

78. Distance Children* and Mothers Live Apart

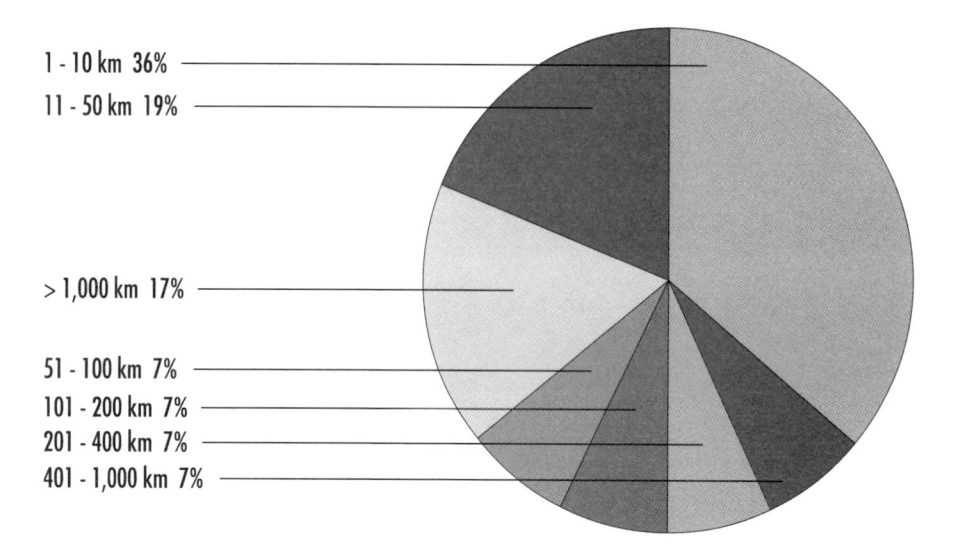

1 - 10 km 36%
11 - 50 km 19%
> 1,000 km 17%
51 - 100 km 7%
101 - 200 km 7%
201 - 400 km 7%
401 - 1,000 km 7%

Distance Children* and Fathers Live Apart

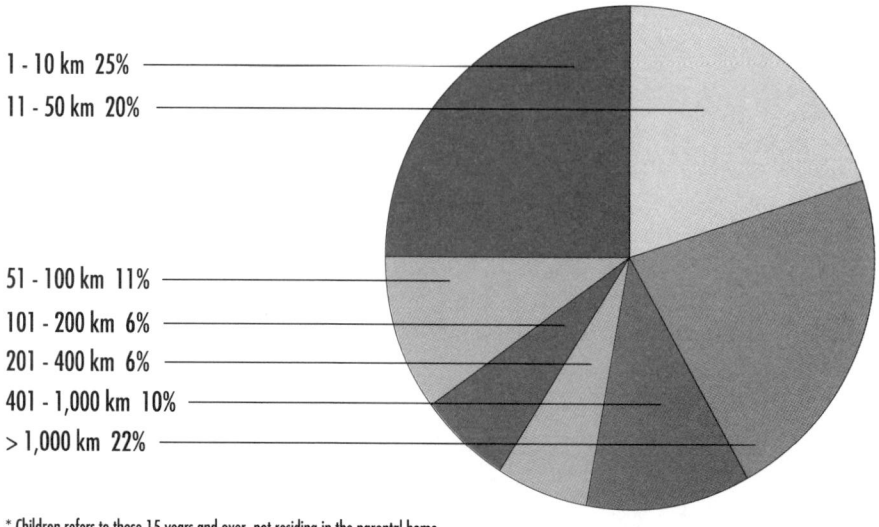

1 - 10 km 25%
11 - 50 km 20%
51 - 100 km 11%
101 - 200 km 6%
201 - 400 km 6%
401 - 1,000 km 10%
> 1,000 km 22%

* Children refers to those 15 years and over, not residing in the parental home

Calculated by the Centre for International Statistics

The patterns of contact between children and their mothers and fathers follows a similar pattern to that of the distances they live apart. No matter how far they live from their parents, children visit their fathers less frequently than their mothers.

79. How Often Mothers and Children* Visit by the Distance Between Them

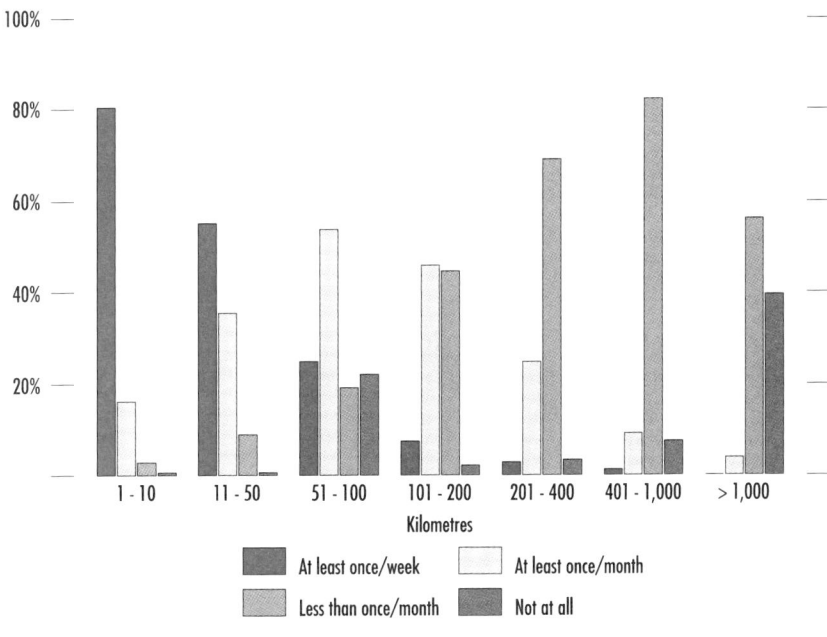

■ At least once/week □ At least once/month
▨ Less than once/month ▨ Not at all

*Children refers to those 15 years and older, not residing in the parental home

Calculated by the Centre for International Statistics

80. How Often Fathers and Children* Visit by the Distance Between Them

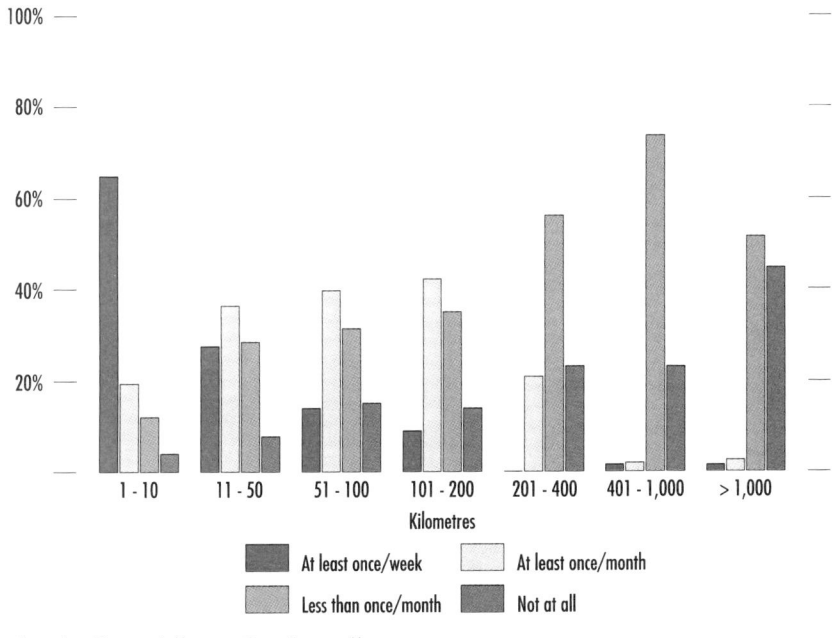

■ At least once/week □ At least once/month
▨ Less than once/month ▨ Not at all

*Children refers to those 15 years and older, not residing in the parental home

Calculated by the Centre for International Statistics

The Vanier Institute of the Family

When children who are on their own live further than 10 kilometres away, the frequency of weekly visits decreases substantially. It becomes more likely that they will see each other monthly, rather than weekly. As the distance increases to between 100 and 200 kilometres, the frequency of monthly visits begins to decline. Visiting less than once a month becomes more common. When the distance between children and parents increases to over 1,000 kilometres, it becomes quite common for children not to visit with their parents at all.

The difference between the amount of contact children who no longer live at home have with their mothers and fathers shows up even more strongly in how often they contact their parents by phone or letter. Children write or phone their mothers at a much greater rate than they do their fathers, regardless of the distance between the child and the respective parent. One out of five such children who live over 1,000 kilometres from their mother communicate with her at least weekly. That's more than twice as often as those who live more than 1,000 km from their fathers contact them. On the other hand, fewer than 10% of these children never phone or write to their mothers. Yet nearly 20% of children never write or phone their fathers, regardless of the distance between them.

And how often do grandchildren visit with their grandparents? While it is known that the frequency of contact gradually decreases as the grandchildren grow older, even when they reach their late teens, a large proportion (almost 40%) see their grandparents at least once a month. However, one-fifth of grandchildren never visit their grandparents and over one-quarter never phone or write.

Contact between these generations provides the grandchildren with the opportunity to gain a sense of their family's history, background or culture. When that contact is lost, many miss the love and security that grandparents can provide, and the grandparents miss out on the hope, fun and togetherness of watching their grandchildren grow. As for the parents in the middle, they lose out on a valuable source of parenting experience and advice, when their parents and their children lose touch with one another.

Canadians have found various ways to deal with the "grandparent gap". Some communities encourage intergenerational programs in order to give children without nearby grandparents and elderly people with no young relatives a chance to benefit from one another's company. A growing problem is the number of grandparents who become cut off from grandchildren after a divorce. Some have even organized in order to help them gain access to their grandchildren. This is another illustration of how the ties of family remain, regardless of where family members live, or with whom.

81. How Often Grandparents and Grandchildren* Visit with One Another

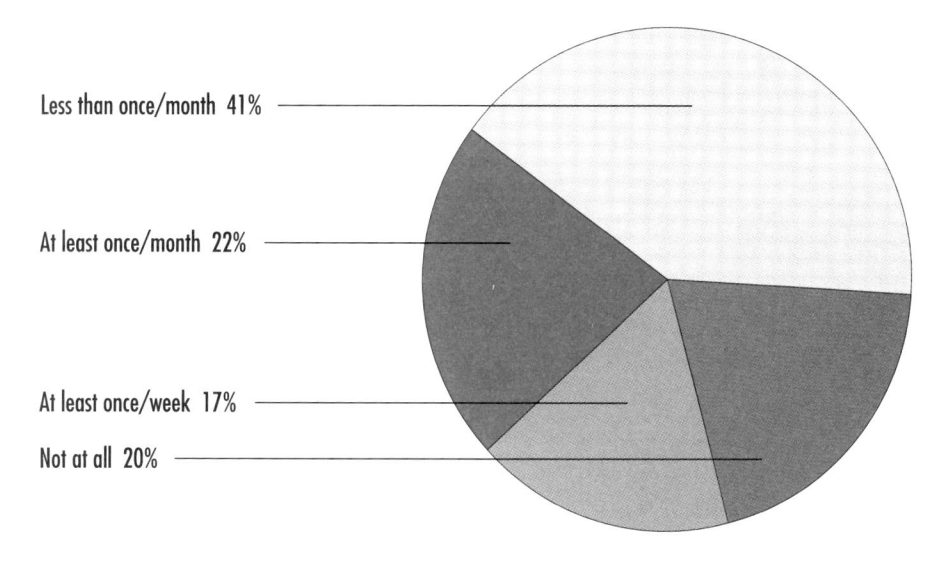

Less than once/month 41%

At least once/month 22%

At least once/week 17%

Not at all 20%

How Often Grandparents and Grandchildren* Phone and Write to One Another

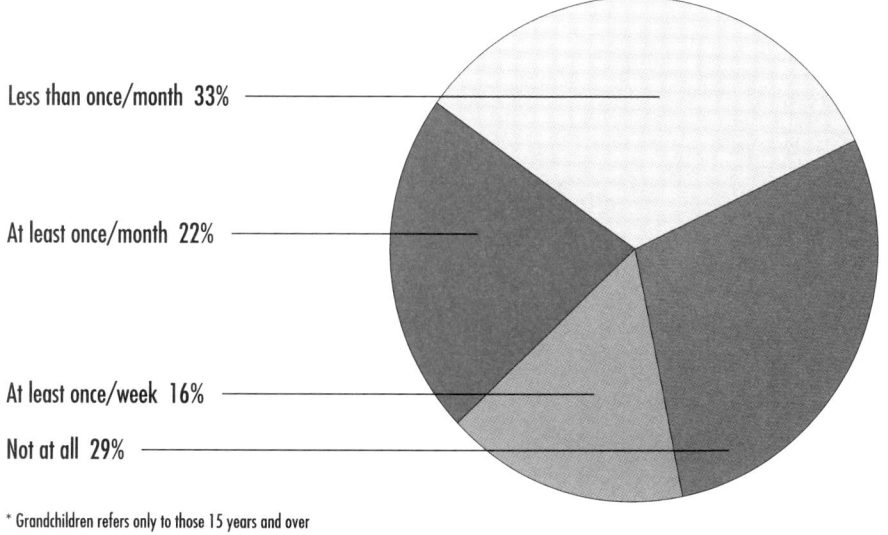

Less than once/month 33%

At least once/month 22%

At least once/week 16%

Not at all 29%

* Grandchildren refers only to those 15 years and over

Calculated by the Centre for International Statistics

The Vanier Institute of the Family

In the presence of grandparents and grandchildren, the past and the future merge in the present.
    Margaret Mead[163]

82. How Often Siblings Visit with One Another

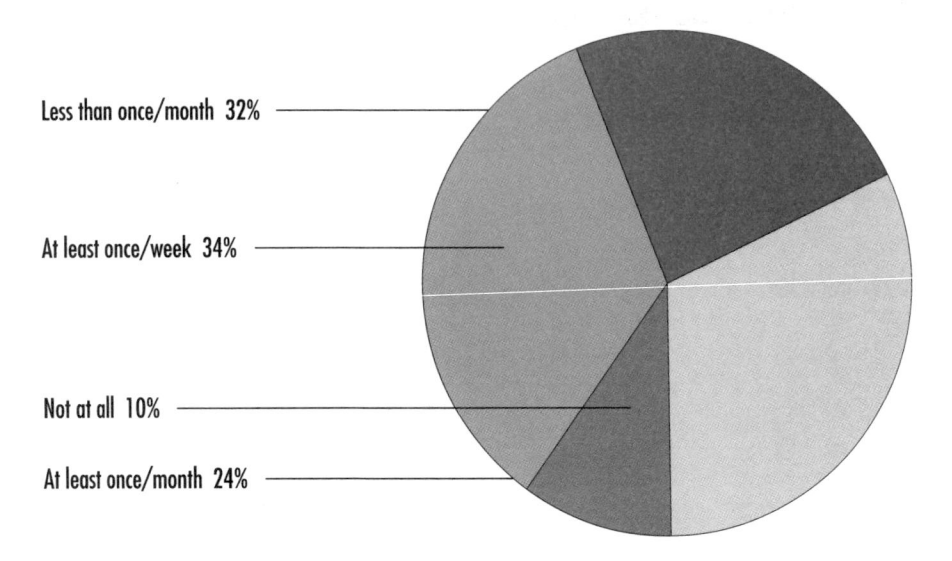

- Less than once/month 32%
- At least once/week 34%
- Not at all 10%
- At least once/month 24%

How Often Siblings Phone and Write to One Another

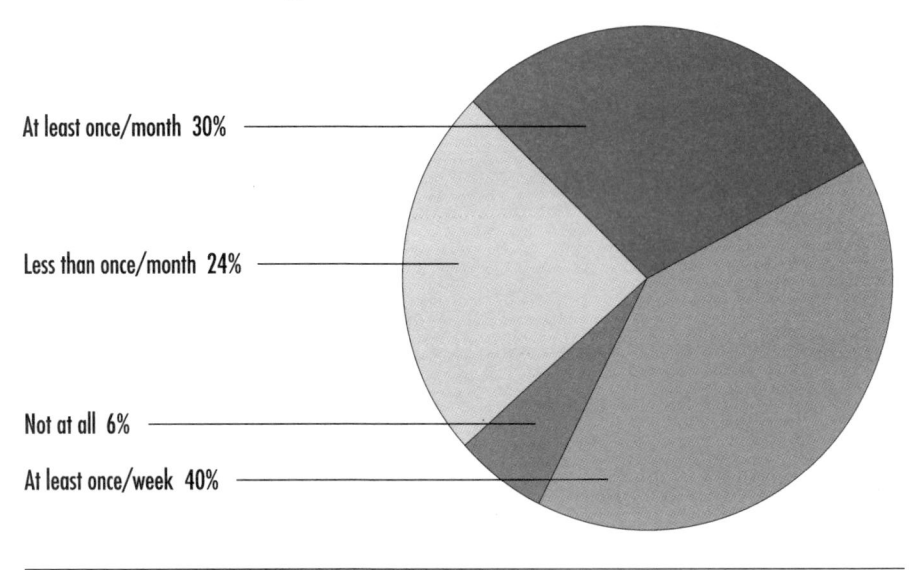

- At least once/month 30%
- Less than once/month 24%
- Not at all 6%
- At least once/week 40%

Calculated by the Centre for International Statistics

Siblings manage to maintain somewhat more contact with one another than with their parents.

Over one third of siblings who live apart visit with one another at least once a week. An even larger portion write or phone their siblings weekly. Only one in ten never visit with their siblings and even a smaller portion never write or phone.

For many people, the word family conjures up a rather limited image: two parents and their children. The reality of families has much more variety and texture. Our connections with one another do not dissolve simply because children grow up and move away. Which roof we sleep under does not determine who we help or from whom we receive support.

Troubled homes: the down side of family

At best, family can be a source of strength and support, joy and love. Sadly, it is not for a great many Canadians. The life of a family takes place somewhere between the public world of work, school and society and the private world of the individual. World events, social trends, cultural beliefs, economic pressure, the conflicts between old ways and modern times – all the things that affect individuals are played out on the family stage.

Many people feel that their families are not as harmonious or as pleasant as they would like. Members of the various generations may find themselves in conflict over fundamental issues such as child-rearing, work, or money matters. Siblings and other family members can carry resentments and grudges that go on for decades. In families, people can develop hurt feelings, guilt or low self-esteem. These emotions can haunt them through their adult lives. Such things happen in many, if not most families. Overall, most of us feel that we must take the bad along with the good, and we attempt to work things out, smooth things over, or simply ignore minor family aggravations in order to get on with the more positive aspects of family life.

Some family problems, however, cannot be swept under the rug. Wife assault, child or elder abuse, or living with someone who abuses alcohol or drugs can make family life awful. For too long, society has attempted to ignore these serious issues. Today, most Canadians finally realize that these problems are far more common and serious than had been previously believed. If we truly care about families, we must act to prevent and end all forms of abuse.

Families and abuse

Abuse of many kinds takes place in a great many Canadian families. This reality has received increasing attention in recent years, mainly because women started speaking out against the assault of women. Now that the extent of such assault has been brought out in the open, other forms of violence and abuse within families have been acknowledged and exposed.

Abuse within families goes beyond the injury inflicted by one family member – most often a man – on another, usually a woman, child or elder. It is about the abuse of power, a more powerful person taking advantage of a less powerful person. In most cases, the perpetrator uses assault or the threat of it to keep the victim in a state of intimidation and fear. In this way, he controls both the victim and, often enough, everyone else in the family as well.

It is hard to gauge the extent of violence and abuse within Canada's families. What is known is that many Canadian women, children and old people are not safe within their own families.

Victims of abuse are constantly intimidated. Many, perhaps most, fear for their lives, the lives of their children or both. Daily news reports of domestic murders confirm the validity of their fears. In many cases, victims come to accept the blame their abusers heap upon them. In abusive families, it is not uncommon for victims to blame themselves for the abuse, nor is it uncommon for victims to maintain a sense of loyalty and commitment to family members who abuse them. Blame, shame and loyalty combine with raw intimidation, making it hard for victims to take the steps necessary to end the abuse.

The Vanier Institute of the Family

Canadians like to imagine the family as a refuge from the stresses and strains of the outside world. While this is true, there is another reality. The family is both the most loving and supportive of human groups and also by far the most violent group or institution.
Child at Risk Report[164]

Alcoholism in the family is a problem for about 10% of all children under the age of 18, and being raised in such a family is one of the most stressful conditions experienced by children (Roosa, Geusheimer, Short, Ayers and Shell, 1989).
Barbara M. Settles[165]

Proportion of all murders in 1992 committed by a member of the victim's own family: 32%
Centre for International Statistics[166]

The Vanier Institute of the Family

Proportion of female murder victims in 1991 murdered by current or former husbands (including common-law): 31%
   Centre for International Statistics[168]

Number of women murdered in Canada in 1992 by family members or acquaintances: 190
   Centre for International Statistics[169]

Proportion of assaults on mothers witnessed by their children: 68%
   Barry Leighton[170]

Proportion of children of abused women who have witnessed assaults on their mothers: 80%
   Deborah Sinclair[171]

Proportion of abusive husbands found by Canada's Correctional Services to have grown up in violent, abusive families: 75%
   Barbara Appleford[172]

Wife assault

Accurate figures on wife assault are hard to obtain because so many cases of wife assault are not reported to the police. Statistics Canada reports, however, that fully one half of all Canadian women have experienced at least one incident of violence since the age of 16. The same survey indicated that one-quarter of all women have experienced violence at the hands of a current or past marital partner. One in six currently-married women reported violence by their spouses. One-half of women with previous marriages reported violence by a previous spouse.[167]

Until recently, wife assault and male violence against women in general were openly or tacitly accepted throughout most of our society. It was assumed that wives and women played a subservient role to husbands and men.

Old ways die hard. Despite changed social values and increased awareness, women and girls are too often still valued on the basis of their ability to attract and keep a man. Teenage boys still pressure, coerce or force their dates to have sex. Large numbers of married men still use all kinds of excuses to justify beating or killing their wives.

Wife assault affects the whole family. Children witness it and they live with the consequences. Growing up in a violent home can hurt children in many ways, including:
- low self-esteem, lack of self-confidence, insecurity, fear, anxiety
- guilt and a sense of responsibility for their mother's suffering and their father's anger
- shame, social isolation, inability to express feelings
- nightmares, sleep disturbances, bed-wetting, poor impulse control
- imitative behaviour including aggression towards the mother and other women
- delinquency
- increased responsibility within the family (for mother or younger siblings), sometimes resulting in severe distress
- difficulties at school.

Elder abuse

Seniors are often at risk of violence and abuse because they are more vulnerable, and in many cases dependent on others. The perception and fear of violence among the elderly, however, may be higher than the actual level of violence they experience.

The elderly were victims of 3% of all violent crimes reported in 1991, while making up 16% of the population. Thus, the elderly were, in fact, less likely to be victims of violent crimes than were the non-elderly.

In 1989 a national study surveyed 2,000 seniors (over 65) who lived in private dwellings about elder abuse. Approximately 4% reported some type of abuse. Financial abuse was the most common form and was more likely to be committed by distant relatives or non-relatives than by close family members. Verbal abuse was widespread, and physical abuse was experienced by a smaller, but not insignificant number of seniors, most of whom were abused by their spouses.

As Rachel Schlesinger reminded us, "We must be aware of the crime of elderly abuse, and we must begin to initiate programs and attitudes to prevent it. We support rape-crisis centres, we fight to help the battered wife, and we speak out against child abuse in all forms. We fight for quality of life. Why are we silent when our mothers and grandmothers struggle alone and in silence in their battle for survival, for growing old in an atmosphere of dignity and understanding? We must provide the strength for those who no longer have much strength. We must hear the silent cries, and our voices must help them speak. We too will grow old, and we too want to live in a world of mutual respect, love, and care, not increased elderly abuse, not a world of 'granny-bashing.'"[174]

Child abuse

Child abuse is the mistreatment or neglect of a child by a parent, guardian or caregiver, resulting in injury or significant emotional or psychological harm. It can take the form of physical abuse, sexual abuse, emotional abuse or neglect.

Child abuse, like other kinds of abuse within families, is vastly under-reported. Neglect is more prevalent than physical abuse.

The effects of child abuse are profound. It can lead to delinquency, criminality, mental illness, developmental delays and increased risk-taking, among other personal and social problems. Victims are at risk of suffering from learning disabilities, brain damage, malnutrition and language delays. Researchers and front-line professionals report that a huge proportion of prison inmates, and mental hospital patients experienced abuse as children.

Child abuse happens in all kinds of families, regardless of their economic status, their heritage, or their structure. There are more reports of child abuse, however, among lower-income families. In part this may be due to greater willingness on the part of teachers, other professionals and neighbours to report such families, greater willingness on the part of child welfare agencies to intervene, and greater willingness on the part of the justice system to prosecute. It may also be partly due to the higher levels of stress, frustration, isolation and despair experienced by poor or vulnerable families.

The Vanier Institute of the Family

Will the evidence of family violence ever end? Following the issues of child abuse, spouse abuse and sexual abuse which have been addressed in sequence over the past 20 years, we must now face the painful facts of abuse of elderly people by their caregivers, in the home. Most of the abuse goes unreported because of the embarrassment and fear of reprisal by the elderly people affected.
    Mish Vadasz[173]

Proportion of teenage runaways in Toronto who had been beaten as children: 75%
    Janus, McCormack, Bugess and Hartman[175]

Proportion of male adolescent prostitutes found by one study to have been physically or emotionally abused by family members: 72%
    D.K. Weisberg[176]

Proportion of families in which the woman is assaulted and the children have also been abused: one third
    Jaffe, Wolfe and Wilson[177]

...because some families have financial, personal, social or family resources in reserve, they can better resist the stress of poverty, and so, do better than others. But that should not make us forget that the risk of discord or violence is no less high for families living in poverty. The data are pitiless: as with dangerous highway curves, we can use the rates of poor families in a district to predict very accurately where the most family violence will occur in the next six months.
    Camil Bouchard[178]

Proportion of female adolescent runaways in Toronto who had experienced childhood sexual abuse: 75%
Proportion of male adolescent runaways in Toronto who had experienced childhood sexual abuse: 38%
Janus, McCormack, Burgess and Hartman[179]

Child sexual abuse

Child sexual abuse can have devastating long-term consequences. Many teenage run-aways leave home on account of it. Adult women survivors of childhood sexual abuse are more likely than others to experience depression, self-destructive behaviour, poor self-esteem, substance abuse, anxiety, and feelings of isolation and stigma.

Nine times out of ten, children who are sexually abused know their abuser…as father, stepfather or uncle or brother or neighbour. Parents, in street-proofing young children, often focus exclusively on the dangers posed by strangers. While strangers can and do abuse children, it is far more common for children to be sexually abused by people they know and trust.

Reports of child sexual abuse are on the increase. The federal government reports that in five study sites (Calgary, Edmonton, Regina, Saskatoon and Hamilton) between 1988 and 1992, there was an increase in the number of cases of child sexual abuse reported to police, more charges were laid, more cases involving very young victims were prosecuted, and more younger victims testified in court. During this period, 70-80% of the victims were female, most victims were under the age of 12, and 15-22% were under the age of five. The vast majority – over 94% – of accused abusers were male. Most of them were adults but approximately one-quarter of them were under the age of 18.

It is clear that abuse and assault occur in many families and that women and children are the main victims. It is also clear that few hard facts exist to document the dimensions and extent of the problem. What *is* known is that its causes and consequences are complex and that the effects are often tragic, profound and far-reaching. It affects their future relationships and families. Individuals and society pay enormous costs when people's lives are altered or misshapen by abuse. Violence and abuse within families is not merely a personal or family problem. It is a serious social problem that affects all of us.

And in the end...
Supporting family life in Canada

It would be wrong to overlook or underestimate the significance of problems that occur within families. The family is a stage on which we play out all kinds of dramas, our greatest sorrows and trials as well as our greatest joys and successes. We dare not gloss over the real problems that family members bring home and, in some cases, continue within the privacy of the home. Yet despite the many problems, family today remains incredibly popular. The vast majority of us feel we cannot live without it. And the enduring strength of families is that together, they cope, adapt, and, in most cases, survive.

Canada's families today maintain the age-old tradition of caring and sharing. At the same time, they face many challenges. They're more rushed and have less time. They're more spread out and see each other less often. They have more obligations and opportunities vying for their time and attention.

Employers, governments, schools, community organizations, service providers and family members themselves can all help to support Canada's families as they cope with their commitments and stresses. How best can we establish the kinds of support for families that are most effective and sustainable in the long term? Finding a balance between support and intruding on privacy and independence is tricky. It is equally challenging to get all the parts of the community pulling together in a coordinated way.

There are a variety of approaches to supporting families. One is to **increase resources available to all families** to help them carry out their family responsibilities. This is a broad category. Examples at the community level include anything from a recreation program to a Neighbourhood Watch to a food-buying co-op. At another level, governments provide resources through such measures as income security programs, tax exemptions, and subsidies for recreation or child care.

The voluntary sector has always played a strong part in providing resources to families. In an age of "donor fatigue," however, it is important to be mindful of the limits of what can be done by volunteers. Public institutions such as schools and hospitals have also provided a great deal of family support. Will they be able to continue this role in an age of cutbacks? Increasingly, employers are beginning to recognize the important contribution they can make in assisting their employees to balance the often-conflicting demands of work and family. Moreover, as the Conference Board of Canada has concluded:

"Organizations that respond to the changing needs of the labour force will no doubt be in a better position to attract, retain and motivate the employees necessary for their success. ...Those organizations that implement various family-responsive supports, particularly in the areas of child care (especially in emergency situations), personal and family-responsibility leave and flexibility in working hours, may be rewarded through an increase in employee morale; reductions in employee stress, absenteeism and turnover; and fewer promotion and transfer refusals."[180]

It is also vitally important to **assist vulnerable families or vulnerable family members**. This kind of high-profile help includes everything from service clubs helping people with disabilities to special income support programs from governments. Examples include transportation or housing subsidies, clothing and food banks, support groups for disease victims, and targeted "head-start" programs for young children from poor neighbourhoods.

The Vanier Institute
of the Family

> There must continue to be crisis-oriented services because the ambulance at the bottom of the cliff can sometimes save the wounded. But it is the fence around the top that really matters, and no approach to family policy that ignores the universal needs of families for assistance can succeed.
> Don Edgar[181]

> Families mattered in the past; they continue to matter in the present; and they will matter still, in the uncertain years of our future.
> C.P. Cowan and C.A. Cowan[182]

It can be sticky, though, to determine just who "deserves "help and how that determination will be made. Again, a balance must be struck between treatment and prevention. Finding effective interventions is not straightforward. Establishing programs that work in an age of business and government austerity requires imagination and political will.

There is a growing preference for support that can **improve the capacity of families and family members** to fulfill their responsibilities. Education, self-help and health promotion are good examples. If new parents can learn parenting techniques, for example, with the help of parent resource centres, a night school class or an employee assistance program, it may prevent child development problems later in life. Such problems can disrupt families and result in long-term costs for communities and governments. Empowering families to prevent problems can be a cost-effective – and popular – form of support.

Another way to support families is to **provide them with supplemental services and supports**. If a company or a community group can assist families in obtaining child care or elder care, for instance, families may experience lower stress, which will enable them to get on with their other important work, both at home and on the job. As Canadians contemplate the costs of such programs, we must also consider what the negative impact of *not* providing such services would be. For example, employees who cannot find adequate child care may be forced to take unauthorized leave or quit prematurely, at great cost to their employers.

One successful approach to family support is to **assist families through transitional stages**. Getting married, having a new baby, moving to a new town, or having teenagers in the house can be stressful. Programs such as marriage preparation, parenting classes, Welcome Wagon or Parents Without Partners can help family members through difficult or new stages in the family life cycle.

An indirect, yet effective, means to help families is to **strengthen the supports to family functioning provided by neighbourhoods and communities**. If communities, governments, and employers can establish and support recreation facilities and programs, family resource centres, and community development initiatives, these can be of tremendous benefit to all kinds of families.

As they have always done, families change and adapt as their world changes. The world will never go back to the "simpler" times that may have existed yesterday. Today, our families face new challenges. We depend on families for so much. It is not sufficient to simply ask the question "What's wrong with families?" Instead, we must ask: "How best can all of us enrich and support the lives of families so they can keep on doing the important things they have always done?"

Chart References

1. Statistics Canada (1992). *Families: Number, Type and Structure.* Cat. #93-312. Ottawa.

2. Statistics Canada (1992). *Age, Sex and Marital Status.* Cat. #93-310. Ottawa.

3. Statistics Canada (1993). *Aboriginal Data: Age and Sex.* Cat. #94-327. Ottawa.

4. Statistics Canada (1993). *Ethnic Origin.* Cat. #93-315. Ottawa.

5. Statistics Canada (1992). *Current Demographic Analysis: Report on the Demographic Situation in Canada, 1991.* Cat. #91-209E. Ottawa.

6. Statistics Canada. *Profile of the Immigrant Population.* Cat. #94-312. Ottawa (not yet released).

7. Statistics Canada (1992). *Mother Tongue.* Cat. #93-313. Ottawa.

8. Statistics Canada (1993). *The Daily* (June 1). Ottawa.

9. Statistics Canada (1987). "Urban Canada," in *Canadian Social Trends* (Winter). Ottawa; Statistics Canada (1992). *Population and Dwelling Counts.* Cat. #93-301. Ottawa.

10. Statistics Canada (1992). *Families: Number, Type and Structure.* Cat. #93-312. Ottawa.

11. Ibid.

12. Statistics Canada. 1992 Survey of Consumer Finances (microdata). Ottawa.

13. Ibid.

14. Statistics Canada (1992). *Age, Sex and Marital Status.* Cat. #93-310. Ottawa.

15. Ibid.

16. Statistics Canada (1992). *Selected Marriage Statistics 1921-1990.* Cat. #82-552.

17. Statistics Canada (1992). *Age, Sex and Marital Status.* Cat. #93-310. Ottawa.

18. Statistics Canada (1967-1986). "Marriages and Divorces," in *Vital Statistics.* Ottawa; and Statistics Canada (1987-1989). *Marriages.* Ottawa: Canadian Centre for Health Information.

19. Statistics Canada (1992). *Current Demographic Analysis: Marriage and Conjugal Life in Canada.* Cat. #91-534. Ottawa.

20. Statistics Canada (1992). *Selected Marriage Statistics 1921-1990.* Cat. #82-552. Ottawa.

21. Ibid.

22. Statistics Canada (1992). *Age, Sex and Marital Status.* Cat. #93-310. Ottawa.

23. Ibid.

24. Statistics Canada (1992). *Current Demographic Analysis: Marriage and Conjugal Life in Canada.* Cat. #91-534. Ottawa.

25. Statistics Canada (1992). *Selected Marriage Statistics 1921-1990.* Cat. #82-552. Ottawa; Statistics Canada. Health Reports, Supplement #17. Cat. #92-003517. Ottawa; and Statistics Canada (1992). *Current Demographic Analysis: Marriage and Conjugal Life in Canada.* Cat. #91-534. Ottawa.

26. United Nations. *Demographic Year Book 1989*; Statistics Canada (1990). Supplement #17. Ottawa: Canadian Centre for Health Information; and Statistics Canada (1992). *Health Reports.* Ottawa: Vol. 4, No. 4.

27. Statistics Canada (1989). "Marrying and Divorcing: A Status Report for Canada," in *Canadian Social Trends* (Summer).

28. Statistics Canada (1992). "Age Structure in Transition: Two Centuries of Demographic Change," in *Report on the Current Demographic Situation in Canada 1992.* Ottawa.

29. Ibid.

The Vanier Institute of the Family

30. Statistics Canada (1993). *The Daily* (June 1). Ottawa.

31. Statistics Canada (1992). *Families: Number, Type and Structure.* Cat. #93-312. Ottawa; and Statistics Canada. *Report on the Demographic Situation in Canada, 1992.* Cat. #91-209E. Ottawa.

32. A. Romaniuc (1984). *Fertility in Canada: From Baby-Boom to Baby-Bust*, in Current Demographic Analysis Series. Ottawa: Statistics Canada; and Statistics Canada (1992). "Age Structure in Transition: Two Centuries of Demographic Change," in *Report on the Current Demographic Situation in Canada 1992.* Ottawa.

33. The Demographic Review (1989). *Charting Canada's Future: A Report of the Demographic Review.* Ottawa: Health and Welfare Canada: 20; and updated figures provided by the Social Statistics Development Project, Statistics Canada.

34. Statistics Canada (1993). *Births 1992.* Cat. #84-210. Ottawa.

35. A. Romaniuc (1984). *Fertility in Canada: From Baby-Boom to Baby-Bust*, in Current Demographic Analysis Series. Ottawa: Statistics Canada; and Statistics Canada (1993). *Births 1992.* Cat. #84-210. Ottawa.

36. Statistics Canada (1993). *Births 1992.* Cat. #84-210. Ottawa.

37. Daly, K. and Sobol, M. (1991). "Adoption in Canada," in *National Adoption Study.* Ontario: University of Guelph.

38. Statistics Canada. General Social Survey 1990 (microdata). Ottawa.

39. Eichler, Margrit (1983). *Families in Canada Today.* Toronto: Gage Publishing; and Statistics Canada (1993). *Historical Labour Force Statistics 1992.* Ottawa.

40. Statistics Canada (1993). *Historical Labour Force Statistics*, 1992. Ottawa.

41. Eichler, Margrit (1983). *Families in Canada Today.* Toronto: Gage Publishing; Statistics Canada (1989). *Labour Force Annual Averages, 1981-1988*; and Statistics Canada (1992). *Labour Force Annual Averages, 1991.* Cat. #71-220. Ottawa.

42. Statistics Canada. Survey of Consumer Finances (microdata). Ottawa.

43. Statistics Canada. General Social Survey 1990 (microdata). Ottawa.

44. Statistics Canada (Various years). *Labour Force Annual Averages.* Cat. #71-220. Ottawa.

45. Statistics Canada. *Labour Force Annual Averages.* Cat. #71-220. Ottawa; and McKie, Craig (1993). "An Overview of Single Parenthood in Canada," in *Single Parent Families.* Joe Hudson and Burt Galaway (eds.). Toronto: Thompson Educational Publishing.

46. Statistics Canada (1993). *Selected Income Statistics.* Cat. #93- 331. Ottawa.

47. Statistics Canada. Survey of Consumer Finances (microdata). Ottawa.

48. Statistics Canada (1993). *Selected Income Statistics.* Cat. #93- 331. Ottawa.

49. Ibid.

50. Ibid.

51. Galarneau, Diane (1993). "Alimony and Child Support," in *Canadian Social Trends.* Ottawa: Statistics Canada (Spring); and Galarneau, Diane (1992). "Alimony and Child Support," in *Perspectives on Labour and Income.* Ottawa: Statistics Canada (Summer).

52. Statistics Canada (1992). *Income Distribution by Size in Canada 1991.* Cat. #13-207. Ottawa.

53. Ibid.

54. National Council of Welfare (1993). *Poverty Profile Update for 1991.* Ottawa.

55. National Council of Welfare (1992). *Poverty Profile 1980-1990 Update for 1991.* Ottawa; and National Council of Welfare (1993). *Poverty Profile Update for 1991.* Ottawa.

56. Statistics Canada. Social Policy Simulation Database and Model. Ottawa; and Statistics Canada. 1990 Survey of Family Expenditures (microdata). Ottawa.

57. Statistics Canada (1993). *Housing Costs and Other Characteristics of Canadian Households.* Cat. #93-330. Ottawa.

58. Ibid.

59. Ibid.

60. Marshall, Katherine (1990). "Household Chores," in *Canadian Social Trends.* Ottawa: Statistics Canada (Spring); and Marshall, Katherine (1993) "Employed Parents and the Division of Housework," in *Perspectives on Labour and Income.* Ottawa: Statistics Canada (Autumn).

61. Statistics Canada. *The Value of Housework in Canada, 1986.* Ottawa.

62. Ross, David and Shillington, David (1989). *A Profile of the Canadian Volunteer.* Ottawa: National Voluntary Organizations.

63. Statistics Canada (1993). Initial Data Release from the 1992 General Social Survey on Time Use. Ottawa.

64. Ibid.

65. Ibid.

66. Statistics Canada. 1988 National Child Care Survey (microdata). Ottawa.

67. Ibid.

68. Ibid.

69. Health and Welfare Canada (1985-1991). *Status of Day Care in Canada.* Ottawa.

70. Child Care Resource and Research Unit (1993). *Child Care: The Provinces and Territories, 1993.* Toronto: University of Toronto.

71. Statistics Canada (1992). *Families: Number, Type and Structure.* Cat. #93-312. Ottawa.

72. Statistics Canada. 1986 Health and Activities Limitations Survey (microdata). Ottawa.

73. Statistics Canada. 1990 General Social Survey (microdata). Ottawa.

74. Ibid

75. Ibid.

76. Ibid.

77. Che-Alford, Janet (1992). "Canadians on the Move," in *Canadian Social Trends.* Ottawa: Statistics Canada (Summer).

78. Statistics Canada. 1990 General Social Survey (microdata). Ottawa.

79. Ibid.

80. Ibid.

81. Ibid.

82. Ibid.

The Vanier Institute
of the Family

End Notes

1. Eichler, Margrit (1988). *Families in Canada Today: Recent Changes and Their Policy Consequences*. (2nd Edition). Toronto: Gage: 4.

2. Reproduced with the kind permission of Demographic Review Secretariat (1990). "Family Research Report." Ottawa: 10.

3. The Vanier Institute of the Family (1992). *Transition* (March): 8.

4. Statistics Canada (1992). *Families, Number, Type and Structure*. Cat. #93-312. Ottawa: 133.

5. The United Nations (1991). *Building the Smallest Democracy at the Heart of Society*. Vienna: The United Nations.

6. Government of Quebec (1984). *For Quebec Families: A working paper on family policy*. Government of Quebec: Standing Committee on Social Development.

7. Social Sciences and Humanities Research Council and Health and Welfare Canada's joint initiative on Family Violence and Violence against Women (1992). "Definition of Family." In *Transition* (March): 3.

8. Dafoe Whitehead, Barbara (1990). "The Family in an Unfriendly Culture." *Family Affairs*. (3) (1-2).

9. Moore Lappé, Frances (1984-85). "What do you do after you turn off the TV?" *Utne Reader* (December/January).

10. Stacey, Judith. "Disinfecting the Family Values Debate." Prepared for *Insight Magazine*.

11. Zimmerman, Shirley L. (1988). *Understanding Family Policy: Theoretical Approaches*. Beverly Hills, CA: Sage: 75-76.

12. Insight Canada Research (1993). "Aspirations Project Qualitative Research Report prepared for Children and Youth Project." Toronto: Premier's Council on Health, Well-Being and Social Justice (February).

13. Jackson, Marnie (1989). "Bringing Up Baby." *Saturday Night* (December).

14. Katz Rothman, Barbara (1989). *Recreating Motherhood: Ideology and Technology in a Patriarchal Society*. New York: W.W. Norton: 32.

15. Boulding, Elise (1981). *The Place of the Family in Times of Transition: Imaging a Familial Future*. Ottawa: The Vanier Institute of the Family: 8.

16. Badets, Jane (1993). "Canada's Immigrants: Recent Trends." *Canadian Social Trends* (Summer): 11.

17. Statistics Canada (1993). *The Nation*. Cat #93-313. Ottawa: 1.

18. The Vanier Institute of the Family (1976). *Learning and the Family: A Conceptual Framework on Learning*. Ottawa.

19. Bibby, Reginald (1990). "The Poverty and Potential of Life in Canada." In *The True North Finally Free*. Toronto: Stoddart: 84-85.

20. Ibid.

21. Kettle, John (1993). "Fifth Column." In *The Globe and Mail* (September 16).

22. Statistics Canada (1992). *Families: Number, Type and Structure*. Cat. #93-312. Ottawa.

23. Skolnick, Arlene (1991). *Embattled Paradise, The American Family in an Age of Uncertainty*. New York: Basic Books: xix.

24. Mead, Margaret (1990). Cited in *Today's Families: A Critical Focus*. Phyllis Meiklejohn, Annette Yeager and Lenore Kurch (eds.). Toronto: Collier MacMillan Canada Inc.: 40

25. Glossop, Robert (1990). "Today's Families: Continuity, Change and Challenge." *Transition* (September): 4.

26. Steinem, Gloria. Cited in *Today's Families: A Critical Focus.* Op. cit.: 209.

27. Hayford, Alison. Cited in *Today's Families: A Critical Focus.* Op. cit.: 209

28. Skolnick, Arlene. Op. cit.: 8.

29. Bombeck, Erma. Cited in *Today's Families: A Critical Focus.* Op. cit.: 153.

30. Cottin Pogrebin, Letty. Cited in *Today's Families: A Critical Focus.* Op. cit.: 202.

31. Statistics Canada (1992). *Families: Number, Type and Structure.* Cat. #93-312. Ottawa.

32. Skolnick, Arlene. Op. cit.: 14.

33. Sussman, Marvin B. (1993). "Families in Time to Come: Taking Position on Trends and Issues." In *Marriage and Family Review* 18 (3/4): 305.

34. Sauvé, Roger (1990). *Canadian People Patterns.* Saskatoon, SK: Western Producer Prairie Books: 8.

35. Baker, Maureen (1993). *Families in Canadian Society* (2nd Edition). Toronto: McGraw-Hill Ryerson: 5.

36. Ibid: 9.

37. Ibid: 253-254.

38. Priest, Gordon E. (1993). "Seniors 75+: Living Arrangements." In *Canadian Social Trends.* Ottawa (Autumn): 24.

39. Sauvé, Roger. Op. cit.: 42.

40. Cooney, Teresa M. (1993). "Recent Demographic Change: Implications for Families Planning for the Future." In *Marriage and Family Review* 18 (3/4):42.

41. Inuit proverb. Cited in *Today's Families: A Critical Focus.* Op. cit.: 101.

42. Kantrowitz, Barbara and Wingert, Pat. Cited in *Today's Families: A Critical Focus.* Op. cit.: 209.

43. Johnson, Samuel. Cited in *Today's Families: A Critical Focus.* Op. cit.: 193.

44. Kettle, John (1992). *John Kettle's Future Letter* (December 1): 13.

45. Scott, Judge J. Wilma (1990). *In Cohabitation: The Law in Canada.* Winifred H. Holland and Barbro E. Stallbecker-Poutney (eds.). Toronto: Casswell: vii.

46. Baker, Maureen. Op. cit.: 153.

47. Statistics Canada. 1990 General Social Survey (microdata). Ottawa.

48. Sauvé, Roger. Op. cit.: 41.

49. Ibid: 44.

50. Skolnick, Arlene. Op. cit.: 194.

51. As cited in Skolnick, Arlene. Op. cit.: 181.

52. Department of Justice, Bureau of Review (1990). *The Divorce Evaluation, Phase II: Monitoring and Evaluation.* Ottawa (May): 94-95.

53. Stacey, Judith. Op. cit.

54. Epstein, Phillip. Cited in *Today's Families: A Critical Focus.* Op. cit.: 198.

55. Freeman, Rhonda (1989). "Divorce and children: A transition experience." In *Transition* (September): 8-11.

56. Richardson, C. James (1993). "Divorce In Canada." In *Marriage and the Family in Canada Today* (2nd Edition). G.N. Ramu (ed.). Toronto: Prentice Hall Canada: 208-209.

57. Ibid: 192.

58. Cooney, Teresa M. Op. cit.: 46.

59. Moore, Maureen (1989). "How long alone? The duration of female lone parenthood in Canada." In *Transition* (March): 4-5.

60. Ibid.

61. Marcil-Gratton, Nicole (1989). "Growing up within a family: Canadian children and their parents' new lifestyles." In *Transition* (September): 4-7.

62. Jones, Charles, Marsden, Lorna and Tepperman, Lorne (1990). *Lives of Their Own: The Individualization of Women's Lives.* Toronto: Oxford University Press: 168.

63. Skolnick, Arlene. Op. cit.: 154.

64. Ibid.: 14.

65. Marcil-Gratton, Nicole. Op. cit. : 6.

66. Ibid.: 7.

67. Royal Commission on New Reproductive Technologies (1993). *Proceed with Care, Executive Summary.* Ottawa: Ministry of Government Services Canada.

68. Couchman, Robert. Cited in *Today's Families: A Critical Focus*: 127.

69. Ramu, G. N. (1993). "Profiles of Marriage and the Family." In *Marriage and the Family in Canada Today* (2nd Edition). G.N. Ramu (ed.). Toronto: Prentice Hall Canada: 69.

70. Kettle, John (1991). *John Kettle's Future Letter* (January 1): 13.

71. Ibid.:12.

72. Nett, Emily M. (1980). *Canadian Families: Past or Present.* Toronto: Butterworths: 145.

73. Beaujot, Rodrick (1991). *Population Change in Canada: The Challenges of Policy Adaptation.* Toronto: McClellan and Stewart: 206.

74. Cooney, Teresa M. Op. cit.: 45.

75. Kettle, John (1992). Op. cit.: 14.

76. Jones, Charles, Marsden, Lorna and Tepperman, Lorne. Op. cit.: 12.

77. Ibid.: 14.

78. Marcil-Gratton, Nicole. Op. cit.: 6.

79. The Vanier Institute of the Family (1992). "Adoption in Canada: A Profile." In *Transition* (September): 5.

80. Spronk, Terri (1992). "Abandoning Ownership...a philosophical approach to adoption." In *Transition* (September): 6-7.

81. Ibid.

82. Mehren, Elizabeth. Cited in *Today's Families: A Critical Focus.* Op. cit.: 109.

83. Cited in *Today's Families: A Critical Focus.* Op. cit.: 109.

84. Thompson-Guppy, Airdie (1986). "A stepmother on step mothering." In *Transition* (December): 5-7.

85. The Demographic Review (1989). *Charting Canada's Future*. Cat. #H21-105/1. Ottawa: Health and Welfare Canada: 16.

86. Statistics Canada (1990). *Women in Canada: A Statistical Report* (2nd Edition). Cat. #89-503E. Ottawa: Supply and Services Canada: 73.

87. Jones, Charles, Marsden, Lorna and Tepperman, Lorne. Op. cit.: 99.

88. Settles, Barbara H. (1993). "Expanding Choice in Long Term Planning for Family Futures." In *Marriage and Family Review* 18 (3/4): 20.

89. Armstrong, Pat and Armstrong, Hugh (1988). "Women, Family and Economy." In *Reconstructing the Canadian Family: Feminist Perspectives*. Nancy Mandell and Ann Duffy (eds.). Toronto: Butterworths: 163.

90. Jones, Charles, Marsden, Lorna and Tepperman, Lorne. Op. cit.: 156.

91. Statistics Canada (1990). Op. cit.

92. O'Toole, Chris and Prud'homme, Marc (1993). "Are Young People Farming?" In *Canadian Social Trends* (Autumn): 33.

93. Douthitt, Robin A and Fedyk, Joanne (1990). *The Cost of Raising Children in Canada*. Toronto: Butterworths: 60.

94. Marshall, Katherine (1993). "Employed parents and the division of housework." In *Perspectives on Labour and Income* 5 (3) (Autumn): 23-24.

95. Moore, Maureen (1990). "Dual-earner Families: The New Norm." In *Canadian Social Trends*. Craig McKie and Keith Thompson (eds.). Toronto: Thompson Educational Publishing: 162.

96. Armstrong, Pat and Armstrong, Hugh. Op. cit.: 163.

97. Status of Women Canada (1986). *Report of the Task Force on Child Care*. Cat. #SW-1/1986E. Ottawa: Supply and Services Canada: 11.

98. Sauvé, Roger. Op. cit.: 80.

99. The Economic Council of Canada (1989). *Legacies: Summary, 26th Annual Review of the Economic Council of Canada*. Ottawa: 15.

100. Morazain, Jeanne (1992). "The Accumulation of Dissatisfaction: Deciding between home and the workplace is never an easy choice." In *Transition* (June): 4.

101. Skolnick, Arlene. Op. cit.: 12.

102. Mirabelli, Alan of the Vanier Institute of the Family (1993). Cited in *The Ottawa Citizen* (November 20): A2.

103. Ross, David P. and Lochhead, Clarence (1993). "Changes in Family Incomes and Labour Market Participation in Post-War Canada." In *Transition* (March): 5.

104. Statistics Canada (1993). *Family Incomes, Census Families 1991*. Cat. #13-208. Ottawa.

105. Grady, Patrick (1992). "The Burden of Federal Tax Increases under the Conservatives." In *Canadian Business Economics* (1) (Fall).

106. Ross, David P. and Lochhead, Clarence. Op. cit.: 7.

107. Nett, Emily M. Op. cit.: 60.

108. The Economic Council of Canada (1989). *Annual Review*. Ottawa: 39.

109. Statistics Canada (1993). *Selected Income Statistics*. Cat. #93-331. Ottawa.

110. Statistics Canada (1993). *Selected Income Statistics*. Cat. #93-331 and Statistics Canada (1992). Age, Sex and Marital Status. Cat. #93-310. Ottawa.

111. Ibid.

112. Federal/Provincial/Territorial Family Law Committee (1989). *Child Support: Public Discussion Paper.* Ottawa: Department of Justice: 3.

113. Ibid.: 7-8.

114. Statistics Canada. Social Policy Simulation Database and Model (5.0). Ottawa.

115. Fortin, Bernard (1993). "Fifteen Years Old and Already Working." In *Transition* (March): 9.

116. Bibby, Reginald W. and Posterski, Donald C. (1992). *Teen Trends: A Nation in Motion.* Toronto: Stoddart: 88.

117. The National Council of Welfare (1993). *Poverty Profile: Update for 1991.* Ottawa (Table 12).

118. Child Poverty Action Group and the Social Planning Council of Metropolitan Toronto (1991). *Unequal Futures: The Legacies of Child Poverty in Canada.* Toronto: 20.

119. Canadian Child Welfare Association, et al. (1988). *A Choice of Futures: Canada's Commitment to Its Children.* Ottawa: 3.

120. Ross, David P. and Lochhead, Clarence. Op. cit.: 7.

121. The Vanier Institute of the Family (1993). "Lone-parent families, low incomes." In *Transition* (March): 13.

122. Senate Committee on Social Affairs, Science and Technology (1991). *Children in Poverty: Toward a Better Future.* Cat. #XC28- 342/1-01. Ottawa: Supply and Services Canada: 6.

123. The National Council of Welfare (1975). *Poor Kids: A Report of The National Council of Welfare on Child Poverty.* Ottawa.

124. Statistics Canada. Social Policy Simulation Database and Model and Statistics Canada 1990 Survey of Family Expenditures (microdata).

125. *The Ottawa Citizen* (1993). (November 20): A2.

126. Statistics Canada. 1990 Survey of Family Expenditures (microdata).

127. Ross, David P. and Lochhead, Clarence. Op. cit.: 6-7.

128. Blumstein, Phillip and Schwartz, Pepper (1983). *American Couples: Money, Work, Sex.* New York: William Morrow: 77.

129. Douthitt, Robin A. and Fedyk, Joanne. Op. cit. : 36.

130. Manitoba Agriculture. As cited by Bruce Cohen (1993). In *Financial Post* (March 6).

131. Hewlett, Sylvia Ann (1991). *When the Bough Breaks: The Cost of Neglecting Our Children.* New York: Harper Perrenial: 354.

132. Kluck Davis, Christine (1991). "Children's Habitat." In *The State of the Child in Ontario.* Richard Barnhorst and Laura C. Johnson (eds.). Toronto: Oxford University Press: 185.

133. Spector, Aron N. and Klodawsky, Fran (1993). "The Housing Needs of Single Parent Families in Canada: A Dilemma for the 1990s." In *Single Parent Families: Perspectives on Research and Policy.* Joe Hudson and Burt Galaway (eds.). Toronto: Thompson Education Publishing: 242.

134. The National Advisory Council on Aging (1993). Aging Vignettes #13. Ottawa.

135. Spector, Aron N. and Klodawsky, Fran. Op. cit.: 252.

136. Statistics Canada. *1992 Household Facilities and Equipment Survey.* Ottawa.

137. Nett, Emily M. Op. cit.: 49

138. Ibid.: 248.

139. Marshall, Katherine. Op. cit.: 24-25.

140. Jackson, Chris (1992). *The value of household work in Canada 1986.* Ottawa: Statistics Canada: 7.

141. Nett, Emily M. Op. cit.: 48.

142. Stretton, Hugh (1977). "Seeing Our Economy Whole: Satisfying Personal, Familial and Community Needs," as cited by James Robertson. Ottawa: Vanier Institute of the Family: 17.

143. The National Voluntary Organization (1989). *A Profile of the Canadian Volunteer.* Ottawa: 13.

144. Statistics Canada (1993). Initial Data Release from the 1992 General Social Survey on Time Use. Ottawa.

145. Dafoe Whitehead, Barbara. Op. cit.: 4

146. Friedman, Dana of the Families and Work Institute, New York (1989). In a presentation during "Work and Family Symposium" convened by the Child Youth and Family Policy Research Centre. Toronto: George Brown House: 18.

147. Cooney, Teresa M. Op. cit.: 83.

148. Hewlett, Sylvia Ann. Op. cit.: 18.

149. Dennis, Wendy. Cited in *Today's Families: A Critical Focus.* Op. cit.: 217.

150. Goelman, Hillel (1992). "What do we know about daycare kids?" In *Transition* (June): 8.

151. Galinsky, Ellen (1988). "Toward New Partnerships." In *Work and Family: New Partnerships*, Work and Family Conference Proceedings. Toronto: Ryerson University (Nov. 30-Dec. 2).

152. MacBride-King, Judith (1990). *Work and Family: Employment Challenge of the '90s.* Ottawa: The Conference Board of Canada: ix.

153. Meir, Golda. Cited in *Today's Families: A Critical Focus.* Op. cit.: 218.

154. Settles, Barbara H. Op. cit.: 10-11.

155. Ibid.: 13.

156. Cooney, Teresa M. Op. cit.: 76-77.

157. Cooney, Teresa M. Op. cit.: 40.

158. Health Promotion Directorate (1993). *A Vision of Health for Children and Youth in Canada: Discussion Paper.* Ottawa: Health Canada (April): 6.

159. Prasil, Sandrine (1993). "Seniors 75+: Lifestyles." In *Canadian Social Trends* (Autumn): 26.

160. Brody, Elaine (The Philadelphia Geriatric Center) (1989). As cited in *Failing America's Caregivers: A Status Report on Women Who Care.* Washington: Older Women's League: 10.

161. Prasil, Sandrine. Op. cit.: 28.

162. Ibid.

163. Mead, Margaret. Cited in *Today's Families: A Critical Focus.* Op. cit.: 149.

164. *Child at Risk Report*, Government of Canada. Cited in *Today's Families: A Critical Focus.* Op. cit.: 180.

165. Settles, Barbara M. Op. cit.: 13.

166. Statistics Canada's Centre for Justice Statistics. *Homicide Survey, 1992.* Ottawa.

167. Statistics Canada (1993). "The Violence Against Women Survey." In *The Daily* (November 18): 1.

168. Statistics Canada's Centre for Justice Statistics. *Homicide Survey, 1992*. Ottawa.

169. Ibid.

170. Leighton, Barry (1989). *Spousal Abuse in Metropolitan Toronto: Research Report on the Response of the Criminal Justice System* (Report No. 1989-02). Ottawa: Solicitor General of Canada: 40.

171. Sinclair, Deborah (1985). *Understanding Wife Assault: A Training Manual for Counsellors and Advocates*. Toronto: Ontario Government Bookstore.

172. Appleford, Barbara (1989). "Prevention and Treatment of Abusive Behaviour." In *Family Violence Review*. Ottawa: The Correctional Service of Canada.

173. Vadasz, Mish (1988). "Family Abuse of the Elderly." In *Abuse of the Elderly: Issues and Annotated Bibliography*. Toronto: University of Toronto Press: 91.

174. Schlesinger, Rachel (1988). Cited in "Abuse of the Elderly: Knowns and Unknowns." By Benjamin Schlesinger and Rachel Aber Schlesinger. In *Abuse of the Elderly: Issues and Annotated Bibliography*. Benjamin Schlesinger and Rachel Schlesinger (eds.). Toronto: University of Toronto Press: 110-111.

175. Janus, Mark-David, McCormack, Arlene, Wolbert Burgess, Ann and Hartman, Carol (1987). *Adolescent Runaways – Causes and Consequences*. Toronto: D.C. Health and Co.: 57.

176. Weisberg, D.K. (1985). *Children of the Night: A Study of Adolescent Prostitution*. Toronto: D.C. Health and Co.: 49.

177. Jaffe, Peter, Wolfe, David and Wilson, Susan Kaye (1990). *Children of Battered Women*. Newbury Park, N.J.: Sage Publications: 22.

178. Bouchard, Camil (1989). "Poverty : A Dangerous Curve." In *Transition* (September): 11.

179. Janus, Mark-David, McCormack, Arlene, Wolbert Burgess, Ann and Hartman, Carol. Op. cit.: 57.

180. MacBride-King, Judith. Op. cit.: x.

181. Edgar, Don (1989). "Strengthening Families in the 1990s." In *Family Matters* (23) (April): 5.

182. Cowan, C.P. and Cowan, C.A. (1992). *When partners become parents: The big life change for couples*. New York: Basic Books: 481.